Let's Talk!

201.855.TALK

TIC TALK
PROMPT 7 OPTION 7

Enrich **your** friendships and relationships as the lessons of *Positive Word Power* for Teens come to life through stories, contests, interviews, facts, and trivia on the TIC TALK Hotline!

201.855.8255 PROMPT 7 OPTION 7

Special for our European listeners – 44-203-375-1580 then 9,9 and then 7,7

BE A PART OF IT
MISHMERES!
The High School Division of CCHF

מסורה

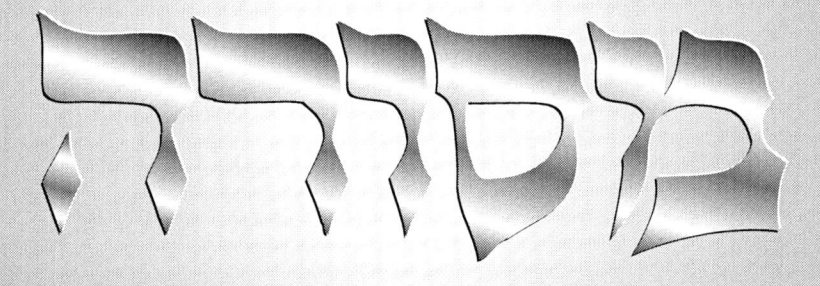

ArtScroll® Series

Rabbi Nosson Scherman / Rabbi Meir Zlotowitz
General Editors

A Project of
THE
CHOFETZ CHAIM
HERITAGE
FOUNDATION

Published by
ARTSCROLL®
Mesorah Publications, ltd

THE AVIGAIL RECHNITZ EDITION

Positive Word Power*

The Language of Friendship and Happiness

*for Teens

The Torah's Wisdom on Human Interaction
Arranged for Daily Study

By: Chana Nestlebaum

Editorial Director: Shaindy Appelbaum

FIRST EDITION
First Impression ... May 2014

Published and Distributed by
MESORAH PUBLICATIONS, LTD.
4401 Second Avenue / Brooklyn, N.Y 11232

Distributed in Europe by
LEHMANNS
Unit E, Viking Business Park
Rolling Mill Road
Jarow, Tyne & Wear, NE32 3DP
England

Distributed in Australia and New Zealand
by **GOLDS WORLDS OF JUDAICA**
3-13 William Street
Balaclava, Melbourne 3183
Victoria, Australia

Distributed in Israel by
SIFRIATI / A. GITLER — BOOKS
Moshav Magshimim
Israel

Distributed in South Africa by
KOLLEL BOOKSHOP
Northfield Centre, 17 Northfield Avenue
Glenhazel 2192, Johannesburg, South Africa

ARTSCROLL® SERIES
POSITIVE WORD POWER FOR TEENS
© Copyright 2014, by MESORAH PUBLICATIONS, Ltd.
4401 Second Avenue / Brooklyn, N.Y. 11232 / (718) 921-9000 / www.artscroll.com

---

A project of
THE CHOFETZ CHAIM HERITAGE FOUNDATION
361 Spook Rock Road / Suffern, N.Y. 10901 / (845) 352-3505

ALL RIGHTS RESERVED
The text, prefatory and associated textual contents and introductions
— including the typographic layout, cover artwork and ornamental graphics —
have been designed, edited and revised as to content, form and style.

No part of this book may be reproduced
IN ANY FORM, PHOTOCOPYING, DIGITAL, OR COMPUTER RETRIEVAL SYSTEMS
— even for personal use without written permission from
the copyright holder, Mesorah Publications Ltd.
except by a reviewer who wishes to quote brief passages
in connection with a review written for inclusion in magazines or newspapers.

THE RIGHTS OF THE COPYRIGHT HOLDER WILL BE STRICTLY ENFORCED.

ISBN 10: 1-4226-1492-1 / ISBN 13: 978-1-4226-1492-1

Typography by CompuScribe at ArtScroll Studios, Ltd.
Printed in the United States of America by Noble Book Press Corp.
Bound by Sefercraft, Quality Bookbinders, Ltd., Brooklyn N.Y. 11232

לע"נ אביגיל מימא רחל ע"ה בת חיים אהרן יבלח"ט

In Loving Memory
of Avigail Rechnitz, *a"h*

Capturing the essence of Avigail Rechnitz, *a"h*, is like trying to capture the fire of a diamond. Each facet of her life shone with its own pure brilliance. The love of family, community and Hashem that burned in her heart brought warmth, light and sparkle to everyone whose life she touched. As a wife, her wisdom, strength and lively, loving nature were the foundation upon which she built her home together with her beloved husband, Reb Yisroel Zev. As a mother, she was the ultimate *mechaneches*, teaching through example the true, eternal priorities in life. Her joyful, can-do approach to every challenge inspired the many women in her community who worked with her in her wide world of *chesed* endeavors. Her enthusiasm spread to everyone around her and spurred them on to achievements they never knew they could accomplish.

Avigail Rechnitz, *a"h*, is an everlasting example of the heights one person can reach, using every asset with which Hashem blessed her to do Hashem's will and to better improve the lives of others. Through this book, may her legacy expand to instill her virtues of sensitivity, kindness, honesty and *ahavas Yisrael* into a whole new generation of Jewish women, and from there, to all of *Klal Yisrael*.

Dedicated by Shlomo Yehuda and Tamar Rechnitz

Letter of Approbation from HaRav Aharon Leib Shteinman שליט"א

As everyone knows, the mitzvos of our holy Torah fall under two categories: mitzvos between man and his Creator, and mitzvos between man and his fellow. The *Aseres HaDibros*, as well, contains mitzvos between man and his Creator and mitzvos which command man to be careful not to hurt his fellow human being.

The Gemara teaches that *ona'as devarim*, causing pain through hurtful words, is more serious than *ona'as mamon*, wronging someone in monetary dealings [i.e. overcharging him] (see *Bava Metzia* 58b). Regarding verbal abuse in marriage, there is no difference if the husband is the guilty party or whether it is the wife (both are included in this prohibition). In fact, the Gemara says that as women cry more easily than men, hurting their feelings is even more serious (see *Bava Metzia* 59a). This includes anything that might cause them emotional pain. To cause pain to a widow or orphan is especially severe.

Conversely, one cannot imagine what he can merit through acts of *chesed* toward his fellow man. In fact, *Rosh* writes (*Mishnah Pe'ah* 1:1) that Hashem values mitzvos through which we benefit our fellow, more than mitzvos that are between man and G-d.

Many sources indicate that although, generally, punishment for sins takes place primarily in the Next World, nevertheless, for hurting someone's feelings people suffer retribution in this world.

Therefore, every person must pay careful attention to everything he does or says that affects others—to ensure that he does not cause pain to others.

In truth, suffering retribution in the Next World is worse than suffering in this world. However, human nature is that one is not so affected by that which his eyes do not see and therefore (the fear of that punishment) does not move one as much. Therefore, we have mentioned that which people better understand.

One who is careful to avoid hurting another person will merit all the blessings mentioned in the Torah, and will have a good life in this world and in the next.

Aharon Yehudah Leib Shteinman

מכתב עוז ממרן ראש הישיבה שליט"א

בס"ד

הנה ידוע שבתורתינו הקדושה יש דינים בין אדם למקום וגם מה שבין אדם לחבירו, גם בעשרת הדברות יש גם דינים שלו לקונו וגם מה שאדם יוזהר מלעשות רע לבריות.

ואונאת דברים מבואר בבא מציעא נ"ח ע"ב שזה יותר חמור מאונאת ממון. וזה אין חילוק בין איש לאשתו או אשה לבעלה. ובגמ' ב"מ נ"ט שם כתוב שכיון שאשה דמעתה מצוי' אז אונאתה יותר חמור מה שמצערין אותה. וזה כולל בכל הדברים שגורם צער, ובפרט לצער אלמנה או יתומים חמור מאד.

ולהיפך חסד אין לשער מה שיכולין לזכות עי"ז, ומבואר ברא"ש בריש מסכת פיאה כי הקב"ה חפץ יותר במצות שיעשה בהם גם רצון הבריות מבמצות שבין אדם לקונו.

והנה בכמה מקומות משמע שאע"פ שבדרך כלל עיקר העונש הוא בעוה"ב ובעוה"ז לא נענשים על עבירות כ"כ, אבל על צער אנשים נענשים גם בעוה"ז.

כל א' ישים לב על כל מה שעושה או מדבר שלא יהי' דבר המצער חבירו.

והנה באמת כשנענשים בעולם הבא העונש יותר גרוע, אבל היות שאנשים מה שלא רואים כעת לא מתפעלים כ"כ, לכן אנו מדברים מה שכל א' מבין יותר.

והנזהר מלפגוע באנשים יחולו על ראשו כל הברכות האמורות בתורה, ויזכה לעונג בזה ובבא.

אהרן יודא לייב שטיינמן

Letter of Approbation from Rabbi Shmuel Kamenetsky שליט״א

בס״ד

שמואל קמנצקי
Rabbi S. Kamenetsky

Study: 215-473-1212
Home: 215-473-2798

2018 Upland Way
Philadelphia, Pa 19131

    While we all know that being a positive person and speaking to others in a positive tone leads to stronger, healthier relationships, many do not realize that this is an imperative of the Torah itself. It is the Torah that warns not to "aggrieve your fellow" (Rashi: with words), and forbids us to remind others of their past mistakes. *Sefer Hachinuch* teaches that we must be especially careful to avoid hurting young children with our words.

    We therefore see clearly that saying what we have to say in a way that is positive, that avoids hurting the other person, is not just for people who are naturally soft-spoken. It is a Torah requirement for every Jew, and a key to all the *mitzvos bein adam lachaveiro*.

    That is why the Chofetz Chaim Heritage Foundation has undertaken the task of producing the book you are about to read. The goal is to make the young women in our high schools, the very ones who will soon be building the next generation, familiar with these important *halachos* and *hashkafos*. Who better than the future wives and mothers of *Klal Yisrael* should be armed with the tools to build homes of *shalom bayis* and raise children with healthy, positive attitudes? And what better time to start sharpening these tools than while one is in high school, interacting with family, friends and classmates on an ongoing basis?

    It is my hope that through reading this book and internalizing its message, those who will soon establish Jewish homes will be prepared to do so upon a strong foundation of *bein adam lachaveiro*, thereby creating a brighter future for *Klal Yisrael*. May all who take it to heart be *zocheh* to a life of *shalom* and *brachah*, and to a share in bringing the Final Redemption very soon.

לע"נ

שיינדעל בת אברהם משה ע"ה

Dedicated in loving memory of

Shaindel Lax *a"h*

By her children

In honor of my dear granddaughters —
those who are ב"ה such a special part of my life, as
well as those who have yet to be born, בעז"ה

Dear Girls,

My hopes and brachos are not only for "my girls," but for all of you who are fortunate enough to read this special book; it is not just to be read, it is to be learned and lived. May its teachings inspire you to implement them as lessons for life. True happiness is the satisfaction we feel when we fulfill our potential. The following beautiful insight by Rav Eliyahu Dessler reminds us to constantly be aware of the power of our own potential.

> Every Act, Thought, Word
> is either
> Giving or Taking,
> Building or Destroying,
> Enhancing or Detracting.

May we always choose our words carefully and wisely, empowering our words to **give** chizuk, **build** strong bonds of friendship, and **enhance** relationships by not demanding more of others than we do of ourselves.

Love, your grandmother, "Ma"

P.S. "My Girls," always remember that in doing so you will be zocheh to emulate your grandfather and great-grandparents, z"l, who lived and taught these lessons so well. They saw both life and people in a positive light. They knew that a radiant smile or even silence could sometimes say much more than words.

לע"נ
יוסף יעקב לייב בן שלמה ז"ל
Rabbi Yaakov Deitsch z"l

נתן בן אריה דב ז"ל ואשתו לאה בת מאיר ע"ה
Mr. Nathan and Mrs. Lena Seiler z"l

שלמה בן משה ז"ל ואשתו פריידל בת פרץ ע"ה
Mr. Samuel and Mrs. Freida Deitsch z"l

ת.נ.צ.ב.ה

Dedicated by Zahava Deitsch

לזכר ולעלוי נשמת

אברהם בן משה ז"ל
ואשתו אסתר מינדל בת מרדכי יעקב הלוי ע"ה

In memory of
Albert and Elaine Moskowitz *z"l*

לע"נ משה בן אברהם ז"ל
*In memory of **Dr. Mark Moskowitz** z"l*

לע"נ אברהם משה בן רפאל הכהן ז"ל
*In memory of **Arnold Krause** z"l*

In memory of those we will always cherish

Dedicated by
Stuart Krause, Renee Moskowitz and family

In honor of Our Grandchildren,
*whose exceptional middos and sensitivity
are a shining example for their peers*
Dedicated by Rabbi Sheldon and Zelda Goldsmith

In honor of our dear daughter
Ariella Kutoff
*May you continue to grow.
We are so proud of you!
Love,
Daddy and Jessica Kutoff*

לע"נ אברהם בן משה ז"ל
נלב"ע י' מנחם אב תשע"ג
Dedicated by Zev & Susan Munk and family

In loving memory of our grandparents

לע"נ
הרב הגאון חיים יהוסף בן הרב יצחק שלום ארי-ה ליב זצ"ל
זאב בן יהודה ז"ל
רבקה מאטיל בת ר' יעקב ע"ה
שמואל שמחה בן אלתר געצעל הכהן זצ"ל
בתי-ה בילה בת צבי הערש ע"ה

May their holy neshamos continue to watch over us and protect all of Klal Yisrael.

Dedicated by the Fuchs family

לע"נ
ישראל דוב בן אהרן יעקב ז"ל
נלב"ע ה' אדר תשס"ב

In memory of
Irving Shimoff *z"l*
Dedicated by Robin and Warren Shimoff

Table of Contents

Acknowledgements	*xxiii*
Foreword	*xxviii*
Note to the Reader	*xxxiii*

Chapter 1: Introduction   5

DAY
1. Know Your Own Power ~ What speech really does
2. What Makes It God ~ Our guide to happiness
3. What Did You Say? ~ Ripple effect of words
4. 40,000 Words a Day ~ The impact of quantity
5. Plan to Succeed ~ Practical steps toward change
6. Paint Job ~ Designing our own world
7. Loved by Others ~ Making and keeping friends
8. In Style ~ Changing the norm

Chapter 2: What Fuels Hurtful Speech   23

DAY   ~ Middos

9. About to Burst ~ Anger
10. The Great and Powerful Me ~ Arrogance
11. The Blame Game ~ Blaming others
12. And the Winner Is... ~ Competitiveness
13. Down a Few Notches ~ Deflating others to inflate oneself
14. "I Rule!" ~ Desire to dominate
15. Heart Surgery ~ Hatred
16. Long-Term Health ~ Hatred 2: Blind to spiritual impact
17. A Thin Disguise ~ Hatred 3: Hidden hostility
18. Your Honor ~ Honor seeking

DAY		
19	Holy War	~ Idealism
20	Danger of Explosion	~ Impatience
21	The Price of an Impulse	~ Impulsive speech
22	Wearing Armor	~ Insecurity
23	Feeling Green	~ Jealousy
24	Kicking the Habit	~ Lack of thought
25	The Perfect Problem	~ Perfectionism

DAY	~ Situations	
26	The Picky Patient	~ Illness/lack of sleep
27	Imaginary Enemies	~ Imagined insults
28	"Well, What Do You Expect?"	~ Justification
29	Misunderstood	~ Miscommunication
30	Ha-Ha	~ Misguided humor
31	Protecting the Border	~ Need for privacy
32	Either-Or	~ Negating the positive

Chapter 3: Insults of Character and Reputation   77

DAY		
33	Bursting Their Bubble	~ Undermining others' pride
34	Free to Move Ahead	~ Reminders of past mistakes
35	My Interesting Past	~ Revealing past sins
36	Not Normal	~ Causing others to feel self-conscious
37	Who Do You Think You Are?	~ Insulting family background
38	Photoshop	~ Damaging others' self-image
39	Ulterior Motives	~ Doubting sincerity

DAY		
	Chapter 4: **Offensive, Disrespectful Speech**	**93**
40	Bursting With Blessing! ~ The urge to shout	
41	Use Only as Directed ~ Making others feel inferior	
42	Talking Funny ~ Ridiculing accents, pronunciation	
43	Looking Good ~ Insulting physical appearance	
44	Nothing Left to Lose ~ Humiliating criticism	
45	The Speaker ~ Embarrassing a speaker/performer	
46	What's in a Name ~ Unwanted/negative nicknames	

DAY	*Chapter 5:* **Statements that Damage Self-Image**	**109**
47	The Absentminded Professor ~ Criticizing forgetfulness	
48	Creating an Undertow ~ Deflating confidence	
49	Threads of Brilliance ~ Coloring others' self-image	
50	Their Pride and Joy ~ Finding the negative	
51	The Career Critic ~ Belittling someone's profession	
52	Recipe for Disaster ~ Criticizing the cook	
53	To Each Her Own ~ Ridiculing others' taste	
54	Nothing to Celebrate ~ Pleasure in others' misfortune	
55	"I Told You So" ~ Unhelpful reminders	
56	Loaded Questions ~ Insults hidden in questions	
57	Don't Ask ~ Nosy questions	
58	Boasting or Sharing? ~ Relating good news	
59	The Happy Buyer ~ Too-late shopping advice	
60	Helpful Hints ~ Killing with kindness	

Chapter 6: Manipulative, Defensive Tactics — 143

DAY
- 61 The Dark Side ~ Spreading pessimism
- 62 Enough Said ~ Overly long rebuke
- 63 "I Can't Say" ~ Anonymous rumors
- 64 "Boo!" ~ Frightening others
- 65 Who's Laughing? ~ Practical jokes
- 66 Really Pushing It ~ Nagging
- 67 "Don't Ask Me" ~ Harsh refusal to help
- 68 Or Else ~ Threats
- 69 The Last Word ~ Adding insult to injury

Chapter 7: Counterproductive Comments — 163

DAY
- 70 How Dare You ~ Dramatizing
- 71 Seeing the Future ~ Lashing out
- 72 Just Trying to Help ~ Dealing with unwanted help
- 73 The Eggshell Skull Rule ~ Causing unforeseen damage
- 74 In His Shoes ~ Specific sensitivities
- 75 Spilled Milk ~ Irritation at clumsiness
- 76 Amazing Praise ~ Tainted praise
- 77 Get Over It ~ Belittling others' problems
- 78 My Favorite Things ~ Rerouting a conversation
- 79 The Nitpicker ~ Correcting small details
- 80 Just Testing ~ Testing others' limits

Chapter 8: Mocking — 187
DAY 81 — The Mimic's Weapon ~ Mocking personal traits

Chapter 9: Revealing Private Information — 191
DAY 82 — Betrayed ~ Violating trust
DAY 83 — The Word's Out ~ Disclosing confidential information

Chapter 10: Misinforming and Misleading People — 197
DAY 84 — False Hope ~ Unfulfilled offers of help
DAY 85 — Chain Reaction ~ Delayed impact
DAY 86 — Just Browsing ~ Asking prices under false pretenses

Chapter 11: Subtle Negative Statements — 205
DAY 87 — Beware the Undertone ~ Muttering
DAY 88 — Get the Hint? ~ Insulting hints and sayings
DAY 89 — The Cutting Edge ~ Sarcasm
DAY 90 — A Day at the Zoo ~ Comparing people to animals
DAY 91 — Music to Their Ears ~ Tone of voice

Chapter 12: Nonverbal Ona'as Devarim — 221
DAY 92 — In Your Face ~ Angry expression
DAY 93 — Unsend ~ Written communications
DAY 94 — In Your Hands ~ Hand gestures
DAY 95 — The Deadly Stare ~ Scornful looks and expressions

DAY		
96	Is Someone Saying Something? ~ Ignoring someone	
97	The Silent Treatment ~ Silence as a weapon	

Chapter 13: Everyday Challenges — 235

DAY		
98	Hello, Goodbye ~ Cell phone etiquette	
99	Just Say "No" ~ Navigating the negative	
100	Same Story, New Ending ~ Recurring challenges	

Chapter 14: Strategies — 243

DAY	~ Think	
101	The Big Payoff ~ Envision your reward	
102	Prepared for Landing ~ Preparing our responses	
103	Fork in the Road ~ Thinking before speaking	

DAY	~ Feel	
104	Image Transplant ~ Cultivating love for others	
105	Human Like Me ~ Developing empathy	
106	Variety ~ Accepting differences	

DAY	~ Act	
107	Be A Visionary ~ Focus on others' potential	
108	The Remedy ~ Caring for others	
109	Word Exchange ~ Choosing the softest words	
110	Reading the Signs ~ Picking up non-verbal cues	
111	Pass It Along ~ Relating others' praises	
112	Going Another Round ~ Avoiding pointless conflicts	

DAY	~ React	
113	Take 15 ~ Cooling down from anger	

DAY		
114	No Offense ~ Overlooking insults	
115	Bouncing Back ~ Dealing with insults	

Chapter 15: Starting Now — 275

DAY		
116	Creating a Pearl ~ Teshuvah	
117	Sorry About That ~ Forgiveness	
118	The Sure Cure ~ Daily learning	
119	In Other Words ~ Test your understanding	

Don't Shut the Book Yet

On the Receiving End	289
Afterword	292

The Positive Revolution

~ More pathways to happiness

Shmiras Haloshon Yomi	298
Machsom L'fi	300
How to Live a Happier Life	303
Spreading the Language of Ahavas Yisrael	304
Tefillah al Hadibbur	306

Acknowledgments

Our gratitude to Hashem *Yisbarach* is inexpressible for His having permitted us to produce this book and continue to spread the concept of *shmiras haloshon* in all its facets to communities throughout the world. At the urging of HaRav Pam, *zt"l*, and with the enthusiastic support of HaRav Shteinman, *shlita*, in 2009 we produced **Positive Word Power**, a work focused on eradicating *ona'as devarim*, hurting others with the words we speak. With astounding *siyata d'Shmaya*, that book has been eagerly embraced by tens of thousands throughout *Klal Yisrael*. Its message has brought self-awareness, understanding, improved family relationships, stronger friendships and real positive change.

With the teen version of **Positive Word Power**, we hope to once again have *siyata d'Shmaya* to spread and firmly implant these blessings within the hearts of our precious daughters.

As this book is the "offspring" of the original, we must begin by acknowledging the groundbreaking work on this subject, *The Power of Words*, by **Rabbi Zelig Pliskin**, whose original treatment of this subject was the launch-point for the first edition of *Positive Word Power*; **Rabbi Eliyahu Lamm** and **Rabbi Eliyahu Klugman** who meticulously reviewed the **original** version to ensure its accuracy; **Rabbi Henoch Moshe Levine** who provided invaluable help in researching sources, and **Mrs. Tzivia Nagelberg** whose outline of the concepts in Rabbi Pliskin's work formed the book's structure.

Mrs. Chana Nestlebaum, the writer of this book and the original **Positive Word Power**, has been the voice of our organization since it began 24 years ago. In this and the original volume, she has created clear, believable scenarios and insightful postscripts that turn a daily learning text into a readable and engaging daily boost.

Mrs. Shaindy Appelbaum, editor/editorial director, is directly responsible for the carefully crafted, progressive flow of this book and the original, designed to elevate the reader step-by-step. In this and countless other Chofetz Chaim Heritage Foundation projects, she has used her talent, wisdom and perseverance to inspire *Klal Yisrael* and change the world.

In gearing this volume to teenage girls, we relied upon **Mrs. Devoirelle Hager** of our **Mishmeres** program, whose careful review and insights greatly enhanced this edition, and **Mrs. Sarah Weiss** of *Bais Yaakov d'Rav Meir*, who has truly embraced the cause of *ona'as devarim* awareness, and provided her wise guidance to ensure that this book reaches its readers with maximum impact.

We thank **Mrs. Tova Finkelman** and **Mrs. Miriam Margoshes** for their efficient editing and accurate proof-reading.

The eye-catching cover and engaging layout bears the unique stamp of the incomparable graphic designer, **Ben Gasner**.

The inside cover by **Mrs. Chani Finkelstein** of **Masterpiece Design** is the perfect finishing touch.

Many people have given of their time and expertise to review samples and ensure that *Positive Word Power for Teens* would speak with an authentic voice to a wide range of teens. We gratefully acknowledge: **Rabbi Avi Bernstein, Mrs. Chani Juravel, Mrs. Brocha Esther Bard, Dr. Ruchama Fund, Mrs. Risa Gross, Mrs. Yael Kaisman, Mrs. Bila Kviat, Mrs. Zlata Press and Mrs. Lynda Zentman** and the many others who offered their help and advice during this book's development.

We would also like to thank the many teens who gave their opinion on everything from cover design to page layout to appropriateness of the scenarios to language usage. Thank you—this is your book!

Chofetz Chaim Heritage Foundation reaches over 50,000 people through its many programs, yet it is only as strong as the people who comprise it. We gratefully acknowledge the staff, volunteers and leaders who work tirelessly to create a culture of caring and spread the language of *Ahavas Yisrael* throughout the world.

Our success flows from the Torah leaders who map out our path:

The Manchester Rosh Yeshivah, HaGaon HaRav Yehudah Zev Segal, *zt"l*, the founding Rabbinic Advisor of our organization; HaGaon HaRav Shmuel Kamenetsky, *shlita*, the Chairman of our Rabbinical Board; and HaGaon HaRav Avraham Pam, *zt"l*, and *yblc"t* HaGaon HaRav Yaakov Perlow, *shlita*, members of our Rabbinical Board of Advisors.

Rabbi Hillel Litwack, Rabbi Eliyahu Lamm, Rabbi Eliyahu Brog and Rabbi Mordechai Klein, who volunteer their time to answer questions on our

Shaila Hotline, guiding those who seek to properly fulfill the mitzvah of *shmiras haloshon*.

Much of our impact emanates from our many publishing projects which reach schools, *shuls* and communities throughout the world. We thank **Rabbi Moshe Mordechai Lowy**, *shlita*, Rav of Agudas Israel of Toronto, who consistently gives of his precious time to review and answer questions regarding our publishing projects. He also regularly contributes halachic responses to educators' *shmiras haloshon* questions in **Impressions**, our popular newsletter for teachers.

We have also gained immeasurably from the involvement of **Rabbi Avi Shulman** in **CCHF**. For the past 12 years he has lent his wise counsel and expertise to the enhancement of **Impressions**, ensuring that its message represents the true ideals of Torah *chinuch*.

We are deeply grateful to the outstanding people of the Chofetz Chaim Heritage Foundation:

To our Chairman of the Board, **Reb Shlomo Yehuda Rechnitz** and his devoted wife **Tamar**, whose vision, enthusiasm and generosity of spirit has helped us spread the language of *ahavas Yisrael* further than ever before. Reb Shlomo Yehuda's involvement in mapping a strategy to conquer *loshon hora* and *ona'as devarim* is indispensable! The dream of "Every Child, Every Day" truly belongs to him, and we are forever indebted to him for partnering with us to fulfill this dream. May Hashem reward him for his great generosity and grant him much *nachas* from his family, and *hatzlachah* in all his endeavors.

To our board of directors who have been a tremendous help in forging our path: **Rabbi Raymond Beyda, Abraham Biderman, Aba Claman, Nachman Futterman, David Lobel, Yitzchok Mashitz, Ari Parnes, George Rohr, Kurt Rothschild, David Shweky, Gedaliah Weinberger** and **Moshe Zakheim**.

To the many dynamic speakers who have inspired us over the years, we offer our sincere thanks.

If you have benefited from a *shmiras haloshon* program or publication over the past few years, it is thanks to the selfless dedication of our staff: **Rabbi Yonah Koenig, Mr. Dovid Kogel, Mr. Velvel Kunofsky, Mr. Joshua Last, Mr. Ahron Lieberman, Rabbi Levi Yitzchok Novoseller, Rabbi Shlomo Ornstein, Rabbi Yosef Pruzansky, Mr. Boruch Reiss, Rabbi Elchonon Snyder, Rabbi Shea Steinberg, Mrs. Chany Bernstein, Mrs. Tehila Danziger, Mrs. Yitty Derbaremdiger, Mrs. Machla Eichenstein, Mrs. Leah Fischer, Mrs. Tziri Frank, Mrs. Blimi Friedman, Mrs. Ruchy Friedman, Mrs. Rivky Goldstein, Mrs. Rivky Goldwurm, Mrs. Sara Leah Gordon, Shevi Greenfeld, Mrs. Miriam Grossman,**

Mrs. Devoirelle Hager, Mrs. Kaila Halpern, Mrs. Michalle Hammer, Mrs. Tzirel Honig, Mrs. Hindy Housman, Mrs. Tamar Hutman, Mrs. Chaya Israel, Mrs. Gitty Kalikstein, Mrs. Batsheva Kaplan, Chasie Kaplan, Mrs. Breindy Kertzner, Mrs. Estie Koot, Mrs. Shira Lazar, Mrs. Esther Leibowitz, Mrs. Blimi Lesser, Rivky Levi, Mrs. Suri Levy, Mrs. Chava Londinski, Mrs. Simi Mandelcorn, Mrs. Sara Gila Margulies, Mrs. Rochel Mendlowitz, Chaya Meth, Mrs. Shoshana Miller, Mrs. Tziporah Esther Mittler, Mrs. Esther Mohr, Mrs. Chana Moskowitz, Mrs. Leah Ozeri, Mrs. Ruchy Perlstein, Shira Rothschild, Mrs. Chayie Schachter, Mrs. Rivka Schwartzberg, Mrs. Leah Sekula, Mrs. Rivka Sherwinter, Mrs. Sara Stern, Mrs. Chavi Twersky, Mrs. Yitty Zehnwirth, Mrs. Faigy Zelcer, Mrs. Sima Zinnes.

We would also like to thank our staff in Eretz Yisrael: **Rabbi Binyomin and Mrs. Shoshana Cohen, Mrs. Tzippy Gottlieb, Mrs. Rochel Orloweck and Mrs. Naomi Rottman.**

The Chofetz Chaim Heritage Foundation is forever grateful to **Rabbi Mendel Kessin**, whose penetrating taped *shiurim* on *shmiras haloshon* inspired us to start our organization.

Our thanks to **Rabbi Heshy Leiner, Rabbi Nochum Stilerman** and **Rabbi Heshy Augenbraun** for their crucial advice.

To our 450 local coordinators—the *rabbanim*, principals and lay people who have lifted the banner of *shmiras haloshon* in their shuls, schools and communities—thank you so much.

We wish to acknowledge the special partnership we have enjoyed with **ArtScroll/Mesorah Publications**, which began in 1995 with *The Chofetz Chaim: A Lesson a Day*. Since then, this visionary publishing house has been instrumental in our effort to spread the message of *Ahavas Yisrael* throughout the world. **Rabbi Nosson Scherman** and **Rabbi Meir Zlotowitz**, general editors of ArtScroll/Mesorah, took a strong interest in this project, and their vast expertise added much to the final product. A special thanks to **Avrohom Biderman** who has always been a crucial link in the production of our *sefarim* and to **Mendy Herzberg** and the entire typesetting/graphics department at ArtScroll, who went far beyond the call of duty to complete this project in a timely manner.

To those who have supported us financially—the major supporters who wish to remain anonymous, the main sponsors of this book and the families who have helped bring this book to publication by sponsoring a day—may the great *z'chus* of *shmiras haloshon* stand by you and your families, bringing abundant *brachah*, *shmirah* and *shalom* into your lives.

Above and beyond all of those mentioned here is the clear *siyata d'Shmaya* that has consistently transformed our ideas and visions into truly momentous forces of positive change throughout *Klal Yisrael*, and this *brachah* is without a doubt the result of the enthusiastic way in which so many individuals from across the country and around the world have embraced our goals. To all of those who have united under the banner of *ahavas Yisrael* and have generously given your support to our organization's projects, your idealism and positive vision of *Klal Yisrael's* future is what inspires us to forge onward.

May all who work toward the dream of a Jewish nation living together with *achdus*, compassion and kindness merit to see the realization of that dream with the coming of the Final Redemption, may it be very soon!

The Chofetz Chaim Heritage Foundation
Nissan 5774

Foreword

A Message From The Chofetz Chaim Heritage Foundation

It's hard to imagine now, but 30 years ago a person would rarely hear the words "*shmiras haloshon*" used among friends, or even in school. Many people thought of *lashon hara* as something impossible to avoid. Learning *Sefer Chofetz Chaim* was not widespread. Shmiras Haloshon Yomi was barely known.

But all that began to change in 1989, when the Chofetz Chaim Heritage Foundation took up the mission of Rav Yehudah Zev Segal, *zt"l*, the great Manchester Rosh Yeshivah, who saw the damage that *lashon hara* was doing to *Klal Yisrael* and sought a way to spread awareness of this far and wide. His Shmiras Haloshon Yomi calendar, through which thousands of Jews came to learn the *halachos* of speech every day, has become a standard learning tool in schools, yeshivos and homes around the world. Today, *baruch Hashem*, the message is out. No one would think it odd for someone to stop a conversation and say, "Maybe that's *lashon hara*." The war is not yet won, but at least we all have joined the battle.

Yet there remains another area of *shmiras haloshon* that has only recently begun to receive attention, and that is *onaas devarim*. We have become educated in how we may or may not speak *about* others, but many of us do not give a great deal of thought to the way we speak *to* others. Of course we know that harsh words can sting; we've all felt that sting ourselves. But in the fast back-and-forth of conversation, in the heat of anger or irritation, in the face of someone else's seemingly thoughtless or hurtful act against us, we may find it difficult to stop and think about the long- and short-term impact of our words.

Just as many people once thought *lashon hara* was impossible to stop, many people believe *onaas devarim*—hurting others with words—cannot be stopped.

We get annoyed, frustrated, hurt or tense, and the words pop out. Can a normal human being prevent that from happening?

The beloved Rosh Yeshivah Rav Avrohom Pam, *zt"l*, believed that we can and we must. In 1998, he urged the Chofetz Chaim Heritage Foundation to undertake the mission of raising awareness of *ona'as devarim* in *Klal Yisrael*, and in 2009 **Positive Word Power** was published in response to the Rosh Yeshivah's request.

That original version of **Positive Word Power** was written to inspire as much change in the area of *ona'as devarim* as we have seen in other areas of *shmiras haloshon*. In the five years since then, we have witnessed a revolution. Tens of thousands of people have used this *sefer* to learn how to eliminate the destructive effects of negative words from their lives. They've learned to recognize the difference between constructive criticism and insult, pleasant humor and bitter sarcasm, caring inquiries and intrusive questions, and much more. They've learned how to think before they speak, and to speak in a way that protects the other person's dignity. Thousands of readers have testified to how this book has improved their family life, friendships and spirituality.

As more and more people discovered these benefits, educators began asking for a version that would speak directly to teens, so that they too could share the gifts that positive speech brings to one's life. The result, the volume you are now holding, is written for you. In the scenarios that start each lesson, you'll recognize all the various types of teens you know—the popular and the introverted, the sensitive and the brash, the friendly and the snobbish—as they deal with the day-to-day events and challenges of a teen's life. You'll find that this book presents very few outright villains; it's about nice, normal, well-meaning people like you, who sometimes say things that hurt someone else.

Our goal is that everyone learning this book will come to realize that those "words that hurt" cause much more than temporary damage. Little by little they create barriers between us and our friends, us and our siblings, even us and our parents. But when we become aware of what we're saying and take seriously the impact of our words, when we learn positive ways to express our needs and thoughts, we take down those barriers and replace them with live, vibrant, loving connections.

Life can be filled with happiness and friendship, even when it's also filled with challenge. **Positive Word Power** teaches us how to grasp this priceless gift of love and friendship–the gift every human heart desires more than anything else in the world.

A Message From Rav Avraham Pam
~ Excerpts from a 1998 address

The crucial importance of guarding one's power of speech—*shmiras hadibur*—has become very well known as it relates to *lashon hara*. However, another prohibition in *shmiras hadibur* is rarely addressed, and that is *ona'as devarim*—hurtful speech... It is comprised of words that cut deeply and cause a great deal of pain, and is the underlying cause of many tragedies.

The source of this prohibition is the *passuk* (*Vayikra* 25:17): *"V'lo sonu ish es amiso*—one may not cause pain to one's fellow." Rashi defines this as *ona'as devarim*, specifying that it refers to using words to hurt the people in our lives with whom we interact.

The *Sefer HaChinuch* describes *ona'as devarim* as a prohibition against "saying to another Jew words that cause pain and suffering, from which he can find no relief." They are words that leave their victim defenseless.

As Shlomo HaMelech says in *Mishlei* (12), words can cut deeply, "like a sword," but they are an equally potent force for good, for "the language of the wise heals." This is the contrast between careless speech, and the healing power and happiness that speech can bring.

Like swords, words are sometimes used as weapons, wielded in anger or outright malice. More often, *ona'as devarim* results from simple carelessness, from speaking without regard to what the consequences might be. **Nevertheless, just as a sword swung carelessly can cut as deeply as one that is wielded with purpose, so can a careless word hurt as much as a deliberate insult.**

Unfortunately, people say brutal things, often with no forethought: insulting remarks, demeaning expressions, derogatory statements, and name-calling are not uncommon at all... These words leave a tragic imprint on the spirit and soul of the person who is the object of such torrents of insults... It doesn't matter whether it's done deliberately to hurt, or out of uncontrolled anger, or out of carelessness. Sometimes the insult comes in the form of a joke, but the joke hurts; the other party doesn't see it as funny—it leaves a scar.

The Torah's prohibition against afflicting one another goes a step further, adding the words "and you shall fear Hashem, your G-d." Why is this statement made here? Perhaps a person has enough self-control to avoid harsh words when he is with outsiders. Perhaps, when there's company around, he is genial and polite. But what happens when the audience goes home and the door shuts behind him?

Some people feel free to use abusive language in private. It seems to them that nobody is listening. The Torah reminds us that this is not so: Someone is listening; Someone is recording every word. If a person were able to find the strength to control his speech in front of other people, then these words, "and you shall fear Hashem, your G-d," should help him maintain the sense of being seen and heard even when he is in the privacy of his home.

The Vilna Gaon describes this graphically in his famous *Iggeres HaGra*, which he wrote to his Rebbetzin while en route to Eretz Yisrael. Included among the advice and blessings he gives her is his urging to carefully guard against improper speech: "They [Hashem's emissaries] accompany each person regularly, and they never separate from him. Wherever he goes they go—and they record every word."

Can you imagine? A person talks in private. He makes sure that nobody is around. Yet in reality he is surrounded by "secretaries" who record everything, word for word. One day it will be played back to this person, and he will find it difficult to believe that he ever said such things.

Therefore the Torah says, "Do not afflict your fellow, and fear your G-d, for I am Hashem your G-d."

Once the words leave one's mouth, it is too late. I would suggest this advice. One should ask oneself: **"Was I sent down from Heaven to this world to make life miserable for someone, for anyone? Is that why the Divine gift of speech was given to me?"** To degrade and defile this gift of G-d—speech—is an insult to the Creator, especially when the same power can be used to heal and soothe a depressed spirit.

Much more needs to be said publicly about the tragedies spawned by *ona'as devarim*. This concept needs the kind of exposure that has been given to *lashon hara* in recent years. More yeshivos and Bais Yaakovs should be teaching their students to recognize this type of speech and restrain themselves from using it....Powerful words should be written about this topic and circulated widely to encourage people to use the gift of speech wisely. **Certainly, everyone should understand the imperative to be extremely careful in avoiding words that inflict wounds that may linger for a long, long time, or perhaps never heal.**

In contrast to the devastation wrought by unkind words, the Chofetz Chaim writes of the magnificent reward for one who thinks before he speaks (*Shmiras HaLoshon, Shaar Zechirah*, Ch. 11, citing *Iggeres HaGra*). He writes: "One who keeps his mouth closed merits the *or haganuz*, the light of Creation that the *Ribbono Shel Olam* set aside for the righteous to enjoy in the World to Come." This light is so radiant that not even an angel can imagine its beauty or the joy of basking in it. Yet this is the reward for simply sealing one's lips when necessary.

May the *Ribbono Shel Olam* give us the *siyata d'Shmaya* to appreciate the great gift of speech, which bears such golden blessings, and to use it properly, so that we will be worthy to witness the *geulah,* speedily in our days.

Note to the Reader
Ona'as Devarim ~ Hurtful Speech

Ona'as devarim is a verbal attack in which other people are hurt by the weapon of harsh, angry or insensitive words. The Torah contains several prohibitions against this type of speech.

The first is the commandment, "*Lo sonu ish es amiso* ~ You shall not cause pain to your fellow" (*Vayikra* 25:17). Rashi explains that this prohibition applies to the words we speak in our personal relationships.

And it is a total prohibition; we violate this commandment even if we cause the slightest pain for the briefest moment, unless there is no other way to accomplish an important constructive purpose.

Harsh words also violate the Torah's commandment of "*V'ahavta l'reiacha kamocha* ~ And you shall love your fellow as yourself" (*Vayikra* 19:18). Because we certainly would not want to be the victim of harsh words, we are not allowed to use such words against others. Finally, the embarrassment *ona'as devarim* may cause violates the Torah's unequivocal prohibition against shaming others.

In the lessons that follow, you will come to see how *ona'as devarim* subtly seeps into so many of our daily interactions. In this way, you will have the chance to build your awareness of the attitudes, situations and expressions that can cause harm, and learn ways to avoid doing so.

But what do you do with this awareness? At the end of each day's lesson, the "**Reality Check**" section guides you to think about how the specific topic being discussed applies to your own life. It offers a practical suggestion for improving your interactions in that area and invites you to take action. When you decide to follow through on a particular commitment, it is recommended that you do so with the words *"b'li neder,"* so that your commitment does not have the force of a vow.

You will also see a feature of each day's lesson called "**What if....**" Here you will have the opportunity to discuss the issue at hand more fully, considering other ways it may have been handled or other variations of the scenario that might have rendered a different result.

Tishrei

*In honor of our children Joseph, Ezra, Julie Bibi
and Albert & Adele Pardo*

Dedicated by Ruth and Reuben Bibi

As a z'chus for our family

Dedicated by Mr. and Mrs. Joel Greenman

---

*As a z'chus for our children
Eliyahu Binyomen Menachem, Moshe Daniel,
Sarah Chana Simcha and Rivkah Shirah
Dedicated by Daddy and Mommy*

Shevat

As a z'chus for our family

Dedicated by Rabbi and Rebbitzen

Yitzchok Frankel

Dedicated as a z'chus for our family

by Joel & Andy Schochet

לע"נ חנה שרה בת יחיאל זאב ע"ה נלב"ע כ' שבט תשע"ג

Sivan

לע"נ אברהם אליעזר בן יעקב צבי ז"ל

In memory of Mr. Abraham Himmel z"l

Dedicated by Rivka & Martin Himmel and family

הצלחה בכל ענינים: יעל ליבא בת יוכבד תחי'

מאיר דוד בן יוכבד נ"י חנה בת יוכבד תחי'

נפתלי בן יוכבד נ"י

נטע יצחק בן גיטל נ"י ויוכבד בת רות תחי'

Dedicated to the most amazing
Shoshana Schwartz
In honor of your bas mitzvah

Love,
Bubby and Upachka

Chapter 1

Introduction

We are about to set out on a guided tour. The place we will be visiting is a place you go to every day: the familiar landscape of person-to-person interaction. What we'll notice on this tour is that this potentially peaceful, beautiful landscape is strewn with litter: the careless comments, hurtful "jokes," tactless questions and insulting criticism that we toss out into the world without much thought. Because this "litter" is everywhere, we don't even notice it, and we don't think anyone will really notice what we add to it. Yet it doesn't just blow away; little by little, it poisons the environment and distorts everything that is beautiful in our lives.

Like someone tossing litter out of a car window, when we toss out a careless word we rarely look back to see where it has landed. We cannot imagine that it had much impact. However, the Torah teaches us right from the beginning that words have a boundless impact. It teaches that Hashem created the entire universe with ten utterances—words—illustrating for us in the clearest possible way that words create worlds. Our own words are a continuation of Hashem's creative work, forming the environment of our families, classrooms, schools, communities and ultimately all of *Klal Yisrael*.

As we travel the familiar landscape of relationships between siblings, families, classmates and friends, you will recognize words you've said and heard, situations you've experienced, and people who are like some you know. But you'll view the landscape with new eyes as you are awakened to the ripple effect of these common conversations and comments. With *siyata d'Shmaya*, you'll learn how to beautify the environment of your world by spreading words of respect, kindness and praise. In doing so you will acquire the tools to plant your own Gan Eden, right here on earth.

DAY 1

Know Your Own Power
~What speech really does

א תשרי
1 Tishrei/Cycle 1

א שבט
1 Shevat/Cycle 2

א סיון
1 Sivan/Cycle 3

> *Your classmate is helping out at her parents' clothing shop. You walk up to the counter to pay for your new skirt and sweater. As you lay your items down, you say, "Hi, Mindy. How are you?"*
>
> *Those two short sentences contain five words. They are said so often that they might seem to have no real meaning. We all know that Mindy is not going to tell you about the store's loss of business or her recent asthma attack. In fact, as she busily presses various buttons on the cash register, she might not even hear your question.*
>
> *It would seem, then, that those five words came out of your mouth and simply evaporated into the air like a puff of breath on a cold day. You spoke, but in essence, nothing happened.*
>
> *Is this true?*

We learn in *Bereishis* that Hashem created the entire world with ten utterances. That means that words are the prime creative force.

We might think, "Fine; Hashem's words can create the universe, but *my* words are just words." That's how it seems, but it's not how it is.

Our G-d-given ability to speak is the result of the breath that Hashem blew into Adam. It was a breath that came from within Hashem, a tiny transfusion of Hashem's own essence which equipped mankind to recognize Him, communicate with Him and sanctify His Name in the world. Therefore our speech is a part of Hashem and carries that creative force. What seems like nothing much—five ordinary words—is in reality nothing less than Divine. Those five words are five little bits of your own personal spiritual essence, pushed out of your mouth and released into the world.

Just as Hashem created His world through words, so do we. If our life is filled with friendship and happiness, it is because we speak to people in a way that brings others close to us. If our life is filled with conflict, it may be because our words create divisions between ourselves and others. The key to creating a world filled with love, friendship, respect and acceptance is to recognize the incredible power and value of our words.

Imagine each of your words as the wood, bricks, paint and furniture that make up the home in which you live. When you build a home, you are creating your surroundings: the place where you dwell, think, study, sleep, eat, *daven*, laugh and cry. Naturally, you want that dwelling to be a pleasant, serene, inviting place. Your words build the dwelling you will inhabit in this world, and inherit in the World to Come. If you learn to choose your words with care, to choose what is positive, beautiful and fine, you will build untold goodness into every day and every relationship in your life.

> **Reality Check:**
> How well do I use my power of speech when I feel challenged? I will think of five ways I could benefit by gaining better control of my power of speech.

> **What If...**
> a person finds it very difficult to think before she speaks? How would this affect her life? How might she help herself improve?

---

1 Tishrei — מלמד זכות על עם ישראל
Dedicated by Perach Gabay and family

1 Shevat — As a *z'chus* for our family
Dedicated by Mr. and Mrs. Joel Zipper

1 Sivan — In memory of Murray Niedober z"l לע״נ מרדכי בן יצחק ז״ל
Dedicated by his wife, children and grandchildren

DAY 2

What Makes It Good
~ Our guide to happiness

ב תשרי
2 Tishrei/Cycle 1

ב שבט
2 Shevat/Cycle 2

ב סיון
2 Sivan/Cycle 3

> Yaffa arrived at her seminary classmate's wedding. The hall, the most elegant one in town, looked like the ballroom of a royal palace. Music was provided by a well-known singer and a six-piece, highly professional band. The food was bountiful, all cooked and presented with gourmet perfection.
>
> But Yaffa found the evening difficult and depressing. Having come late, she had to take a seat at a table of girls from the kallah's high-school class. Yaffa didn't know any of them, and they were so excited to catch up with each other that they barely gave Yaffa a second glance. She left the wedding early, feeling like a social misfit.
>
> The next night, Yaffa went with a group of girls to help a different friend move into a new apartment. The night was spent in hard labor, lifting boxes, unpacking, stacking dishes in the cabinets, cleaning out the refrigerator and other such chores. The girls took a break to eat some lukewarm pizza served atop an inverted cardboard carton—a far cry from the previous night's feast. But to Yaffa, the evening was perfect. Surrounded by the warmth of her friends, immersed in conversation and laughter, she wished the night didn't have to end.

How could a night of hard work moving into an apartment be so much more enjoyable than an evening spent as a pampered wedding guest? The answer is that nothing gladdens a person's heart and soul like the feeling of being connected. We all need to have "our people" who know us well: who we are, what matters to us, what challenges we face, what makes us happy, what we need

8 Chapter One: Introduction

and what we have to give. We need people with whom we feel comfortable being ourselves, for they value us for ourselves.

The most ordinary circumstances, or even difficult situations, can fill us with happiness if our personal feeling of connection is present. On the other hand, the most exquisite event can leave us cold if we experience it with a feeling of isolation or rejection. **If there were a formula for human happiness, by far the main ingredient would be "positive relationships."** Nothing is a stronger indicator of a person's happiness than the quality of her friendships and family relationships. In other words, a person with good relationships usually feels she has a good life, even if she faces many challenges. When we connect in a positive, loving way with each other, we feel happy and alive.

Since Hashem provides us with all our needs, it would make sense that He has provided us with a way to fulfill this most essential need—and He has. It is a precise tool for building and maintaining our relationships, filling us with the sense of happiness and energy that we all crave. That tool is the Torah, the "tree of life," and specifically the laws of *shmiras haloshon* and *ona'as devarim*. **Because words are so powerful a creative force in this world, Hashem has given us instructions on how to use them with care.** He has fenced off dangerous territory that can lead to the damage and destruction of our relationships, and has left open to us a wide world of kind, caring, bond-building words that create good will and positive feelings between us and others.

The Torah provides us with perfect guidance and the *halachos* enable us to apply the Torah's teachings to every facet of our daily lives. If we learn these laws and use them, we are guaranteed to build a life surrounded by caring friends, loving family and a warm, supportive community.

2 Tishrei — לע"נ אבא בן לאה ז"ל
לזכות פארטונה שלומית בת מיסה שתחי'
2 Shevat — לע"נ דוב בער בן אברהם יעקב ז"ל
לע"נ אהובה בת יעקב ע"ה נלב"ע י"ח כסלו
2 Sivan — In memory of Isser *ben* Yaakov z"l
Dedicated by his daughter Betsy Schrott

Reality Check:

If there are people with whom I don't get along, I will think about the types of conversations we have. Is there a more positive approach I could take? Are there words or attitudes I should modify to avoid generating negativity?

What If...

the girls at Yaffa's table had recognized her discomfort? What might they have done to help her feel connected? What might Yaffa have done to connect to the girls?

DAY 3

What Did You Say?
~ Ripple effect of words

ג תשרי
3 Tishrei/Cycle 1

ג שבט
3 Shevat/Cycle 2

ג סיון
3 Sivan/Cycle 3

Ruthie was furious at Nechama, her older sister. What part of "don't tell anyone" did she fail to understand? Just because she was older, did that mean she had to be a spy? An informer? She had to tell their mother everything that happened? Now Ruthie's mother knew that she had lost the gold necklace her grandmother had given her. Couldn't Nechama mind her own business and let Ruthie have a chance to look for it some more?

Nechama walked into the girls' shared bedroom.

"Don't think I don't know what you did," Ruthie hissed. "Mommy already asked me about the necklace. She was so upset!"

"Well, I didn't think it was something you should hide from Mommy," Nechama said reasonably.

"YOU didn't think? YOU decide everything? Now I look like an irresponsible baby and it's all because of YOU! You ruin everything. I HATE you!" Ruthie cried, not realizing that her voice had reached fever pitch.

The girls' mother appeared at the bedroom door. "What did you say?" she asked Ruthie in a voice that offered no room for an explanation.

Ruthie could not evade the question. She had said what she had said; Nechama heard it, her mother heard it and there was no denying it. Furthermore, the tears of shock and hurt shimmering in Nechama's eyes told Ruthie that her sharp words had hit their mark.

The Talmud (*Chagigah* 5b) teaches that when we reach the Next World, we will have to answer the question Ruthie's mother asked: "What did you say?" *Chazal* reach that conclusion through a verse (*Amos* 4:13) that states "*u'magid l'adam*

10 Chapter One: Introduction

mah sicho—He recounts to a person what were his words."

We learn a deeper meaning of this verse from Rav Chaim Volozhiner in *Nefesh HaChaim*. He asks why the verse is phrased "He recounts to a person what were his words," as opposed to simply "He recounts to a person his words." The added *"mah,"* says Rav Chaim, means that **a person not only hears his words, but sees *what* his words caused**. If Nechama in our story feels depressed after her sister's remark, and therefore has no patience to entertain the children for whom she babysits that evening, so that the children complain to their mother and Nechama loses the job and cannot save up money for a ticket to visit her cousins in California, Ruthie will someday have to account for all this spin-off from her words.

By the same token, the *"mah"* can refer to the trail of happiness set in motion by a positive word. Had Ruthie responded differently, her words might have made Nechama feel good about her role as an older sister. She might have gone to her babysitting job re-energized and given the children a fun-filled night. Their mother might have recommended Nechama to other families, enabling her to not only buy her ticket, but give extra money to *tzedakah* as well.

Not only are our words a reality in *what* they cause to occur in the world, but they also create a reality within the people to whom we speak. They are like a permanent marker, capable of marking others' self-image with confidence and optimism, or the opposite.

"What did you say?" is a question that each of us will have to answer some day. Keeping that in mind can inspire us to think before we speak, so that the words we say in our lifetimes will generate good things in this world, and sound sweet to our own ears in the World to Come.

---

3 Tishrei — May we see much *nachas* from our children and grandchildren.
Dedicated by Dov and Peral Solomon

3 Shevat — לע"נ ר' אברהם בן ר' יהושע ז"ל

3 Sivan — May today's learning be a *z'chus* for our family.
Allen & Susan Black and Pinchus & Ariella Chayne and family

Reality Check:

If everything I say in the course of a day were recorded and played back to me each night, would I be embarrassed? If so, I will try to pay more attention to my choice of words.

What If...

Ruthie had handled the situation differently? How could she have expressed, without *ona'as devarim*, her disappointment in Nechama's decision to reveal her secret?

DAY 4

40,000 Words a Day
~ The impact of quantity

ד תשרי
4 Tishrei/Cycle 1

ד שבט
4 Shevat/Cycle 2

ד סיון
4 Sivan/Cycle 3

> *One termite cannot do much harm. But thousands of them can take down a whole house. On the other hand, one atom bomb can do incredible harm. Fortunately, however, there are not many of them in this world. There are very few things in existence that are both very powerful and very plentiful.*
>
> *Words have this rare trait.*

In the past few days, we've learned about the power of words. Now, let's spend a few minutes thinking about the *quantity* of words in our day-to-day lives. Counting the number of words the average person speaks in a day is a task not too many people would wish to undertake. However, it was undertaken by an expert on sales and marketing named Hal Urban, who wrote a book about using positive words to sell products successfully.

As part of his research for his book, he devised a way to arrive at an estimate of words spoken per day. He made his calculation by singing the song "A Hundred Bottles of Beer on the Wall" at a normal pace. In the space of one minute, he sang 140 words, which adds up to 8,400 words per hour. Then he subtracted the hours normally spent sleeping, eating, working and listening to others speak, concluding that a person speaks about 40,000 words a day.

From what we now know about the power of words, we can understand that the combined force of 40,000 of them a day will define the entire shape and texture of a person's life. **The Chofetz Chaim describes each word we speak as a thread that ties us to either positive or negative habits of speech.** While one thread is easy to break, a mass of hundreds of threads together can be considered almost indestructible, even though it is composed entirely of slim, breakable threads. Someone who habitually speaks in a hurtful, insensitive way creates a mighty rope of intertwined threads that ties her to negative words, relationships and spiritual forces.

On the other hand, someone who pays attention to the nature of each thread of speech also builds a thick rope; it ties her to positive habits and all the positive relationships and experiences that are consequences of those habits. **The more a person speaks with care and compassion, the stronger the habit becomes.**

Each time we open our mouths to speak to someone, we choose to tie ourselves a little more tightly to one side or the other. Every negative choice strengthens the hold of the negative and every positive choice strengthens the hold of the positive. Repeating that choice becomes easier each time, just as a well-worn path is easier to follow.

From this description, it might seem that once the habits are formed, they cannot be broken. However, our free will is the most powerful force of all. Imagine the rope that holds a gigantic cruise ship to its mooring at the pier. The rope is made to withstand crashing tides, winds and storms. Nevertheless, if the captain wants to take the ship in a new direction, he simply has someone lift the heavy rope and set the ship free to sail.

In the same way, Hashem can set us free from the negative habits of speech. No matter how tightly we have bound ourselves to this negativity, we are still the captains of our ship. If we choose to sail in a new direction, Hashem will set us free from our moorings, giving us the *siyata d'Shmaya* we need to begin our journey.

Reality Check:

How aware am I of the impact of my words, especially those I speak in ordinary conversation? I will try to stop every so often and consider which "rope" I am strengthening as I speak.

What If...

the people around you tend to insult and criticize each other? How can you build your ties to positive habits when you are surrounded by negativity?

---

4 Tishrei — Mrs. Bessie Weiss a"h לע״נ חי׳ פעסיל בת יששכר דוב הכהן ע״ה
Dedicated by Mr. and Mrs. Heshy Jacobs, Los Angeles, CA

4 Shevat — In memory of our father לע״נ הרב רפאל בן החכם רבי חייא ז״ל
Dedicated by Ralou & Ronnie Stern and Shireen & Alfred Ohebshalom

4 Sivan — In honor of our children, Miri, Shlomo and Esti Greenberger
Dedicated by their loving parents

DAY 5

Plan to Succeed
~ Practical steps toward change

ה תשרי
5 Tishrei/Cycle 1

ה שבט
5 Shevat/Cycle 2

ה סיון
5 Sivan/Cycle 3

When Sara's sister got engaged in June, Sara went straight to her friend Tova and asked to borrow the lilac satin gown that Tova had made for her own sister's wedding. Sara tried it on and it fit perfectly. She brought it home, hung it in her closet, and one week later set off for camp.

In late July, when Sara returned from camp, the wedding was three weeks away. She tried on the gown again to be sure it didn't need alterations. To her horror, the gown wouldn't zip! One month of late-night ice cream and potato-chip parties with her co-counselors had added six pounds to Sara's small frame, and now, the gown was too small.

"That's it!" Sara told herself. "Nothing but cottage cheese and vegetables until the wedding!" By Day Two, however, the smell of her mother's meatloaf and fried potatoes made her empty stomach growl. She dug in with gusto, and then, figuring the day was "lost" to her diet, topped off the meal with some chocolate cake. In the morning, she awoke too late to sit down to breakfast, so she grabbed a cinnamon bun as she ran to catch a bus to her day camp job. At noon, having forgotten to bring lunch, she treated herself to a slice of pizza. Week One ended with Sara weighing one pound more than she had before the "diet."

Poor habits usually arise out of some real need. Sara's weight gain came from her desire to socialize with her camp friends and share in the party atmosphere. Poor habits of speech also develop out of some deeper need. A person may be trying to assert herself, defend herself, vent frustration, appear sharp and witty, or any of a number of other motivations.

14 Chapter One: Introduction

No matter what the habit and what the reason behind it, the keys to change are the same. The first key is motivation. **Shedding the old habits and building new ones must be important enough for us to exert our willpower where it's needed.**

The second key is to arm ourselves against challenges to our willpower. That means choosing small, reachable goals that will encourage our efforts. Additionally, we must try to modify the old situations and give ourselves the opportunity to practice new reactions.

For Sara that might mean planning a more balanced menu to avoid hunger and cravings. Certainly, it would involve getting up early enough to prepare a healthy breakfast and lunch. She might even ask her mother to steer clear of her favorite high-calorie dinners for the few weeks before the wedding, helping to reduce temptation.

In the same way, **if we want to change our speaking habits, we also have to plan ahead**. The first four days of this book are meant to provide the first key: motivation. We now realize that *ona'as devarim* **is the enemy of friendship, love and happiness**; that its ripple effects fan out over the course of our lives; and that our words are packed with spiritual power. It's hard to imagine better motivations for taking control of our speech.

Then we need to arm ourselves against challenges to our self-control. One way is to continue learning each day, bolstering our awareness of how and why we speak as we do. Another way is to take an honest look at our interactions and choose one small area we can successfully change. Whatever we do, doing it consistently helps to create new habits and ultimately, a new kind of life.

> **Reality Check:**
> What specific situation in my life can serve as a good motivation for mastering the art of positive speech?

> **What If...**
> Sara had been more serious about losing the weight? What would she have done differently? Is it too late for her to succeed?

---

5 Tishrei — לע"נ חי' רחל בת מרדכי צבי ניטקמן ע"ה
Dedicated by Dr. and Mrs. Moshe Nitekman
5 Shevat — לזכות חנה בלה בת יעל רחל ואברהם לב שתחי'
5 Sivan — לזכות יוסף בן מזל נ"י ואשתו בלומא בת שפרינצא שתחי'
Dedicated by their children and grandchildren

DAY 6

Paint Job
~ Designing our own world

ו תשרי
6 Tishrei/Cycle 1

ו שבט
6 Shevat/Cycle 2

ו סיון
6 Sivan/Cycle 3

> *Kayla and her best friend, Shoshana, woke up early and drove to the local home improvement store. They had agreed to work together that entire Sunday to paint Kayla's room.*
>
> *Arriving at the paint department, they scanned a bewildering array of cards bearing small squares of color in every hue and shade imaginable. "I like this one," Kayla said. "'Thundercloud.' Then I could use this deeper gray, 'Battleship,' as the trim. Oh, and wouldn't it be cool to do the door an even darker color, like this one here—'Coal Dust'?"*
>
> *Shoshana looked on in shock, shaking her head vigorously as Kayla laid out her plans.*
>
> *"Why do you want dark gray?" Shoshana asked her. "Do you really want to be surrounded by dark, depressing colors? Imagine waking up every day feeling like it's about to rain. You'll end up being in a bad mood all day. Why don't we do something lighter, like this pale yellow one called 'French Vanilla'?"*

Most people do not wish to surround themselves with darkness. People naturally feel more energetic and cheerful when they are in bright, light, cheerful surroundings. Just as surely as the paint Kayla and Shoshana select will create the atmosphere of Kayla's room, the words we choose to think and speak paint the atmosphere of our world.

When a person is feeling negative, her paint palette may contain "colors" like "wrong, bad, ridiculous, ugly, insulting, selfish, snobby, mean, unfair." She slathers these words across her life, seeing, thinking and speaking of others in these terms. The result is not surprising. Just as it would be impossible for

16 Chapter One: Introduction

Kayla's room not to be gloomy if she paints it with dreary shades of gray, this person's life cannot be anything but dark and gloomy if she "paints" it with negative words.

It is not enough, however, to refrain from choosing the words that paint a grim environment. Kayla can also create surroundings that are light and airy, soothing, comforting and bright. There are hundreds of shades to choose from, shades that evoke happiness, that reflect the beauty of nature, the blue sky, the flowers and trees, the sunlight, the sand, the sea and the silvery light of the moon. Likewise, positive words are a vast palette of shades for us to use to paint a beautiful environment for ourselves. Our words, gestures and facial expressions can color our world with "thanks, good, nice, pretty, helpful, thoughtful, friendly, trying her best, forgiveness, understanding, caring, love."

If given a choice, any emotionally healthy person would prefer to be surrounded by love and happiness. We now know that we hold in our hands the bucket of paint that determines what our world will look like. It takes awareness and honesty to look carefully at what is in that bucket.

Not only do we make our lives vastly better by staying away from the dark, depressing "colors," but as the *Zohar* teaches, we have a positive obligation to use the bright "colors" whenever we can. A positive word left unspoken is not just a missed opportunity; it is an actual transgression of this obligation. Hashem wants us to use our power of speech to beautify His world and uplift each other. And if we think about it, that is what we want as well; because we are the ones who must live in the world we have painted.

Reality Check:

What kind of words are in my "bucket" of usual thoughts and comments? If I tend to be critical, I will make a conscious effort to replace the dark colors with lighter, brighter ones for one specific period of the day—for example, during lunch.

What If...

a person really does live in a difficult, negative environment? For instance, what if someone is sick in the hospital, *chas v'shalom?* Can this "paint bucket" analogy apply, and if so, how?

---

6 Tishrei — לזכות יעקב גבריאל בן לאה ואשתו חנה שיינדל בת חיה לפשא שפרנסקי שיחיו, ובניהם צבי מאיר, אהרן פנחס, אילנה רבקה ומשפחתם

6 Shevat — לע"נ מלכה דבורה סימא ע"ה בת מאיר נתן יבלחט"א נלב"ע ז' שבט
Dedicated by her Aunt and Uncle, Pinchas and Marilyn Newman

6 Sivan — In memory of Sheila Shiffman *a"h* לע"נ שולמית בת מרדכי ניסן ע"ה
Dedicated by her children and grandchildren

DAY 7

Loved by Others
~ Making and keeping friends

ז תשרי
7 Tishrei/Cycle 1

ז שבט
7 Shevat/Cycle 2

ז סיון
7 Sivan/Cycle 3

Miri walked into her class Purim chagigah with Naomi and Rivki by her side. The three girls lived a few doors away from one another, so it made sense that they would carpool to the event. Miri thought of them as "friends of convenience" with whom she would probably spend very little time if not for their living so close to one another.

Within seconds of their arrival, two girls had come to greet Naomi; Rivki had dashed off to some friends who were waving to her from the other side of the room. Miri stood alone, scoping out the room to find someone with whom she could connect. It seemed that everyone was already talking, laughing and joking with one another, and there was no place for Miri.

"Why was it always like this?" she wondered. But she knew the answer. The girls in the school could certainly tell by her facial expressions and sarcastic comments that she felt superior. "I'm lost in a sea of airheads," she thought as she scanned the room. But being smarter than everyone else was little compensation for the isolation Miri felt. Why did people seek out Naomi and Rivki, but not her?

With this glimpse of Miri's inner thoughts, we can imagine how she interacts with others. When they ask a question she considers unintelligent, she lets them know with a roll of the eyeballs or "Really? You never heard of that?" When they discuss topics she finds boring, she groans and walks away. When they include her in their plans, she turns them down. When they exclude her, she stashes away the hurt in her growing bag of grievances. People feel uncomfortable around her, and since no one wants to feel uncomfortable, people avoid her.

18 Chapter One: Introduction

If Miri really wants to know why the other two girls have real, caring friends, she need only listen to their conversations. They focus on the people they are talking to, express sincere interest in their friends' concerns, and find what is good, interesting and admirable in others. When they speak to their friends, their friends feel good. Since people want to feel good, people want to be around Naomi and Rivki.

In the vast majority of cases, the way people feel about us is a reflection of the way we speak to them. **That is why the most powerful thing we can do to make stronger, happier relationships with our friends, family, classmates—and eventually, our own spouses and children—is to build a habit of positive speech.**

It is not a quick project; it takes time to build an awareness of how we see and speak to others, and it takes practice to turn this awareness into a new way of reacting and responding. However, we can make real changes almost immediately by utilizing the many opportunities we have each day to say something positive.

Pirkei Avos (13:3) teaches us that being loved by others is not just an empty quest to be "Miss Popularity," but an important spiritual goal, for "One who is pleasing to other people is pleasing to Hashem." That is because we can only win the love of others by working on our own character traits, which brings us to a higher level of love for our fellow Jews and for Hashem.

Ever since Hashem placed Adam in the Garden of Eden, people have been on a quest to find happiness. Loving others and being loved is crucial to this quest, and by mastering the art of positive speech, we each have the power to find what we want most in our lives.

Reality Check:
Can I imagine myself being that positive, sought-after girl? Would I handle myself any differently than I do now? What, if anything, would I change?

What If...
a girl is ostracized by her class or is simply too shy to make positive connections? What advice would you have for such a girl? What advice would you have for her classmates?

---

7 Tishrei — לע"נ בנימן בן יוסף ב' אב ואשתו מרים בת בצלאל ז"ל ז' תשרי
Dedicated with love by their daughter Joyce and the Mendelsons

7 Shevatm — לזכות שירה דבורה בת העני' דינה תחי' וגבריאל משה נ"י
Dedicated by her great-great aunt, Judy Z. Lane

7 Sivan — In memory of our parents
לע"נ רב שלמה בן רב יעקב ז"ל ואשתו חוה בת משה חיים ע"ה

DAY 8

In Style
~ Changing the norm

ח תשרי
8 Tishrei/Cycle 1

ח שבט
8 Shevat/Cycle 2

ח סיון
8 Sivan/Cycle 3

Tamar sat on the grass eating her picnic lunch. The Lag BaOmer "field day" had been fun for her, an athletic girl in her senior year who still loved a good game of Machanayim. Elisheva and Shani sat down next to her.

"If I were the head of student government," said Elisheva, "this would have been a trip to the mall. What a waste of time!"

"Nothing wrong with getting some exercise," Tamar responded. "It was fun. Anyway, I can't stand the mall. All those stores make me dizzy."

"Ha! You mean you can't afford the mall," Elisheva retorted. "Just your luck that this year the trip was free!"

Tamar gave a half-hearted laugh. "Yeah, right," she said. "You're just mad because your team lost."

Shani squirmed as the conversation turned sour. Tamar pretended not to mind Elisheva's comment, but Shani knew it hurt. Living next door to Tamar, she knew of the struggle her family faced as Tamar's father searched for a job. It was no joking matter.

"No, really, Tamar," Elisheva shot back. "This year we didn't even have to buy lunch. It's a dream vacation!"

"Oh, no," Shani thought. "This is going too far. I don't know what to do. If I try to stop it, I'm going to look like Little Miss Rebbetzin. Well, I guess Tamar can protect herself."

Had Elisheva been punching Tamar repeatedly in the nose, there is no doubt that Shani would have sprung into action to save her friend from injury. Yet something stopped her from saving Tamar from the verbal attack. She knew Elisheva would claim it was "just a joke" and

20 Chapter One: Introduction

Shani would feel like an obnoxious, overzealous fool. Shani's protective instincts were right, but she lacked the confidence and the tools to stand up for her friend. Since Tamar's injury was invisible, Shani could justify her inaction.

Ona'as devarim is often this way. People insult each other as a joke, or they speak in a blunt way that they see as "real," and everybody is expected to accept the insensitivity as normal. It is the person who objects who is seen as abnormal. Little by little, everyone becomes less sensitive to each other's feelings and to the impact of their own words. People become emotionally closed.

Because words create the atmosphere we live in, and everyone contributes to the atmosphere, the best way to encourage a positive atmosphere is to get everyone involved in changing it. Learning together about *ona'as devarim* brings everyone into the same mind-set so that a girl like Shani can comfortably say something to stop a verbal attack. What seems overzealous one day can become completely normal a few weeks later as people begin to pay attention to their words and their impact.

A perfect example of this phenomenon is the anti-smoking campaign. In the 1950s and '60s, smoking was considered an elegant, sophisticated activity. Today, smoking is rightfully considered a terrible habit. People who smoke must stand outside in the freezing cold to indulge, and many who walk by them look at them with pity.

What's "in" can change. The witty jokes and blunt comments that hurt others can become as unacceptable as a smoke-filled room. We can learn the tools to put a halt, in a calm, respectful way, to *ona'as devarim* in our midst. We may think the person being insulted "doesn't care," but if we care and get others to care, we will be living in a much better world.

Reality Check:

If I heard someone speaking to another girl in an insensitive way, would I feel obligated to stop her? I will keep in mind that everyone has a role to play in creating an open, friendly atmosphere at home and in school.

What If...

Shani had chosen to speak up? What might she have said? How might she have handled the situation so that she would not embarrass Tamar or Elisheva?

---

8 Tishrei — In memory of R' Yisroel Farkovits z"l לע"נ ישראל בן דוב ז"ל
Dedicated in memory of our father, by Eli and Esty Stolberg
לע"נ יהושע שמואל בן דוד ז"ל — **8 Shevat**
8 Sivan — May today's learning be a *z'chus* for our family.
Dedicated by Dr. & Mrs. Yaacov Yisroel Goldstein, Yerushalayim

Chapter 2

What Fuels Hurtful Speech

Very few people wake up in the morning and think to themselves, "Who can I hurt today?" The hurtful words we speak to others usually arise out of some flaw in our own personality. Like a cloudy lens, the faulty trait blocks our true view of the situation and prevents us from recognizing the damage our words can cause. At other times, harsh words spring from a stressful situation.

For easily accessible reference, we've listed in alphabetical order some of these challenging traits in Days 9-25, and some challenging situations in Days 26-32.

DAY 9

About to Burst!
~ Anger

ט תשרי
9 Tishrei/Cycle 1

ט שבט
9 Shevat/Cycle 2

ט סיון
9 Sivan/Cycle 3

It was a little past midnight when Chedva arrived home, tired out from her long study session. Finals season was no picnic.

She trudged wearily up the stairs to the bedroom she shared with her sister Brochi. "Ah, to plop myself in bed and drift off…!" Chedva thought blissfully. Her plump down comforter and marshmallow-soft pillow seemed to call to her from the other side of the bedroom door. "Clothes and all," she thought, "I'm just going to collapse on that bed and space out for a while."

When she opened the door, her eyes fell upon Brochi, who had apparently made a late-night decision to reorganize her loose-leaf. Every flat surface in the room was covered with various piles of paper. That included Chedva's bed.

Brochi instantly read the message on her sister's face: "Anger! Warning! Outburst ahead!" it seemed to say. Chedva noticed Brochi's frightened expression. She had told her sister hundreds—no, thousands—of times to respect her space and her belongings. But Brochi just had to spread herself out all over the room. On the other hand, Chedva knew how much Brochi looked up to her and wanted that deeper sisterly bond. "I'll really hurt her if I yell at her," the older girl thought. "She'll cry and I'll feel guilty. It's just not worth it."

Still, Chedva's frustration remained. "Why can't I come home tired and lie down on my own bed like everyone else does?" Chedva thought. "Why can't she stay away from my stuff? It's not RIGHT!" The angry thoughts built up like water against a dam, pushing hard against Chedva's self-control. At last, the dam burst.

"I've HAD IT with you!" she shouted angrily.

Chedva knew better than to yell, and yet she did it anyway. *Chazal* explain why: anger robs a person of his *daas*—his wisdom. Take away the wisdom a person gains through his learning and life's experiences, and he is back to the level of a child. His anger—even if he manages to connect it to some kind of righteous principle—is still nothing more than a child's tantrum. The difference is that the adult's angry reaction really hurts the other person.

Each one of those injuries is like a thin layer of clear plastic separating one person from the other. They don't realize how separate they are becoming until the layers build up.

Nevertheless, anger is a human reaction that rushes in when a person is insulted, hurt or frustrated. The question we face is what to do with that feeling when it floods our minds. The answer is one word: time. **The old trick of counting to ten, or if necessary 50 or 100, is one of the most effective ways to avoid bursting out with angry words.**

Sometimes, while you wait, your anger dissolves. You are then able to speak calmly about what is wrong, or forget it altogether. Other times, the problem is real and needs to be solved. In that case, it is even more important to speak in a way that will ignite a discussion, not a fight.

Even if after waiting and thinking, you still have to tell the other person something he or she may not want to hear, you will at least be able to do so with respect. There will be no explosion, no hurt feelings, and no regrets.

> **Reality Check:**
> Do I have my "hot-button" issues that make me angry? The next time I feel that anger rising, I will stop myself and silently count to ten.

> **What If...**
> instead of thinking about how wrong her sister was, Chedva had thought about what she might be able to do to finally get her sister's cooperation?

---

09 Tishrei — May today's learning be a *z'chus* for our children.
Dedicated by the Wolpe family

09 Shevat — In memory of Isadore and Rose Glorsky *a"h*

09 Sivan — לע"נ משה ניסן בן מנחם מענדל ז"ל
Dedicated by the Weiland, Katz, Grossman and Cohen families

DAY 10

The Great and Powerful Me
~ Arrogance

י תשרי
10 Tishrei/Cycle 1

י שבט
10 Shevat/Cycle 2

י סיון
10 Sivan/Cycle 3

This year, for the first time since Gitti was in ninth grade, the school play was not fun. In fact, it was the opposite of fun. It was torture, and the reason for that change could be summarized in one word: Dina.

Dina, a twelfth-grader with tremendous acting talent, was given the honor this year of being the school's first-ever student play director. Gitti, who won the lead role, quickly found out that her dream-come-true was more like a nightmare. Dina's ego and Gitti's nervousness combined to make every rehearsal a real tear-filled tragedy.

"Listen to me right now," Dina yelled as Gitti stood on stage fumbling for her next line. "Get your lines into your head already! We've been in rehearsal for two weeks and you still don't have your part down!"

"I'm sorry!" Gitti exclaimed almost as loudly. "I'm not perfect!"

"All right, let's move on. Where are the props for the next scene? Props! You girls have to move! You have to be ready!" The props girls scampered out from backstage to replace some living-room furniture with a few fake trees and a large stuffed horse.

"Listen to me, everyone," Dina commanded. "Stay sharp. Stay focused. I'm not putting up with all this spacing out! I'm not directing a play that ends up being the joke of the town!" All the girls at the rehearsal, from the main actresses to the girls in charge of ordering dinner, felt the tension of Dina's demanding presence. Who would be the next one to fail to live up to her standards? Who would get the next earful of criticism? No one felt safe.

26   Chapter Two: What Fuels Hurtful Speech

Dina blamed and shamed her cast so harshly that all the fun and excitement of creating a school play turned sour. Could all this emotion and embarrassment arise out of a school play? What could have driven Dina to treat her cast so harshly? When we analyze her words, the answer is obvious: arrogance. The way she sees things, the world should operate to meet her expectations and standards. There should be well-memorized lines, prompt prop changes and complete devotion to the success of "her" play. And if there isn't, then someone has to pay for Dina's disappointment.

While the example may be extreme, it's not as unique. **In fact, *ona'as devarim* is quite often rooted in our belief that things should be done our way.** Most people trust their own judgment above that of others, especially if we view another person as less experienced or intelligent than we are. In that case, we may not really be concerned about what the other person thinks of us. In fact, for some people, it's a compliment to be considered tough or difficult.

Speaking in a soft, gentle manner displays the trait that is the opposite of arrogance: humility. Someone with humility shows that she does not consider herself superior. She sees her talents and advantages as a gift from Hashem, given to her for the purpose of doing good in the world. Even if she must correct someone, she doesn't attack. She uses words and a tone that the other person can more easily accept. Because of that, her influence accomplishes far more than any amount of intimidation could ever achieve.

Reality Check:

When I get upset about something, do I have in my mind words such as "I don't have to put up with this" or "I deserve better than this"?

If such phrases run through my mind, I will try to remind myself that my expectations are not more important than other people's feelings.

What If...

Gitti was the daughter of the school principal? How might Dina have handled each of the frustrations she experienced at the rehearsal?

---

10 Tishrei — לע"נ יעקב בן יצחק צבי ז"ל ואשתו חנה בילה בת זאב ע"ה
Dedicated by their children Fran and Jerry Weinberg

10 Shevat — In memory of Serach bas Eliezer *a"h*

10 Sivan — Shlomo Imiak נ"י לזכות שלמה בן פיגה נ"י
Dedicated by his wife Esther and children

DAY 11

The Blame Game
~ Blaming others

י"א תשרי
11 Tishrei/Cycle 1

י"א שבט
11 Shevat/Cycle 2

י"א סיון
11 Sivan/Cycle 3

> "I'm not going to be nice about it," Yitzchak told his older sister, Esther. "That's why the world is filled with incompetent people—because no one has the guts to blame people when they mess up!"
>
> Yitzchak stomped out of the house, jumped onto his bike and sped out of the driveway. He was off to fight another battle against incompetence—this time at the dry cleaner. Even though the worker had told him that the paint stain he had gotten on his sleeve would probably not come out completely, Yitzchak was certain that with a little intelligence and effort, his shirt could be restored to perfection.
>
> Of course it wasn't just the dry cleaner that irritated Yitzchak. At yeshivah, he suffered with immature classmates and an ineffective rebbi, which explained the lack of enthusiasm with which he approached learning. Socially, he suffered with inconsiderate friends, which explained his lack of companionship. At home, he suffered with noisy, nosy siblings, which explained his inability to get anything done. Incompetence, in his view, was a worldwide epidemic. How could he achieve success against such odds?

When a person is always right and everyone else is always wrong, two predictions can be made with certainty: The person is not succeeding in his life, and he does not accept any responsibility for his failures. Such people see themselves as victims of other people's flaws and mistakes, and they imagine that all their problems are the result of what others do and say. They feel tremendous

28 Chapter Two: What Fuels Hurtful Speech

frustration and often react by lashing out with *ona'as devarim* at those whom they believe are responsible for their troubles.

Why do people blame others for their own shortcomings? There are two reasons:

- It is easier than having to face our own mistake and do the hard work of fixing it.
- You see in the other person exactly the trait you most dislike in yourself. Rather than disapproving of yourself, you recognize the trait in another person and disapprove of it in him. In that way, you can feel superior in comparison.

Even if another person really does deserve blame for something, rebuking him only has a constructive purpose if your words will help him learn from his mistake. **Ona'as devarim cannot meet this standard, because people seldom accept and learn from harsh words of blame.** A person will, however, learn from a calm, respectful suggestion or from observing a better approach to the situation in question.

When people do what we expect and act as we wish, *ona'as devarim* is rarely a problem. Human beings, however, are so varied in the way they do things, judge things, behave and react that we are almost guaranteed to be confronted with behaviors we do not like or understand. To gain mastery over *ona'as devarim*, a person needs to assemble a full inventory of positive thoughts and reactions. Then we have tools that we can grab and use on the spot when we discover—as we always will—that the people in our lives are only human.

Reality Check:

What is my first reaction to failure? Is it to blame another person or situation? If so, I will take my investigation one step further and try to determine what I could have done differently, even under the same circumstances.

What If...

Yitzchak had admitted to himself that his own carelessness caused the paint stain on his shirt?

---

11 Tishrei — לע"נ ר' משה בן ר' שמואל הלוי ז"ל
לע"נ מרת נחמה בת אברהם ע"ה
11 Shevat — In memory of our loving mother לע"נ הענדל בת רחמאל ע"ה
Dedicated by the Grape family
11 Sivan — אלישבע חי' בת שרה יענטא שתחי'
זכות לחזור בתשובה שלמה, זיווג הגון, בריאות, פרנסה טובה והצלחה

DAY 12

And the Winner Is...
~ Competitiveness

י"ב תשרי
12 Tishrei/Cycle 1

י"ב שבט
12 Shevat/Cycle 2

י"ב סיון
12 Sivan/Cycle 3

> "You got a 93 on your math final?" Chaya asked her classmate. "That's amazing, but would you believe that I got 100 plus five points extra credit! My tutor really paid off!"
>
> "Mommy! I got a speaking part in the school play!" Devorah announced proudly as her mother arrived home from work. "Fantastic!" her mother replied. "Yeah," her older sister added, "being in the play is a lot of work and a lot of fun. I remember how exciting it was when I played the lead."
>
> "I can't believe it! My whole family is going to Israel for my aunt's wedding! I've never been there before!" Aliza told her friend Nechama. "We'll be there for a whole week. We're staying in the middle of Geula in my grandmother's extra bedroom." "That's nice," Nechama answered. "I love it there. Ever since my parents bought a vacation apartment in Yerushalayim, we've been going every summer."

Some people just have to compete. Everything is about them; they fail to think about what a particular fact or situation means to the other person. Competitive people are not really listening to the news their friends share with them; they are simply using it as a connection to bring up their own, even better news. In the process, they belittle and undermine the other person's happiness.

In the scenarios above, the girl who got 93 on her math test is left feeling that her achievement, which might have been an amazing success for her, is really not that great. The girl who tried and succeeded at getting a speaking role now remembers that her sister's accomplishment was far more glorious. The girl who is thrilled about her first trip to Israel now feels like one

30 Chapter Two: What Fuels Hurtful Speech

rushed week in a cramped apartment is nothing compared to entire summers in a luxurious vacation home.

Sometimes, competitive people even compete over bad news. For instance, you complain that you were up until midnight doing homework, and your friend says, "That's nothing. I was up till 3!" When that happens, it seems as if the other person is saying, "I don't care how tired you are because it's nothing compared to how tired I am!" In reality, however, the other person's tiredness has nothing to do with yours. You do not feel any better just because she is also tired. You are looking for a little sympathy, not a fatigue contest, and you should not have to be the most tired person in the world to merit that sympathy.

One reason people are competitive is that they need to feel that they are more important than others. Such people can be so involved with themselves that everything they hear relates back to their own experiences. If you tell them that you failed a test, they will tell you a story of when *they* failed a test. If you tell them that your brother is engaged, they will tell you how they felt when *their* brother got engaged. "It's all about me" is the message of a competitive person.

This need to compete results in *ona'as devarim* because it makes the other person's statement seem unimportant or invalid. Rather than constantly comparing herself to others, a person with a competitive nature can consciously make an attempt to keep herself out of the story. This gives her an opportunity to really listen to the other person's statement and respond to it sincerely. When a person teaches herself to feel real happiness for another person, she is not inclined to dampen it by offering comparisons that make it seem small. Instead, her satisfaction will come from knowing that her friend is happy, and that is good!

> *12 Tishrei* — להצלחת א-לחנן, יצחק אריא-ל, אביטל, אילת ובת שבע
> Dedicated by Benhoor Hanasabzadeh
> *12 Shevat* — Rabbi Chaim Feldberg z"l לע״נ הרב חיים צבי בן ר׳ יהודה ז״ל
> Dedicated by the Feldberg family
> *12 Sivan* — לע״נ מרים ליבא בת אליהו ע״ה

Reality Check:

Do I tend to bring myself into the story when other people tell me what is going on in their lives? If so, I will try to become more aware of this habit and hold myself back from stepping into their spotlight.

What If...

Nechama had shown sincere interest in and happiness for Aliza's news? What questions might she have asked? Could she have helped Aliza benefit from her greater familiarity with Israel? How?

DAY 13

Down a Few Notches
~ Deflating others to inflate oneself

י"ג תשרי
13 Tishrei/Cycle 1

י"ג שבט
13 Shevat/Cycle 2

י"ג סיון
13 Sivan/Cycle 3

Ariella labored long and hard in high school. She was a slow student, but she loved to learn and she was placed in a special, modified classroom where she found great success. She played an important part in the high school's extracurricular activities and looked forward to each day in school.

Rachel also struggled with school. Unlike Ariella, however, Rachel could not stand being anything less than the star. Gradually, she lost any desire to learn and began skipping classes. Better to quit the game, she thought, than to always be the loser. She stopped attending school altogether and was eventually expelled.

One Shabbos, Ariella and Rachel found themselves standing near each other at a Kiddush in their shul. Rachel overheard Ariella's friend praising her. "You know, Ariella, I wish I had the patience to study as hard as you do. I think you're the best student in your class!"

"Anyone can be the best in that class," Rachel interjected. "It's like eighth grade, only with bigger kids. Now, if she were the best student in the top class, like my cousin is, then it's something to talk about."

"Yeah, well, I've never been the sharpest pencil in the box," Ariella agreed. She realized that it was probably true that in another class, she wouldn't be anything special.

The fact that Rachel wasn't even enrolled in school did not prevent her from looking down on Ariella. In fact, anyone with an understanding of psychology would be able to predict that Rachel's feelings of inferiority would make it all the more likely that she would knock down

Ariella. The fastest way to feel taller is to shrink everyone around you.

This is often the reason that someone cuts another person down to size. In whatever area a person feels inadequate, she is most likely to find others whom she can point to as even less accomplished in that area. That way, she feels more "normal." It is as if she is saying, "I might be bad, but I'm not *that* bad!"

In reality, this course of action accomplishes nothing positive at all. Rachel's academic ability has not been improved one iota by making an insulting statement about Ariella. Her sense of inferiority remains the same; she cannot fool herself into thinking that, now that Ariella has been exposed as lacking, she, Rachel, has somehow become smarter.

The true route to soothing feelings of inadequacy is to work on accomplishing real goals. Once a person discovers the satisfaction of trying and succeeding, even in small, achievable steps, she no longer needs to deny others their due. Instead, she can find inspiration in the success others have achieved in overcoming their challenges.

Reality Check:

Are there areas in which I feel inadequate? Do I tend to take comfort in the fact that other people are even less successful in that area? If so, I will turn my attention to setting one very achievable goal in my weak area, and working toward it.

What If...

Rachel was aware enough of her own feelings to realize that she was jealous of the way Ariella was being praised? What might she have said or done with that realization that would have been productive?

---

13 Tishrei — לע״נ מיכאל בן ברוך ז״ל נלב״ע י״ג תשרי
לע״נ הינדא רחל בת אברהם ע״ה נלב״ע ט״ו כסלו
13 Shevat — לע״נ שרה בת אברהם ע״ה נלב״ע י״ד שבט
Dedicated by Dr. and Mrs. Dovid Wayne
13 Sivan — Mendel Herskovits לע״נ חיים עוריאל מענדל בן אברהם ז״ל
In loving memory by Jeffrey and Dorothy Ackerman and family

DAY 14

"I Rule!"
~ Desire to dominate

י"ד תשרי
14 Tishrei/Cycle 1

י"ד שבט
14 Shevat/Cycle 2

י"ד סיון
14 Sivan/Cycle 3

Gila's group of friends occupied a choice table in the lunchroom. Gila arrived late, having spent some time debating with her teacher over the grade on her literature essay. As she approached the table, the girls' laughing and chatter quickly muted, as if someone had turned down the volume. "Move!" she said to one of the girls. Gila said it jokingly, but the girl quickly gave up her seat.

For anyone else, the behavior would be labeled just plain rude. But Gila ruled the clique, and anyone who wanted to be part of her elite group of friends—the ones whose tastes and preferences defined "normal" for the rest of the school—simply had to abide by her domineering ways. Gila decided what styles were "in" and what styles were "out," which jokes were funny and which jokes weren't even worth noticing, which stories were interesting and which deserved her "O.K., next topic" critique.

Gila knew she sometimes hurt people. But in her mind, she was justified. If she didn't set them straight, they would be doomed to nerdhood for the rest of their lives. "How can I let a friend walk around in those shoes?" she would think. "Everyone will laugh at her. She'll never realize how ridiculous she looks!"

People come up with many justifications for being tough and aggressive with other people. The same thinking that gives Gila "permission" to rule her clique could follow her throughout life. She could become a boss, a teacher, or even a mother who thinks that the only way to get cooperation is to make others fear her. She will always tell

34 Chapter Two: What Fuels Hurtful Speech

herself that what she has to accomplish is just so important that she can't afford to let anyone get away with any mistakes.

But the bottom line is that whatever the justification, the motivation behind all the bluster is the sense of power she feels when others shake and quake, agree with her every idea and feed her a steady diet of flattery and praise. It's so much quicker and easier than earning real respect and admiration for traits like intelligence, character and talent.

The problem with this fast track to power is that it ignores other people's value and human dignity. The domineering person believes that he or she has to "step on some toes" to achieve great things in life—yet no one has the right to advance himself by tromping on other people. **Those who justify their bossiness with the idea that "it's a tough job but someone's got to do it" often become a fountain of *ona'as devarim* that gradually poisons every relationship they have.**

It's true that most people want and need a certain sense of power; *Pirkei Avos* teaches how to gain power that is real, not just an illusion. "Who is strong?" the Mishnah asks, and answers, "One who controls himself." Controlling other people is easy compared to facing our own flaws and bad habits, and making the effort to conquer them. Recognizing the value and the feelings of other people is the first step to real, lasting power.

Reality Check:

Do I sometimes treat other people as if they are inferior to me? If so, I will try to become more aware of that attitude and speak—even if at first it's just an act—with more respect for the other person's dignity and feelings.

What If...

there was a new girl in school who dominated Gila the way Gila dominated the other girls?

---

14 Tishrei — In memory of our father לע"נ אביגדור מנחם בן מרדכי צבי ז"ל
14 Shevat — לע"נ אלחנן צבי ז"ל בן ישראל מנחם יבלח"ט
Dedicated in memory of Elchonon Kramer z"l by his loving family
14 Sivan — לע"נ לאה מרים בת ישראל ע"ה
In honor of Sidney Rabin and Alan & Joyce Neff

DAY 15

Heart Surgery
~ Hatred

ט"ו תשרי
15 Tishrei/Cycle 1

ט"ו שבט
15 Shevat/Cycle 2

ט"ו סיון
15 Sivan/Cycle 3

The Frieds and the Steins had been enemies for 15 years, ever since Fried-Stein Realty had gone bankrupt. The Steins had recovered financially, but the Frieds had gone broke. Leah Stein and Mimi Fried were both in 10th grade in the only Bais Yaakov in town. Leah felt that the feud was an emotional drain, and that since she and Mimi were just babies when it began, they had no reason to be angry. She tried occasionally to make conversation with Mimi, but each time, Mimi ignored the effort. In fact, Mimi's bitterness spilled into her entire personality, leaving her with few friends.

Sadly, Mimi's mother became ill. One day, the girls' teacher informed the class that Mrs. Fried had passed away. Leah was determined to be menachem avel Mimi and heal the rift once and for all. It would be a great zechus for Mrs. Fried's neshamah, she reasoned.

When she showed up at Mimi's house and sat down, Mimi stared past her, pretending she wasn't there. Finally, Mimi's hatred pushed its way out of her heart and into the world. "You don't have to come here and feel bad for me," she said coldly. Leah got up in silence and left. "That's it. I tried," she said to herself. And she went on with her life.

Mimi, on the other hand, carried her hatred with her everywhere, gradually destroying the sources of love and friendship that could have filled her life.

Hatred is a poison that hurts the hater as much as, or more than, the person she hates. Once a person sees what it does to her, she often wishes she could be rid of it. Fortunately, there are ways to remove the hatred from our hearts just as a surgeon removes a blockage. The first step is to understand ourselves. **Sometimes, we discover that hatred arises out of our own insecurity.**

Reuven, a yeshivah student, has never been a great learner. He hates his neighbor, Avraham, who is always trying to rub his failings into his face. "What are you learning these days?" Avraham asks every time Reuven comes home from yeshivah. "He just wants to make me feel like an idiot," Reuven thinks. In truth, Avraham is trying to make what he assumes is appropriate conversation. Only because Reuven feels inferior in his learning does Avraham's question offend him.

Another powerful way to rid ourselves of hatred is to realize that everyone has flaws. If we can accept that the other person is flawed in a certain way, as are we and everyone else, we can disqualify the flaw as a cause for hatred.

Sonya comes from a large, financially strained family. She babysits whenever she can and pays for all her own clothing and entertainment. Shana's family lives in a large, comfortable house. Her mother has full-time household help and plenty of time for Shani. It seems they are always out shopping. When Shani tells Sonya about one of her new purchases or her exciting summer plans or some other detail of her rich-girl life, Sonya feels tremendous resentment. In fact, Shani is a sweet and friendly but self-centered person. She has a flaw, but Sonya, too, has flaws. By facing that fact, Sonya can get rid of her anger.

Even without finding merit in the other person, it is important to acknowledge at least that she *is* another person. She doesn't think, live or act as you do. That alone can help a person find and respect the G-dliness that is at the core of every single Jew.

Reality Check:
Do I make an effort to understand the perspective of people whom I find difficult or irritating?

What If...
as in Mimi's case, you find it difficult to get over a deep hurt? How can Mimi get rid of her hatred?

---

15 Tishrei — In memory of Fay Kasmer Broome לע"נ צפורה בת משה דוד ע"ה
Dedicated by Bernard Broome

15 Shevat — לזכות לראות נחת דקדושה מכל יוצאי חלציו שיהו כולם זרע
קודש, ברך ד' הולכים בדרך התורה והיראה תמיד אי"ס

15 Sivan — לע"נ אברהם בן שמואל ז"ל נלב"ע ט"ז סיון
Dedicated by Mr. William and Mrs. Adina Teichman

DAY 16

Long-Term Health
~ Hatred 2: Blind to spiritual impact

ט"ז תשרי
16 Tishrei/Cycle 1

ט"ז שבט
16 Shevat/Cycle 2

ט"ז סיון
16 Sivan/Cycle 3

"If you don't floss your teeth, you'll lose them when you get old," the mother warns her 14-year-old daughter.

"If you smoke, you could end up getting lung cancer when you're older," the rebbi tells his student.

"If you don't exercise, by the time you're middle aged you'll be fat and out of shape, and maybe even have heart problems," the doctor tells the overweight young man.

"If you eat too much sugar, you could get diabetes someday," the school nurse tells a student.

"If you don't drink milk, your bones will be weak when you're old," the babysitter tells the child.

The warnings fall on deaf ears. Why? Because the consequences are far, far away.

Most people think very little about how their habits today will affect their health decades from now. *I'll worry about it when the time comes,* they think. Furthermore, they assume that before things fall apart completely, they will have an opportunity to make the changes necessary to repair whatever has gone wrong. They'll lose weight, start exercising, quit smoking, start flossing, and everything will be fine.

But the Chofetz Chaim tells us that some of our actions in the present can create consequences for our health—our spiritual health—that will last forever. That is because everything in this world has a counterpart in the spiritual world. There is a "This World" you and a "Next World" you. They both exist right now. In the Next World, however, most of a person's physical capacities are not needed. A *neshamah* has no use for powerful muscles or a healthy appetite. **However, two organs do have an eternal role: the mouth, which sings praises**

38   Chapter Two: What Fuels Hurtful Speech

to Hashem, and the heart, which feels the pleasure of being close to Hashem.

The damage done to a person's physical self in this world is left behind in this world. But the damage done to a person's spiritual self lasts forever. **What fatty foods and polluted air do to our physical health, hatred does to our spiritual health.** A dark, negative view of others causes our mouths to speak hurtful words, and our hearts to carry a heavy, depressing spirit.

The effect is not just in the future, after 120 years, but right now, as our spiritual selves respond moment by moment to the choices we make in our lives. As we make our choices, speak our words and do our deeds in This World, we are forming the Next World version of ourselves in real time. As we interact with others in our lives, we are feeding our spiritual selves—either with the wholesome nourishment that makes us radiant and vibrant, or the toxins that make us weak and pale. By cultivating a loving, accepting view of others, we assure ourselves of eternal good health.

> **Reality Check:**
> Do I carry around negative feelings toward some people? What can I do to cultivate a more positive view?

> **What If...**
> your tongue swelled up every time you spoke *ona'as devarim*? Would that help or hurt you in the short term? How about in the long term?

---

16 Tishrei — As a *z'chus* for a *refuah shleimah* for the *cholim* in Am Yisrael
16 Shevat — לזכות שרה חי' בת מירל רבקה אביטן שתחי'
In honor of of our granddaughter, by Debra and Meyer Abittan
16 Sivan — Joseph Jaroslawicz z"l — לע״נ אליהו שרגא פייוויל בן הרב מנחם מענדל ז״ל
Dedicated by his children, Isaac and Shoshana Jaroslawicz

DAY 17

A Thin Disguise
~ Hatred 3: Hidden hostility

י"ז תשרי
17 Tishrei/Cycle 1

י"ז שבט
17 Shevat/Cycle 2

י"ז סיון
17 Sivan/Cycle 3

It was Aviva's first summer as a senior counselor. As a longtime camper and then junior staff member, she had a great reputation among campers, parents and counselors. Funloving, creative and patient with even the most difficult campers, Vivi got along with everyone.

Everyone, that is, except for Shaina, Vivi's junior counselor. For Shaina, Vivi's ever-present smile seemed to evaporate. Vivi's ready-to-help personality seemed to turn stubborn. Whatever Shaina said seemed to irritate Vivi.

One day, Vivi's bunk was scheduled for a trip to a local zoo. Rena, another junior counselor, was assigned to accompany them to provide additional help. The children had boarded the bus and Shaina took a head count.

"I've got to run back to the bunk and get my hat," Shaina told Vivi. "Could you do the second count?"

"I'm busy going over directions with the bus driver," Vivi answered curtly. "Just take a minute and finish the job!"

Rena, who had been standing with Vivi, watched Shaina dejectedly climb the bus stairs.

"What's the big deal with recounting the kids?" Rena asked. "I could have done it. She was just trying to save time."

"I know," said Vivi. "She just rubs me the wrong way. I'm always saying mean things to her and then feeling guilty."

If Vivi would look a little deeper into her reaction to Shaina, she would realize that there was no mystery in the hostility. She knew that Shaina had asked specifically

40 Chapter Two: What Fuels Hurtful Speech

not to be teamed with her. Shaina wanted her chance to shine, and with a superstar counselor like Vivi, she feared she would remain in the shadow. Vivi, a sweet-natured girl, had thought, "I'm not going to let that bother me. I'm going to give Shaina the benefit of the doubt. I'm sure there was some good reason why she felt that way."

She thought she could let the information "roll off her back," and in fact, she thought she was doing a very good job. After all, she had not said one word to Shaina about it. However, Rena's remark made Vivi realize that deep in her heart, the insult had taken root and was coloring every word she spoke to Shaina.

Like Vivi, many people harbor a negative feeling toward someone that they might not be able to express directly. The feelings might come from envy, hurt over a past incident or some other cause. There might be many reasons why they do not just come out and express their hurt directly, but anger that is held inside does not usually just disappear. If it is rooted deeply enough in a person, it can become a constant source of *ona'as devarim*, causing sarcasm, one-word answers or even rudeness in her interactions with the other person.

The first step to repairing the situation is to recognize the source of the negative feelings and try to deal with it in a more straightforward way. If possible, speak directly to the other person in a calm, non-argumentative tone. If there is a dispute, try to work it out. If there is a hurt, try to seek or give forgiveness. Even if you cannot directly express your feeling, or you do so but it doesn't change how you feel, it is valuable just to recognize that the hostile feelings are there. You then have the information you need to make a decision: Will you let your anger, or your best judgment, do the talking?

Reality Check:

Are there people who rub me the wrong way, with whom I have trouble restraining myself from *ona'as devarim*? If so, I will try to get to the root of my negative feelings and deal with it in a more productive way.

What If...

Vivi had expressed her hurt to Shaina? How might the conversation have sounded? What might the outcome have been?

---

17 *Tishrei* — לע"נ זלמן בן משה ואסתר רבקה ומשפחתו ע"ה
17 *Shevat* — לזכות חיים בן מרים נ"י
Dedicated by his חברותא
17 *Sivan* — לזכות חיים יוסף בן ליבא שיינדל נ"י
As a merit for Chaim Yosef *ben* Leba Shaindel *n"y*

A Thin Disguise ~ Hatred 3: Hidden hostility

DAY 18

Your Honor
~ Honor seeking

י"ח תשרי
18 Tishrei/Cycle 1

י"ח שבט
18 Shevat/Cycle 2

י"ח סיון
18 Sivan/Cycle 3

Chaya was gearing up. Every eye was on her as she began explaining her brilliant idea for the senior class fundraising event. It was the make-it-or-break-it event that would pay for the class yearbook and graduation trip, and the Event Committee was getting ready to solidify a plan. Chaya's heart swelled with pride as she thought about being the one to run the most successful event ever. Soon, everyone at the meeting would see how superior her plan was to the ideas that had been proposed by some of the other girls on the committee.

"O.K.," Chaya said as she opened her presentation, "I have a plan. I'll admit that I'm not going to be a big tzadekes like Michal, who wants to run a Tehillim-a-thon for the whole town." She smirked at Michal, who squirmed under the "tzadekes" spotlight.

"And I'm not going to create the event of the year, like Simi, who had a dream that we would run our own Olympic games. I guess she forgot that it takes four years to plan the Olympics," she continued, smiling smugly in Simi's direction. Simi's plan to invite neighboring schools to compete in a day of athletics sounded like the wild idea of an impractical fool.

"Here's what I suggest...," Chaya continued confidently. She carefully unveiled her grand plan step by step, knowing that every girl in the room would simply have to agree that no one was as sharp as she.

For a person like Chaya, honor is everything. It is so precious, in fact, that she is willing to ridicule others' honest efforts in order to boost her own standing. *Pirkei Avos*, however, teaches that Chaya's strategy is sure to backfire.

42   Chapter Two: What Fuels Hurtful Speech

"Who is honored?" *Pirkei Avos* (4:1) asks, and answers, "He who honors others." It would have been a simple matter for Chaya to give credit to the other girls who had put their own time and talent into coming up with fundraising ideas. Even if their ideas were impractical, they did not deserve embarrassment as payment for their efforts.

Why did Chaya completely overlook the opportunity to pay tribute to the others' ideas? The reason is that her only goal was to gain maximum credit and honor for herself. In her eyes, that meant that she had to avoid sharing it with anyone else. She looked at honor as one might look at something tangible, like money. If she gave some away to others, there would be less left for her.

Over the course of time, a person who craves honor insults many people and develops a reputation as an arrogant, self-centered person. She might eventually have her day; she might be named "Volunteer of the Year" for dozens of organizations, but the honor will exist in this world alone. From heaven's view, the people she has hurt with her credit-grabbing ways may far outweigh her achievements.

Reality Check:

Do I do things in order to get honor and recognition? Do I ever step on others in an effort to boost my own reputation?

What If...

Chaya was really concerned about having to reject the other girls' plans in favor of her own? How might she have begun her presentation?

---

18 Tishrei — In memory of my parents, Harold D. Kane *z"l yahrtzeit* 12 Adar and Eleanor R. Kane *a"h yahrtzeit* 18 Tishrei

18 Shevat — *L'ilui Nishmas* Harav Yitzchak *ben* Peretz *z"l* Dedicated for his tenth *yahrtzeit*, by Sandy & Eli Klein and family

18 Sivan — Dedicated by Reva and Gary Ambrose

DAY 19

Holy War
~ Idealism

י"ט תשרי
19 Tishrei/Cycle 1

י"ט שבט
19 Shevat/Cycle 2

י"ט סיון
19 Sivan/Cycle 3

When Rivky was 19, she set off for seminary in Israel with a group of her friends from high school. At first, the girls spent all their time together, which helped to make their strange surroundings seem a bit more familiar. Gradually, however, Rivky and her friends began to part ways.

While they spent their off-time traveling the country and shopping in Geula, Rivky took upon herself one chesed after another: baby-sitting for her teacher's children, helping young Jerusalem mothers cook and clean for Shabbos, visiting children in the hospital, tutoring weaker students. She forged a close bond with her principal and was often seen walking with her, deep in discussion.

"I don't get it," Rivky told her old friends as the group departed for a Friday-afternoon shopping trip. "You're in Eretz Yisrael! You're surrounded by these amazing, holy women! How can you spend your time shopping as if you're still in high school? You're wasting your parents' money." Rivky's friends had heard her rebukes a million times already; their solution was to ignore her. "She's not even human anymore," said one of the girls.

As Jews and as human beings created in Hashem's image, we all have a natural drive to reach for high ideals, not only in our spiritual lives, but in the way we approach our social lives, academic achievement, neatness, health and many other areas of life. Some people see these ideals very clearly, like the signs and traffic signals on the road in front of them. They are able to ignore all the distractions

44 Chapter Two: What Fuels Hurtful Speech

and strive with all their energy for the goals they've set for themselves. Often, these are the ingredients out of which greatness is made.

But there's a danger to such clear vision. This extraordinary person may not be able to see the world the way ordinary people see it. She may see her way as the only way to grow, and the stringencies she has adopted as the only way to succeed. She may not realize that her friends may be growing in ways she can't see, or that they may be heading in the right direction, but on a slower path. She may not understand why they are so tempted by distractions, why they find it so hard to live up to their own goals. Therefore, she may start focusing on other people's flaws. **If she is thinking poorly of others, she is almost sure to begin speaking poorly to them as well, resulting in *ona'as devarim*.**

And there's the irony. In this idealistic girl's efforts to become holier and purer, she actually transgresses the Torah's law against *ona'as devarim*. Yet if she would look at the lives of true *tzaddikim*, she would realize that not only are they devoted to Torah and mitzvos, but they are filled to the core with *ahavas Yisrael*.

Regardless of which ideals bring out the "holy warrior" in a person, this mind-set can stir up intolerance of others who seem deficient. Yet this approach is not only wrong because of the *ona'as devarim* it involves; it is also impractical. It doesn't work. **No one ever inspired other people by insulting them.** On the other hand, a person who strives and achieves, all the while treating others with friendliness, warmth and generosity, can truly inspire everyone in her life. Naturally, they will want to be just like her.

19 Tishrei — In honor of Dr. Bernie & Miriam Adler
With love by their children, grandchildren and great-grandchildren
19 Shevat — In honor of my borther Gabriel *n"y*
Dedicated by Ben Goldstein
19 Sivan — In memory of Yehoshua Chaim *ben* Shabse Pesachya Moskowitz *z"l*
Dedicated by the Moskowitz and Schulman families

Reality Check:

How do I act toward others when I feel that I am so very right and I can see that they are so very wrong? I will try to hold back my criticism and inspire by example instead.

What If...

instead of criticizing her friends, she had invited one or two of them to join her once in a while in a *chesed*, followed perhaps by some shopping or a slice of pizza? How might that have changed Rivky's attitude? How might it have affected her friends?

DAY 20

Danger of Explosion
~ Impatience

כ תשרי
20 Tishrei/Cycle 1

כ שבט
20 Shevat/Cycle 2

כ סיון
20 Sivan/Cycle 3

"Leah, you're such a pest!" Dina scolded her little sister. Leah was dancing around Dina excitedly, trying to tell her a story about her bus ride home from kindergarten. But Dina, who was on the phone with her friend, heard nothing but a squeaky little voice. *"Really, Leah, leave me alone! You're always yelling in my ear! I don't have patience for this!"*

Finally Leah gave up her effort to get Dina's attention. She strolled into the kitchen, found some paper and a pencil, and drew a picture of a big girl holding the hand of a little girl. Both were smiling.

Later that evening, when Leah was already in bed, Dina sat down at the kitchen table and noticed the picture. Her eyes filled with tears. She went up to her sister's room and found her fast asleep. She kissed the little girl gently on her soft cheek and whispered, "Good night." She wished she could have known beforehand what a wound her impatience was going to make in her sister's heart. She would never have fired off those harsh words.

As any older sibling can attest, younger children have a knack for interrupting, breaking things and acting irrationally. When you're in a hurry to go somewhere, he can't find his shoe. When you're on a trip, she's hungry or thirsty or needs the rest room. When you're out shopping, he wants to go home. When you're home relaxing, she wants to go to the park. When you're fast asleep, he wakes you up.

But the most important thing to know about children is that the big people in their lives are giants in their eyes. Whatever the adults in their family say, they take as truth. If you tell a child

46 Chapter Two: What Fuels Hurtful Speech

he's a pest, he believes himself to be a pest. If you treat him as a nuisance, or incompetent, he will eventually live up to your description of him.

If we allow ourselves to think that "I don't have patience" is a valid reason for harsh comments, we can expect to hurt friends, family members and ultimately, our very own beloved children. *Ona'as devarim* coming from an adult is tremendously powerful. Just as a child cannot safely absorb an adult dose of medicine, he cannot absorb an insult that an adult might just dismiss with a shrug and a "what's *her* problem?"

But even with adults, we can never know when our irritable little explosions will hit a sensitive nerve. Someone who is insecure about her place among her friends might feel rejected. A family member may feel unloved or disrespected. Someone who needs our help or attention might feel that she is a nuisance. Worst of all, with each impatient outburst, we are building a trait within ourselves that can only damage the families we hope to raise one day.

As young adults, the time is right to begin building patience. With this tool, we can enter adulthood equipped to succeed at the most important mission of our lives: building a home and a life that fosters a love of Torah, mitzvos and *yiras shamayim*.

Reality Check:
Am I impatient with children or other people in my life? How can I learn to reduce my annoyance and increase my appreciation of those I sometimes find demanding or irritating?

What If...
Dina had focused for just one moment on what her little sister was saying?

---

20 Tishrei — לע"נ מאיר וואלף בן דוב ז"ל
לזכות ישועות ורפואות for all of כלל ישראל.
20 Shevat — In memory of Jeanette Feldman *a"h* לע"נ עדינה בת יוכבד ע"ה
Dedicated by her daughter
20 Sivan — לע"נ מרים חיענע בת ר' אשר ע"ה
Dedicated by her loving son צבי הירש הורן

DAY 21

The Price of an Impulse
~ Impulsive speech

כ"א תשרי
21 Tishrei/Cycle 1

כ"א שבט
21 Shevat/Cycle 2

כ"א סיון
21 Sivan/Cycle 3

As Tzippora lay in bed reviewing the evening's events, she realized that her heart was still beating hard. The emotions aroused by her latest battle with her mother were slow to fade. How had she let herself get caught up in such a tidal wave? She thought back to the early part of the evening, when she had just come home from school.

She had been in a terrible mood: an F on her math test, a lecture from her principal, a fight with her friend… another bad day. She dumped her book-bag on the floor and headed upstairs to the peace and quiet of her room.

"Can't you say hello?" her mother had called out.

"I had a bad day," Tzippora had replied irritably. "I'm going up to my room. Don't make me supper. I'll take my own later."

"Just make sure you wash your dishes," her mother had responded curtly, obviously upset at Tzippora's tone. It was true that Tzippora's late-night suppers often resulted in a mess, but really, right at that moment, did it have to be mentioned? She felt attacked, as if her mother were issuing an order just to prove she was still the boss. Did she need to be made to feel like a child?

Tzippora turned to her mother and screamed, "Stop it! Stop trying to run my life! Leave me alone!" She stomped up the stairs, slammed the door and cried. Somewhere in the background, she heard her mother's outraged response of "Don't you dare speak to your mother like that!"

Now, an hour later, she sat humiliated. Why had she let loose like that? How could she approach her mother after treating her so disrespectfully? Why did she have to make yet another problem for herself, as if the problems with school and friends weren't enough?

48 Chapter Two: What Fuels Hurtful Speech

Tzippora surely did not want to be unhappy. No one does. Therefore, you would think that everyone would avoid hurtful words as much as possible. **You would think that people would realize that many of the problems and hard feelings they experience start as harsh criticism or a cruel comment.** Once someone fires the "first shot," the other party defends herself with the same weapon. Soon, so much pain has been inflicted on both sides that forgiveness seems almost impossible.

Why, then, do people even start on this path? The answer is impulsiveness. **The *yetzer hara* functions best when people speak before they think about the consequences.** As long as their only concern is the momentary pleasure of getting back at the other person, *ona'as devarim* seems to make perfect sense.

But when we stop and think about how important our relationships are to our happiness, we see the great wisdom in holding our fire and finding another way to deal with the irritation of the moment. Eventually, we realize that our angry impulses, like a broken GPS, will always lead us in the wrong direction. With that hard lesson learned, we are far more inclined to turn a deaf ear to what those impulses are telling us.

Reality Check:

How often do I say something that I wish I could take back? If this is a problem for me, I will try to devise a reminder for myself that will help me delay my hurtful words long enough to think about their impact.

What If...

Tzippora had found a more productive way to let her mother know that she needed some time alone? What might Tzippora have said to convey that message?

---

21 Tishrei — Dedicated as a *z'chus* for our dear daughter Michaela Chana שתחי׳
With love, Dad & Mom — Jaron & Shelley Tobias, Johannesburg, South Africa

21 Shevat — לע״נ טובא בת צבי ע״ה נלב״ע כ״ו שבט
Dedicated by Michael and Erica Sommer and family

21 Sivan — May today's learning be a זכות for the Grunfeld family.

DAY 22

Wearing Armor
~ Insecurity

כ"ב תשרי
22 Tishrei/Cycle 1

כ"ב שבט
22 Shevat/Cycle 2

כ"ב סיון
22 Sivan/Cycle 3

> *The long line of Roman soldiers marched for hours in the hot sun. It was 90 degrees outside, but for them the temperature was far higher, because they were covered from head to toe in armor. Not only were they required to wear these terribly uncomfortable, heavy, suffocating uniforms, but in fact, they wanted to wear them. Their armor, they knew, protected them from the spears and swords of their enemies.*

Although it doesn't clank and glisten in the sun, armor is still worn by many people today. It is emotional armor, a tough, hard exterior that hides their lack of confidence in themselves. Just as a soldier puts on his armor to protect his vulnerable body, people who wear emotional armor use it to protect their vulnerable self-image. While most people can accept themselves even if they make the occasional mistake, people with a weak self-image cannot stand being discovered to be wrong or lacking in any way.

Tehilla was not the most motivated student, mostly because she found the work confusing. Instead of admitting to herself or anyone else that she lacked some academic abilities, she taught herself to see academic achievement as a waste of time. When her teacher announced an essay contest, her friends spent recess discussing the topics on which they might write. "This whole thing is so babyish. An essay contest—what are we, second graders?" Tehilla said. "I don't know why you're wasting your time on it. I guess if you don't have a life...."

The problem with "armor" is that it doesn't just protect the person inside, it repels the people outside. People who try to make themselves invulnerable to criticism often do so by displaying character traits that make them more likely to attract criticism. They appear cruel, uncaring and immature, a state which not only discourages anyone from criticizing them but discourages others from befriending them as well. Furthermore, their ferocious front is see through. It doesn't take long for others to realize that the aggressive exterior hides a frightened interior. They soon perceive that the brave words "I don't care what anyone thinks" mean "If I let myself care about what others think, I might be crushed by their disapproval."

Thus, the armor does not succeed in protecting its wearer from the poor opinions others have of her. In fact, it can cause much of that poor opinion.

For a person who uses hostility and aggression as a means of protecting herself, *ona'as devarim* **becomes a way of life.** She "says it how she sees it" and in doing so, alienates so many people that she gradually loses every relationship that might actually help to build real, lasting self-esteem within her.

There's only one way out of this rut: to recognize it and start strengthening the interior so that the armor will not seem necessary. **This can be done by bending in the opposite direction: encouraging and helping others, seeking and accepting advice from others, and most of all, accepting oneself as a unique and worthy creation of Hashem.** When a person follows this path, she finds that she no longer needs to be tough. She can survive the news of her own imperfection and even use it to inspire tremendous personal growth.

Reality Check:

How would I want myself to be described? Is it important to me to be considered particularly tough or individualistic? Do I mind being considered a soft, sensitive person?

What If...

a person develops "armor" because she has experienced a great deal of pain and difficulty in her relations with others? For instance, what if she has some physical trait that has brought her ridicule? How can she learn to live without armor?

---

22 **Tishrei** — As a z'chus for זרע של קיימא for those who are in need
22 **Shevat** — לע״נ בתי׳ רחל בת משה יוסף ע״ה
22 **Sivan** — In memory of Mr. Hirsch Wolf z״l לע״נ צבי יעקב בן ר׳ חיים ז״ל
Dedicated by his children: the Wolf, Dessler and Ginsberg families

DAY 23

Feeling Green
~ Jealousy

כ"ג תשרי
23 Tishrei/Cycle 1

כ"ג שבט
23 Shevat/Cycle 2

כ"ג סיון
23 Sivan/Cycle 3

Riva knew she should be happy for her sister, Batya. There she was, center stage, playing the lead role in the school play. Meanwhile, Riva was terrified of performing in front of an audience. She stayed backstage handling the props, watching her sister shine. Listening to Batya's strong, steady voice singing one of her dramatic solos, Riva admitted to herself that she certainly deserved the role. But why did Batya have all the self-confidence while Riva always had to struggle just to raise her hand in class?

When Batya's solo was over, she ran backstage to prepare for the next act. Riva, who was standing in the wings, rushed over to her sister and smothered her in a hug.

"You were fantastic!" she forced herself to say. She knew she should stop there, but she couldn't. Her jealousy boiled up from her heart and spurted out in words that instantly deflated the praise: "You're so lucky you can do it. But it makes sense, because you just love to be in the spotlight."

When a person feels inferior to others or is jealous of them, she might find herself searching eagerly for their flaws just to prove to herself that others are "not so great." It is reassuring for her to confirm that everyone has their areas of weakness because that makes her own weaknesses seem less important. For instance, someone who feels she is not quite as religious as she should be might look at others who appear more religious, and tell herself that they are not as kind hearted as she is, or as happy. Someone who is jealous of other people's wealth might deride them

52 Chapter Two: What Fuels Hurtful Speech

for flaunting their expensive clothes or accuse them of being a snob. In other words, "She's got nothing over me."

These jealous thoughts become *ona'as devarim* when they seep into our interactions with the other person, and they always do. The negative thoughts fuel negative comments, which cause needless hurt. **Therefore, the way to prevent this kind of *ona'as devarim* is to work on eliminating the jealous thoughts.** When a person understands that each individual receives the portion Hashem has designated for her, and that this portion is exactly what she needs to accomplish her life's purposes, there can be no jealousy. A dentist doesn't long for a carpenter's tools, nor does a carpenter long for a dentist's tools.

When a person masters this attitude, other people's good fortune no longer "hurts." It's no longer a contest of "her or me," because what one person receives has no bearing on what the other person receives. In the story above, if Batya had not won the lead role, Riva still would not have had it.

For many people, it's easier to cry over a friend's sorrow than share the joy of a friend's good fortune. This can only be because we are never jealous of someone else's sorrow. But in reality, we would spend many more happy hours in this world if we could make other people's happiness a source of our own.

Reality Check:

Am I jealous of some people in my life? Would my life be made any better by their lives becoming worse?

What If...

Riva, knowing that jealousy was a problem for her, had prepared exactly what she was going to say to Batya after the performance? What might she have decided to say?

לע"נ ר' יחיאל בן ר' משה ז"ל ואשתו רבקה בת ר' יצחק אייזיק ע"ה — **23 Tishrei**
לע"נ ר' אפרים בן ר' משה ז"ל ואשתו רבקה בת ר' שמואל ע"ה
לע"נ שמואל דן הלוי בן מיכאל יהודה ז"ל נלב"ע כ"ה שבט — **23 Shevat**
By Sophie Polevoy and Chayim, the Shammahs and the Greenfields
לע"נ רב שמאול אביגדור בן רב יצחק מאיר זצ"ל — **23 Sivan**

DAY 24

Kicking the Habit
~ Lack of thought

כ"ד תשרי
24 Tishrei/Cycle 1

כ"ד שבט
24 Shevat/Cycle 2

כ"ד סיון
24 Sivan/Cycle 3

> The phone was ringing somewhere in the house. "Where's the phone?" Esti Reiner shouted to the family at large. "Who's got it?"
>
> By the time the handset was located—as usual, in Mindy's bedroom—the caller had hung up. Checking the caller ID, Esti saw that it was Candy Palace, no doubt calling about her summer-job application.
>
> "How many times have I told you to return the phone to the stand?" Esti complained to her younger sister. "It's not right that every time it rings we have to hunt all over the house!" Calling back the number, Esti discovered that the owner had left for the day. Now she was really furious.
>
> "You're so careless! Don't you ever think about what you're doing?" Esti scolded. "We go through this a hundred times a day and you still can't stop to think of someone else!"

Esti's sister had a bad habit: leaving the phone wherever she happened to be. But Esti had a worse habit. She was quick to criticize, and being a perfectionist by nature, she always found plenty worthy of her criticism. Carelessness was one of Esti's pet peeves. How could people act without thinking, especially when their thoughtlessness ended up causing inconvenience to other people?

What Esti did not realize was that she, too, was guilty of acting without thinking. Whenever a harsh judgment popped into her head, it inevitably ran right out of her mouth without a second's thought. It was only after the words had flown from her mouth that she noticed the look of hurt on the other person's face and wished she had held her tongue. Yet she repeated her pattern over and over again, just as surely as her sister mindlessly left the phone wherever it happened to land.

Most people think that this is the natural way a human being speaks. We say far too many words each day to weigh and measure each one. Our conversations, it would seem, would be awkward and stilted if we had to think about each word. **Nevertheless, the truth is that every word starts out as a thought.** Our brains are already on duty when the process of speaking begins. Are our brains capable of quickly weighing the impact of the words that are forming, and then filtering out the ones that might cause harm?

They are. We know this because in certain situations, such as when we want to impress someone or avoid getting someone angry, we automatically turn on the filter to block out words that might have a negative impact. This fact proves that **when it really matters to us, we can control what we say.**

That leaves us with one challenge: making it matter all the time. **When we take stock of the damage the habit of *ona'as devarim* does to us, to other people and to the important relationships in our lives, we realize that it does matter very much.** With this realization, we can make a sincere effort to form a new habit: to think before we speak. Someone who is really serious about achieving this goal can do simple things, such as posting reminder signs in strategic spots, to keep the idea in mind until it becomes second nature.

The person who tries will not fail; where human effort leaves off, Divine assistance steps in. We can count on Hashem to provide His support to all those who devote themselves to protecting the dignity of their fellow Jew.

Reality Check:

How often do I end up regretting something I said? If that does occasionally happen to me, I will begin to fix the problem by realizing that control is possible.

What If...

Esti's sister's carelessness with the telephone really does need to be addressed? Could Esti address the problem? If so, when and how could she do it without *ona'as devarim*?

---

24 Tishrei — Gavriel Gavrielov *z"l* לע״נ גבריאל בן ברוריא ז״ל נלב״ע כ״א אב ב׳ה
Dedicated by Rabbi and Mrs. Nisan Gavrielov

24 Shevat — May today's learning be a *z'chus* for our parents and grandparents.
Dedicated by the Liberchuk family

24 Sivan — In memory of our parents Bella *bas* Kalman and Abram *ben* Shmuel *a"h*
Dedicated by their daughters

DAY 25

The Perfect Problem
~ Perfectionism

כ"ה תשרי
25 Tishrei/Cycle 1

כ"ה שבט
25 Shevat/Cycle 2

כ"ה סיון
25 Sivan/Cycle 3

"How do I get myself into these things?" said Hindy, half to herself and half out loud. In two hours, the entire school would be arriving for the Chanukah chagigah, and the auditorium looked atrocious. As head of the event, Hindy would be mortified. She couldn't do everything herself, but why was it that no one ever did anything right? She spotted Batsheva pushing a 10-foot-tall cardboard dreidel onto the stage.

"No! Batsheva, what are you doing? I told you, that thing is not going out until the skit!" Batsheva silently pushed the giant dreidel back off-stage. Hindy looked around to see what else needed doing. She spotted a group of girls sampling the cookies they were laying out on the table.

"Hello! Everyone! I don't want the table to look half-empty by the time people get here! And who's supposed to be setting up the chairs? We don't need everyone at the sweet table!"

"Chill out, Hindy!" said one cookie-eating girl. "There's tons of food. We're supposed to be having fun!"

"Yeah, well, it's not you who's going to look like a fool when everyone comes and nothing is ready," Hindy retorted. But in a corner of her mind, she thought a little sadly, "Is this really supposed to be fun? I wish it were!"

Hindy's tension and the *ona'as devarim* it causes arise out of her need for perfection. People like Hindy approach everything in their lives, whether something as important as their studies or as trivial as the color of the paper plates for the *chagigah*, as if it is of life-or-death significance.

56 Chapter Two: What Fuels Hurtful Speech

They place such unbearable pressure on themselves that they are bound to crack, bound to explode and release the pressure onto others. Her non-stop criticism and tension make her impossible to work with. Her siblings, friends and classmates stand clear; there's no pleasing her.

Often, people who are perfectionists do not want to be so hard on people. They recognize that this, too, is an imperfection. Therefore, after berating everyone else, they end up berating themselves for being unkind.

In other ways, as well, the perfectionist makes herself unhappy. No matter how well she does, she knows she could always have done a little better. No matter how high she climbs, there's always a higher peak to push for. She is never satisfied, and sometimes, she is not even willing to try something new, because she knows that her first efforts will, of course, be imperfect.

Any time we strive for perfection, we must realize that we are chasing an illusion. Imperfection is the human condition—the way Hashem created us. In fact, in the *berachah* of *Borei Nefashos*, we thank Hashem for creating a multitude of people *v'chesronan*, "and their imperfections," a clear statement that our deficiencies are a planned part of the fabric of creation. Our job is to do Hashem's will, working with the gifts and deficiencies we have, and to recognize that every person is gifted and flawed in her own, Divinely ordained way. When we stop using perfection as our measuring stick, we find that we and the others in our lives no longer seem to fall short.

Reality Check:

Am I a perfectionist? How does it impact the way I judge and speak to others? How does it affect my contentment with my own life? In what area of my life can I begin to let go of this trait?

What If...

Hindy had the self-control to speak kindly and respectfully when she corrected people, but still demanded perfection? Would the trait of perfectionism still be a problem?

---

25 Tishrei — In honor of my wife Lisa Garfunkel שתחי׳
Lovingly dedicated by her husband Nosson Garfunkel
25 Shevat — לזכות לברכה והצלחה בריאות ושמחה למשפחת סלקין
25 Sivan — לזכות רבקה חנה בת דוידה צביה שתחי׳
Dedicated by her husband

DAY 26

The Picky Patient
~ Illness/lack of sleep

כ"ו תשרי
26 Tishrei/Cycle 1

כ"ו שבט
26 Shevat/Cycle 2

כ"ו סיון
26 Sivan/Cycle 3

Debby could not believe how painful her throat was. Somehow, she had caught strep from her little brother, and she was stuck in bed with a high fever, a boring book to read and the feeling that her head was made of lead. If only she could get a refill of her ice water! She had asked her younger sister Riva to bring it to her—it seemed like hours ago—and here she was, still waiting. On top of all that, she couldn't even call out; it was too painful.

Debby could hear clanking around in the kitchen. Just as Riva had gone to fill up the pitcher, her 2-year-old brother had started emptying out a cabinet full of pots and pans. Riva took a few minutes to put them away.

"I'll bet she's making herself a snack," thought Debby bitterly. "She's probably gonna sit down and eat a whole grand meal before she remembers me. What does she care that I'm waiting here in pain?"

Moments later, Riva arrived with the pitcher and a sympathetic look on her face. "Here, Debby," she said, offering the pitcher. "I hope this helps your throat."

"Well, it's about time you showed up!" Debby responded sourly. "What were you doing down there for so long? My throat hurts so much and I was waiting and waiting!"

Riva understood that her sister felt miserable. But Riva had given up a Sunday at her best friend's house to keep Debby company, and now she felt unappreciated. She was hurt, even though she knew her sister was not really "herself."

The best protection against saying something hurtful to another person is to think before speaking. That takes strength and self-control, two traits that are at their low point when someone is not feeling well, whether from illness, lack of sleep or some other reason. In that condition, everything is annoying: bright light, being too warm or too cold, waiting for help or food, noise, odors—everything!

However, the Torah does not offer a special allowance for people who are sick or tired. **The challenge to avoid *ona'as devarim* in those circumstances is therefore very great.** While some people are "perfect patients" who actually cheer up those who come to help them, many people find their situation overwhelming. They can treat others in a bossy, demanding way that creates a lot of hurt.

The result is sadly ironic; the patient hurts the very people who are trying to help her. To avoid that outcome, the patient has to focus on recognizing the help she is receiving. Even if the help is not perfect, it should not be rewarded with criticism and insults. This situation, though it can be very difficult, is a good opportunity to build patience and appreciation that will benefit the person even when she's in the best of health.

Reality Check:

When I'm sick or tired or under extra stress, do I excuse myself for treating others in an impatient way? If so, I will remind myself in such situations that there is no "health exemption" from the Torah's rule against *ona'as devarim*.

What If...

Riva really was taking her time and making herself a snack? Would that have given Debby a reason to snap at her? How could she have handled the situation without speaking *ona'as devarim*?

---

26 Tishrei — לזכות ברכה, הצלחה, בריאות, פרנסה ונחת
למשפחת אהרן אליהו הרצוג

26 Shevat — In memory of our dear mother ע"ה לע"נ פייגה חנה בת יעקב ע"ה
Dedicated by her loving family

26 Sivan — לזכות ברכה, הצלחה, בריאות, פרנסה ונחת
Dedicated by Mr. and Mrs. Joseph Kahan and children, Idy and Moshe

The Picky Patient ~ Illness/lack of sleep

Imaginary Enemies
~ Imagined insults

DAY 27

כ"ז תשרי
27 Tishrei/Cycle 1

כ"ז שבט
27 Shevat/Cycle 2

כ"ז סיון
27 Sivan/Cycle 3

Ilana's new school had everything she wanted: challenging classes, great extracurricular programs and teachers who really knew their stuff. Even though she had transferred in tenth grade, she already felt right at home with her small group of friends.

The downside was that the girls outside her little group made her very self-conscious. It was a rich-kids' school, and Ilana and her friends were not rich kids. That meant that they had little to add to conversations that revolved around exclusive clothing brands, summers in Israel and the latest electronics. Basically, Ilana's group kept to themselves, happy to take advantage of all that the school had to offer.

Ilana's only irritation was Temmy, a girl from a very wealthy family who had apparently decided to make Ilana her "chesed case." She was always inviting Ilana to study with her and partner with her on class projects. But Ilana wasn't interested in helping Temmy show the world how great she was. "I've already got someone to work with," Ilana replied to all of Temmy's offers.

One day during recess, Temmy was trying to strike up a conversation with Ilana. "I've gotta go," Ilana told her. "I left something in my locker."

"Ilana, can I ask you something?" Temmy replied. Feeling trapped, Ilana nodded.

"Why are you always avoiding me? Why can't we be friends?" Temmy asked.

"I'm not interested in being your 'case'!" Ilana replied hotly. "You don't have to prove how nice you are to the poor kids!"

Temmy was crushed. She felt as if she were wounded in a battle that she didn't even know she was fighting.

Many people spend their energy fighting imaginary fights. They decide, based on their own false impressions or feelings of inferiority, that someone thinks poorly of them and based on that, they build up a case against the other person. They misinterpret words, actions and even facial expressions to support their unfounded assumptions, and in defense, they treat the other person with undeserved hostility.

What creates these false impressions? Often it is our own preconceptions. "Look at her. She's so smart. She probably laughs to herself when I answer a question in class." "She's so gorgeous. She probably wouldn't want to be seen with someone like me." "She lives in a mansion. She would never come to my house for a Shabbos." "Her father is the Rosh Yeshivah. She wouldn't be friends with someone from a regular family."

But it could be that none of these impressions are true. **When we act on our preconceptions, we find ourselves fighting a fight that has only one side.** Eventually, this leads to lashing out angrily at someone who has absolutely no negative feelings about us.

The only way to avoid this kind of *ona'as devarim* is to listen for the thoughts running through our minds. When we look at someone who is simply minding her own business and say to ourselves, *She thinks she's so great,* we are raising the temperature of our emotions. Then all it takes is one wrong look or one wrong word from that person to push our emotions to the boiling point. If we realize that our negative thoughts may be baseless, we can keep our thoughts positive and pleasant and our inner temperature cool, so that even if a possible insult does come our way, we can deal with it calmly.

Reality Check:

Do I sometimes judge others' feelings toward me without a basis in fact? If so, I will do an experiment; I will "break the ice" by making a friendly statement to someone for whom I have an unfounded negative feeling.

What If...

Temmy really was reaching out to Ilana just to be nice? Would Ilana's response have been appropriate then? What might Ilana have told herself about the situation that would have given her a more positive feeling toward Temmy?

---

27 Tishrei — Dedicated as a *z'chus* for the Kahen family
27 Shevat — לע"נ יוסף זיסקינד בן שלמה הכהן גמרמן ז"ל נלב"ע א' אדר
Dedicated by Shlomo Gammerman
27 Sivan — לזכות בנציון בן רות נ"י
Dedicated by Mordechai and Avigail Jaffa

Imaginary Enemies ~ Imagined insults

DAY 28

"Well, What Do You Expect?"
~ Justification

28 Tishrei/Cycle 1

28 Shevat/Cycle 2

28 Sivan/Cycle 3

Aviva Gross was not cut out for dorm life. Back home, she had her own spacious room, which she kept in perfect order. Here in seminary, there were four girls to each small room, and none of those girls shared Aviva's need for private space. They constantly traded skirts and shirts, shampoos and lip gloss as if everything belonged to everyone.

Knowing that this "all for one and one for all" mentality would drive her crazy, Aviva set her boundaries. "I'm just not comfortable sharing my things," she told her roommates. "So if you want to borrow something, please don't take it without asking. I'm telling you, it will really get me mad if you do. And I don't want to get mad."

The other girls thought she must be joking. Who said things like that? The first Shabbos of the school year, Aviva shuffled through her drawer looking for her turquoise hair clip. "I know I stuck it in here when I unpacked," she thought. Then her roommate, Rikki, walked into the room.

"Where did you get that?" Aviva asked accusingly, staring at the turquoise clip holding back Rikki's bangs.

"Oh, you were in the shower and I had to run to get the tables set for Shabbos, so I couldn't ask you about the clip," Rikki said. "I didn't think you'd mind."

"You didn't think I'd mind?" Aviva railed. "I told you the first day of school that I would mind. I can't believe you just helped yourself! How can you be so inconsiderate?"

Rikki felt as though she had opened an oven door and been blasted in the face by the heat. She mumbled "sorry," and slunk out of the room. Aviva gave a

62 Chapter Two: What Fuels Hurtful Speech

satisfied sigh. "I told them not to touch my stuff," she thought, "and now they know I mean it."

People do not usually make hurtful remarks just to be cruel. They usually have some reason behind what they say: "I'm just being honest." "I have to protect myself." "She needs to learn a lesson." "She pushed me too far." "She had it coming."

However, even when someone has what she considers a valid reason, there is still another step to take before speaking. **That is, to find a way to say her piece without using hostile, angry words.** This is especially true when she already knows that a certain person or situation gets under her skin. In that case, she has the opportunity to prepare other ways to react. She can even rehearse different responses.

For instance, if Aviva in the above story is often bothered by people using her belongings, she can think of firm, non-hostile ways to get her feelings across to those who continue to ignore her wishes. "I realize that most people don't mind sharing things, but I am really serious about my personal things. It's important to me." She may have to say it a few times in a few different ways, but she will eventually solve the problem without causing hurt.

When a doctor treats an infection, he starts off with the weakest medicine that can do the job. He only goes to a stronger medication if the weaker one doesn't work. That is how we should go about curing the irritating behaviors of others: **the kindest, softest words that will do the job are the ones we must try first**, no matter how irritated we are, no matter how valid our reason might be.

28 Tishrei — לזכות דוד אברהם בן שרה נ"י
Dedicated by his mother Sarah Friedland
28 Shevat — In memory of Rachel *bat* Victoria a"h - *Yahrtzeit* 29 *Shevat*
Dedicated by her children and grandchildren
28 Sivan — לזכות בתי-ה יהודית בת שרה שתחי'

Reality Check:

Do I sometimes feel that I've been pushed to a point where my angry words are justified? If there is a "pet peeve" or situation that comes up again and again, I will work out a respectful way of dealing with it and practice before the situation arises.

What If...

no matter how many times Aviva expresses herself calmly, her roommates do not respect her privacy? What alternatives should she pursue? Do angry words ever become a legitimate alternative? Why or why not?

DAY 29

Misunderstood
~ Miscommunication

כ"ט תשרי
29 Tishrei/Cycle 1

כ"ט שבט
29 Shevat/Cycle 2

כ"ט סיון
29 Sivan/Cycle 3

Rachel didn't know what hit her. She was having what she thought was a perfectly normal conversation with her co-counselor, Bina, when all of a sudden, Bina became furious at her and stomped out of the bunkhouse yelling, "If that's what you think of me, I don't have to stay here and listen to you anymore!"

And there Rachel stood, alone in the bunkhouse. She re-ran the conversation in her mind.

Rachel: Today was such an unproductive day. Everything I tried to do got messed up somehow.

Bina: I know just what you mean! Every time I started working on the color war poster, one of the campers needed something right that second! I got pretty much zero done.

Rachel: Well, that's nothing new. . .

Bina: Oh, yeah? That's what you think? You are always so self-centered! You really don't appreciate what I do at all!"

Meanwhile, sitting in a private corner near the stream, Bina cried her eyes out thinking of how ungrateful Rachel was for all the time she put into taking care of their campers. It was the youngest bunk in camp and they needed help with everything. Bina had taken that motherly role upon herself while Rachel did most of the planning and organization. Well, let Rachel see what it's like to spend the day tying shoes and buttoning sweaters!

Rachel thought she had been showing sympathy for Bina, who always had to deal with the kind of frustration that Rachel only experienced once in a while. That is why she commented that getting "zero done" was "nothing new" for Bina, who was always busy with the campers' needs. Bina, on the other hand, felt that Rachel was criticizing her, saying that she never got anything done.

Often, if you search for the seed of an argument, you find miscommunication or misinterpretation of something someone said. The person who feels insulted responds with *ona'as devarim* out of a desire to defend herself and return the insult. In doing so, she causes pain to the other person, who may not have even realized there was an argument brewing.

There are several ways to avoid going to war over a mistaken understanding of someone else's words. First, we have to **listen to each other carefully.** Very often, people begin thinking about how they are going to answer before the other person has even finished speaking. The listener is therefore not really listening, and is almost guaranteed to misunderstand what is being said.

The second way is to **become familiar with people's styles of speech.** Some people have a blunt or gruff way of expressing themselves. They may sound angry or aggressive, but they are not.

Finally, **always clarify the other person's intentions.** Ask in a calm, normal tone if they mean what you think they mean.

With these three steps, we can avoid taking offense at words that were never meant to offend. In the course of listening, thinking and clarifying what someone says, even if the words do turn out to be somewhat hostile, the listener's anger will probably lose its edge and her response will be calmer and more reasonable.

---

29 Tishrei — לע"נ חי' בת שמעון צבי ריעדרער ע"ה
Dedicated by Kenneth Ephraim and Julie Pinczower

29 Shevat — לע"נ פעסיל מלכה בת שמואל הכהן ע"ה
Dedicated by her children and grandchildren

29 Sivan — As a *z'chus* for our family and *Klal Yisrael* on our anniversary
Dedicated by Dr. and Mrs. Sam Friedlander

Reality Check:

When I feel that I'm under attack, do I really listen to what the other person is saying or do I start forming my defense and rebuttal before she finishes? If I tend to block out the other person's words, I will try to listen carefully, think and clarify before I respond.

What If...

Bina had responded to Rachel's comment with a question for clarification? What would be a good question for her to ask? What impact might Rachel and Bina's relationship have on the above scenario: What if there was always tension between them? What if they generally got along well?

DAY 30

Ha-Ha
~ Misguided humor

ל תשרי
30 Tishrei/Cycle 1

ל שבט
30 Shevat/Cycle 2

ל סיון
30 Sivan/Cycle 3

The Mendelson family had a sharp, lively sense of humor. They loved to tease one another and they could do perfect impressions of people they knew. Sometimes they would spontaneously create a comical character and launch into a whole hilarious routine. Whenever they got together, their family jokes always wove their way into their conversations.

One day, the oldest sister, Rena, became engaged. Her chassan was planning to spend Shabbos at the Mendelsons, and Rena was filled with panic.

"Not ONE JOKE about him!" she instructed her siblings. "NOTHING! No teasing, no funny comments. His family has a completely different sense of humor and he's definitely not going to realize you're joking, believe me!"

"What do you mean, Rena? Is he the type of guy who can't take a joke?" her younger brother asked in disbelief. It seemed impossible that such a person could be joining their family.

Humor, like ice cream, is a matter of taste. What one person finds incredibly delicious and satisfying can be distasteful to another person. However, there is another, more serious potential problem with humor: it can actually hurt and insult people. The funny, clever comments that pop into a witty person's mind can sometimes be humiliating to the subject of the comment.

This is especially true if the "joke" is said in front of others. In private, the victim might be able to say, "That's not funny." But with a whole group of people laughing and smiling at the joker's great wit, the victim is defenseless. If he admits being hurt, everyone sees him as oversensitive or lacking a sense of humor. People will think or say, "Can't you take a joke?" which only adds to his humiliation.

Even with this potential for inflicting real damage, there are many people who just cannot keep a clever comment to themselves. Often, such people crave the feeling of being admired for their wit. They are like performers who will do anything for applause, and although they do not set out to hurt anyone, they are so focused on getting the laugh that they never consider how others might take the joke. The joke might not even be aimed at a person; it might make fun of a certain trait or group of people.

On the more positive side, sometimes they are motivated by the pleasure of making others laugh; they may even feel that it's a mitzvah to do so. Nevertheless, **if they do not use humor with sensitivity, the laughs they receive may be at someone else's expense.**

But it is not always the joker who commits *ona'as devarim*. Sometimes the joker is simply trying to share a laugh, so he tells a joke or a story that he finds funny. The audience, whether it's one person or several, can inflict great humiliation on the joker by groaning, staring blank faced at the person or giving a clearly fake laugh.

What, then, can a person do to deal with someone who always tells bad jokes? The best way to deal with the situation is to tell the other person that, for instance, "I don't know why, but those kinds of jokes just never make me laugh." In other words, it's your sense of humor, not the other person's joke, which is lacking.

> **Reality Check:**
>
> Do I consider myself a great judge of humor? Do I believe that what's funny to me is funny, and what isn't funny to me is not funny? If so, I might well be hurting other people with my jokes or my reactions to their jokes.

> **What If...**
>
> Rena had not forewarned her family that her *chassan* would likely take offense at their sense of humor? How might the Shabbos meal have unfolded? What could Rena do if her family's jokes got out of hand?

---

30 Tishrei — In memory of Sidney Broome ז״ל לע״נ ישראל יצחק בן ר׳ אברהם שלמה ז״ל
Dedicated by Bernard Broome

30 Shevat — לע״נ הרב מיכאל בן הרב מרדכי הלוי מינקוף ז״ל
Dedicated by his loving children Judy and Bob Pransky

30 Sivan — לזכות אליהו ישראל נ״י בן דבורה קנדל תחי׳

Ha-Ha ~ Misguided humor 67

Cheshvan

Dedicated as a z'chus for our family

By Mr. and Mrs. Leo Berger

---

*In loving memory of Nan Woodrow Mark
and Ansel Mark a"h*

*Dedicated by their children, grandchildren
and great-grandchildren*

In memory of my parents

לע"נ מלך בן אברהם הכהן ז"ל
ואשתו חוה בת נחום הכהן ע"ה

Dedicated by Dr. and Mrs. Charles Forgy

Adar

לזכות ריטה בת לונה שתחי'

In honor of my wife Rita Cohen and for hatzlachah and good health for the whole family Dedicated by her husband Benjamin Cohen

In honor of the bar mitzvah of our twins

אברהם צבי ואיתן יהודה נ"י

Dedicated by Mr. and Mrs. Marc Kwestel

לזכות רינה בת שרה שתחי'

Tammuz

לע"נ אהרן דוד בן שמעון הכהן ז"ל נלב"ע ט"ו תמוז

In memory of
Mrs. Zeesy Klein a"h לע"נ זיסל בת צבי ע"ה
Who survived churban Europe and came to America and built a
Jewish home with emunah and simchah
She was one of the founders of the
"Crown Heights Bikur Cholim."
Dedicated by her daughters
Peri Garfinkel, Ruchy Gottleib and Devora Goodman

Dedicated as a z'chus for my grandchidren

Rena, Temima, Avraham, Benyamin,
Meira and Jasie

DAY 31

Protecting the Border
~ Need for privacy

א חשון
1 Cheshvan/Cycle 1

א אדר*
*1 Adar/Cycle 2

א תמוז
1 Tammuz/Cycle 3

* During Hebrew leap years, a thirteenth month called Adar Sheini is added to the calendar. During those years, the lessons for the days of Adar should be studied during each of the Adars.

א אדר ב
1 Adar Sheini

"Machla! I can't believe you're doing it!" Shira shrieked as her friend walked into the class Purim chagigah. Shira's clown hat bobbed on her head as she ran to intercept Machla at the door.

"What can't you believe?" Machla asked, taking a protective step back from her overexcited classmate. Nosy Shira was at it again, fishing around for the latest scoop.

"You know! Transferring! Going out of town for 12th grade!"

Machla felt anger rising up inside her. She had been thinking, investigating and discussing this move for months. The last thing she wanted was for her carefully thought-out decision to be the latest subject of class gossip, but apparently, somehow, word was out. And with Shira in the know, it was only a matter of time—probably just seconds—before everyone would know.

Not that it was a secret. It was just that Machla had thought long and hard about this. She did not want to have to review her whole process with everyone she knew, answer their questions, debate their objections and so forth. It was her business; she and her parents had made the decision, and that was the way she wanted it to stay.

"It's not up for public discussion," Machla answered Shira coldly.

"Well, O.K., O.K.," Shira said, offended. "It's just 'cause I care about my friends."

"Right now I wish you didn't care so much," Machla retorted as she moved past Shira into the crowd.

"Be that way," Shira mumbled to herself. "What did I do so terrible?"

72 Chapter Two: What Fuels Hurtful Speech

People's sense of privacy varies. Some people are very open with their life; they enjoy bouncing their ideas, goals and problems off others. Others, however, feel more protective of their private lives and they view others' interest in the details as an intrusion. Each person has a boundary between her private life and her public life, and it is a boundary that should be respected. That means finding ways to show interest in others' lives while still making an effort to avoid "nosy" questions.

On the other hand, we don't have to shoot live ammunition at anyone who sets a toe over the border. In most cases, people ask "nosy" questions out of curiosity or to keep a conversation going. There is very rarely any way in which the questioner can force the other person to disclose private information. Therefore, no real harm is done. Her secrets are still hers to keep; she is simply annoyed at what she sees as an invasion of her privacy.

If there is no real harm done by the question, there is certainly no need to strike back in an angry manner. Someone who knows she tends to be more private could avoid these hurtful reactions by thinking in advance of pleasant responses. She could try a little humor: "Sorry, that's top secret." Or she could be simple and direct: "No offense, but I'd rather keep that to myself."

When we give the other person the benefit of the doubt, we come to realize that often, "nosy" questions arise out of care and interest in another person's life. If we respond to such situations by thinking, "She cares about me," then whatever our response might be, it will not be hurtful.

---

1 Cheshvan — לע״נ צפורה הינדא פייגא בת רחל ע״ה
1 Adar — As a *z'chus* for a *refuah shleimah* for all *cholei Yisrael*.
1 Tammuz — לזכות תומר בן דליה שתחי׳ ומשפחתו

Reality Check:
What kind of questions do I consider "nosy"? Is it the question, or the person who asks the question, that arouses my resentment?

What If...
Machla did not consider Shira to be a nosy person? What if, instead, she considered her a trusted friend? What might her reaction have been to Shira's excitement even if she didn't want everyone speaking about her decision?

DAY 32

Either-Or
~ Negating the positive

ב חשון
2 Cheshvan/Cycle 1

ב אדר*
*2 Adar/Cycle 2

ב תמוז
2 Tammuz/Cycle 3

* During Hebrew leap years, a thirteenth month called Adar Sheini is added to the calendar. During those years, the lessons for the days of Adar should be studied during each of the Adars.

ב אדר ב
2 Adar Sheini

"How can you call yourself religious when you don't even say morning berachos while it's still morning?" Mindy asked her teenage sister, who was snug under the covers at 1 p.m.

Mindy was 19, working full-time and taking courses at night. Her sister, Shana, had just returned from a six-week camping program for troubled girls. At just 16 years of age, she had already seen her share of trouble. But now, after an inspiring six weeks surrounded by mentors, counselors and girls like herself, she felt ready to re-engage in religious life. She came home proclaiming herself fully religious, Shabbos-observant, kosher and in love with Hashem.

But to Mindy, a straightforward girl who had always done what was expected of her, Shana's problems were hard to understand, and her "big change" seemed phony. She still dressed in clothes that brought her curious stares on the street. She still slept half the day, and rarely opened a siddur. So what if she kept Shabbos? There was more to being religious than that!

"Either you're religious, and you do what the Torah and the rabbis tell us to do," Mindy told her sister, "or you're not religious and you do what you want."

Shana had come home from camp feeling like she was on the way to winning the gold medal. Now her accomplishment seemed very much in doubt. Perhaps she really hadn't changed. Perhaps she never would.

"Either-or" is a false idea that causes us to identify a person according to her flaws. If someone is "either kindhearted or selfish," then

74 Chapter Two: What Fuels Hurtful Speech

her one selfish act is enough to overturn dozens of kind acts. If someone is "either calm or temperamental," then the one time she loses her temper undoes all the times she has remained calm. Those who witness her outburst may say, "See? She's really got a temper! She just keeps up a good act!"

The problem with this framework is that it does not provide an accurate picture of the personality of human beings. **We are all a combination of every trait Hashem has placed into mankind.** Different personalities result from the different proportions of these traits within the person. **But if we judge someone on an "either-or" basis, we strip away their positive traits, which are the basis of their potential to grow.** Instead of finding and feeding the seeds of greatness that exist in every person, the "either-or" approach lets those seeds wither, and feeds the weeds instead.

To avoid identifying people as their worst selves, we have to change our focus. For instance, if a friend refuses to lend a classmate her notes, the classmate might respond, "You're so selfish!" which casts the spotlight on her negative trait. Instead, the classmate can say, "Your notes are always so clear and helpful. I could really use the help now, too." The second response recognizes the other girl's hard work and careful note-taking, identifying her by her positive traits and encouraging her to express them further.

The best way to break out of "either-or" thinking is to look inside ourselves. How many times do we fight off the urge to say "no" to a favor? To skip or speed through a mitzvah? To get in that one funny but hurtful remark? Those urges prove that even the most helpful, zealous, soft-hearted person has another side. No one is "either-or." We are all "this and that."

> **Reality Check:**
> When I see "the other side" of someone, how much does it influence my opinion of her? Do I tend to see the negative as the "true person"? I will try to readjust my opinion by thinking about how I, too, am a mixture of positive and negative traits.

> **What If...**
> Mindy really wanted to be a positive influence on her sister? What else could she do besides showing her, as in the scenario, the seeming contradiction between her lifestyle and her desire to live a religious life?

---

2 Cheshvan — לע"נ רחל בת שמחה בונים ע"ה נלב"ע א' חשון
Dedicated by Fay & Chaim Fortgang and family

2 Adar — לע"נ ישראל יצחק רפאל בן ברוך משה יבלח"ט

2 Tammuz — לע"נ הרה"ג ר' פלטיאל בן ר' דוד ישעיהו ז"ל
Dedicated by his family

Either-Or ~ Negating the positive

Chapter 3

Insults of Character and Reputation

Our good name and reputation are among our most precious possessions. They are the key to many of our goals, from the immediate concerns of acceptance into high school, camp, and seminary and finding our marriage partner to long-term goals of giving our children a sense of pride in their family and making a positive impact on our communities. Words that stain someone's reputation or cast doubt on her character can cause far-reaching damage, even when none is intended.

DAY 33

Bursting Their Bubble
~ Undermining others' pride

ג חשון
3 Cheshvan/Cycle 1

ג אדר*
*3 Adar/Cycle 2

ג תמוז
3 Tammuz/Cycle 3

* During Hebrew leap years, a thirteenth month called Adar Sheini is added to the calendar. During those years, the lessons for the days of Adar should be studied during each of the Adars.

ג אדר ב
3 Adar Sheini

"The house was flying!" Dafna told her friend Bracha. "The kids were climbing the walls. The baby was screaming, and the 2-year-old kept walking on the kitchen table. The twin boys were throwing Lego pieces at each other and the older sister, who's only 6, was begging me to read her a story. And the parents weren't going to be home for another three hours."

"Oh, I know just what you mean," said Bracha. "Those Levin kids are crazy. I'm so strict when I babysit them. They're scared to death of me!"

"Well, you're not going to believe it, but it turned out amazing. I was so desperate. I figured I had to do something radical to get things under control. So I found a nice loud CD of wedding music and I turned it on full blast. I grabbed the 2-year-old off the table and started dancing like mad with him and the baby.

"The next thing you know, the twins are joining in, and then the little girl. We danced through the whole CD and when we were done, the baby was fast asleep and the other kids were so exhausted they were begging to be put to bed. I studied for the rest of the night!"

"Well," said Bracha, "I guess it's the best thing to do if you don't know how to get kids to listen to you. If you let them know who's boss, you don't have to do tricks like that."

Suddenly, Dafna's sense of sweet victory went sour. She wasn't a creative babysitting genius; she was a failure who couldn't command respect.

78 Chapter Three: Insults of Character and Reputation

When people share their moments of pride with us, we sometimes have a tendency to burst their bubble with a negative comment. Someone passes her driver's test and her friend says, "Great. I guess the third try is lucky!" Now instead of enjoying her moment of accomplishment, the new driver is mentally shoved back in time to her two previous failures.

Why do people do this to each other? Envy is one reason. For instance, Bracha in the above story might be jealous that Dafna had such a friendly, easy-going relationship with the children. In the case of a sarcastic comment, sometimes people cannot pass up the chance to demonstrate how sharp they are. In other situations, the remark might come from good intentions: by bringing up past errors, the speaker might feel she is putting the current success into its proper perspective. Sometimes people are so self-absorbed that they don't even realize the other person is trying to share a proud moment.

In all cases, however, **the negative response to someone else's success says something negative about the speaker**: She does not know how to sincerely share another person's happiness. If someone else's happiness is your happiness too, you would never want to dampen it. At the moment when someone is offering you a taste of her success, the best response is to take a taste and, without any other agenda, just appreciate its sweetness.

Reality Check:

How do I react to other people's success? Is there a tinge of envy or a desire to bring up previous failures? I will try to tune myself in more completely to the happiness my friends are feeling and to share that feeling more wholeheartedly.

What If...

Bracha had a sincere constructive criticism to offer, for instance, about the danger of allowing the 2-year-old to stand on the table? When and how should she make that comment?

---

3 Cheshvan — לע"נ משה דוד בן שלמה דוב ז"ל נלב"ע כ' חשון
לע"נ רב חיים בן נחום ז"ל ואשתו בתי-ה בת אברהם אבא ע"ה

3 Adar — לע"נ ר' מנשה בן ר' דוד ז"ל
Dedicated by Debbi & Hesh Granik

3 Tammuz — לע"נ יצחק ועלוול בן אהרן ז"ל ואשתו גיטא רייזל בת דוד ע"ה
Dedicated in loving memory by Trudi and Irwin Kabak

Bursting Their Bubble ~ Undermining others' pride

DAY 34

Free to Move Ahead
~ Reminders of past mistakes

ד חשון
4 Cheshvan/Cycle 1

ד אדר*
*4 Adar/Cycle 2

ד תמוז
4 Tammuz/Cycle 3

* During Hebrew leap years, a thirteenth month called Adar Sheini is added to the calendar. During those years, the lessons for the days of Adar should be studied during each of the Adars.

ד אדר ב
4 Adar Sheini

> *The hikers were lost in the forest. They rested by a little stream, gathered their packs and began heading in the direction they thought would lead them back to the main road. But the forest looked the same in every direction. Trees and more trees, bushes, fallen logs, small swampy patches all spread out before them, behind them, to the right and to the left. They lost their bearings as they trudged along.*
>
> *At last, they saw a small clearing ahead. "Maybe that's the way out," one hiker said to the other.*
>
> *"Oh, no!" said the second hiker. "That's the stream where we started out!"*
>
> *"No, it's not," said the first hiker. "It's different... it's bigger... it's... oh, no, you're right!"*
>
> *"We've gone in one big circle," the second hiker moaned. "We haven't gotten anywhere in an hour of walking. I give up!"*

"Walking in circles" is a well-known metaphor for a feeling of futility, a feeling of despair that overcomes us when our efforts seem to produce no results. For this reason, **one of the most painful forms of *ona'as devarim* is the kind that forces people back into roles they've outgrown and problems they've overcome**. Such *ona'as devarim* tells a person that no matter how far she has traveled, she really hasn't gotten anywhere.

Sometimes, people make such comments out of jealousy or frustration. **When a person sees growth and change in a friend, she may feel inferior.** For instance, a woman meets up with an old friend from high school who is now, 10 years later, a popular rebbetzin and speaker in the community. "Some rebbetzin!" the friend comments. "I remember when you and I used to skip school to go stroll on the boardwalk in the middle of the winter. Remember when we got suspended for a week?"

This woman is essentially saying, "Even though you have gained much respect during the past decade, you're no better than I am." The woman who has done so much with her life is then cast back into the role of a mischievous high-schooler.

Some people mistakenly think that reminding people of past errors is also a way of setting them straight: A girl who has successfully lost a lot of weight is at a birthday party slicing herself a large piece of cake. "You're right back to your old eating habits! You don't want to put the weight back on, do you?" her friend warns her. The friend believes her reminder will scare her friend into staying away from the sweets that caused her so much grief in the past.

Instead, however, the girl feels as if all the effort and self-control she has exercised for the past six months account for nothing. She is being seen as the same out-of-control overeater she was before. Rather than relishing her success, she is harnessed to her past failures.

Nobody is born perfect. We are taught (*Sefer HaBris* 2:4-18) that man is constantly in motion, and his mission in life is to keep moving forward. As we move forward, there will always be habits, places and mistaken ideas that we leave behind. When we remind people of the things they are trying to leave behind, we force them to continue carrying them along in life as part of their identity. In doing so, we increase, rather than lighten, the burden of our fellow Jew.

Reality Check:

Do I look at my siblings and friends as people who have grown, or do I hold onto my image of them as they were when they were less mature? I will try to notice and give credit to the accomplishments of others and encourage their greater accomplishments in the future.

What If...

someone has headed downward, rather than upward, in her life? Is it *ona'as devarim* to remind her of her past in that case?

לע"נ ר' יונה בן שלמה יוסף ז"ל — *4 Cheshvan*
ואשתו רבקה בת מנחם ע"ה נלב"ע ו' ניסן
לע"נ אסתר חי' בת חיים דוד ע"ה — *4 Adar*
Dedicated by her husband, children and grandchildren
לע"נ מנחם מענדל בן חיים ז"ל נלב"ע ד' תמוז — *4 Tammuz*
לע"נ וילצא בת ר' משה ע"ה נלב"ע כ"ב כסלו

Free to Move Ahead ~ Reminders of past mistakes   81

DAY 35

My Interesting Past
~ Revealing past sins

ה חשון
5 Cheshvan/Cycle 1

ה אדר*
*5 Adar/Cycle 2

ה תמוז
5 Tammuz/Cycle 3

* During Hebrew leap years, a thirteenth month called Adar Sheini is added to the calendar. During those years, the lessons for the days of Adar should be studied during each of the Adars.

ה אדר ב
5 Adar Sheini

> "Why does Devorah pronounce Hebrew so funny?" Chana asked her friend Shaindy. "Did you ever hear her say 'halachah'? She says 'halakah.' And 'boruk Hashem.' She sounds like she isn't really Jewish."
>
> "Oh, don't you know? Devorah only became religious when she was in ninth grade!" Shaindy said wisely. "Her family's not even religious. Some kiruv organization got her the lifeguard job here at camp so she could meet more girls."
>
> Just as the two finished talking, Devorah approached on her way back from the pool.
>
> "Hey, Devorah!" Chana called, applying an extra-thick coat of friendliness to her greeting. "How're things at the pool?"
>
> "Great!" she replied. "The girls are so cute. But it's a lot of work. I'm starving!"
>
> "Do you like the food here?" Chana asked. "Is it as good as non-kosher food?"
>
> "Huh?" Devorah responded.
>
> "Oh, you know, I heard that you weren't always religious," Chana explained matter-of-factly. "So I guess you must have eaten things like cheeseburgers and bacon and all that. I think it's amazing that you made such a big change!"
>
> "That was four years ago," Devorah said. "I don't really remember."

Before our words pop into the world, they exist **in our minds as thoughts**. But not all thoughts should be spoken. There is an intermediate step that must be taken before our thoughts get all the way from our

82   Chapter Three: Insults of Character and Reputation

brains to our tongues, and that is to decide if they are in fact worthy and appropriate of expression. The Torah teaches us that one particular type of thought that should not be spoken is one that reminds a person of her past sins.

In some ways, that seems confusing. We might think that Devorah, in the above story, would be proud to let people know that she has successfully made a major change in her life. In fact, that idea is supported by *Chazal's* well-known saying that a *tzaddik* cannot even stand in the place of a *baal teshuvah*.

But when we think of it from a personal point of view, we see the wisdom in prohibiting such comments. Devorah has remade herself; she does not want to be reminded by random people at random moments of how she used to live. She may worry that this information will lower her image in other people's eyes. She may not want to think about it. It's her information to share or withhold as she pleases.

Imagine the situation this way: What if there were a journal sitting on a bookshelf in the school library that detailed all the sins and misdeeds of each student? Even if those sins were long ago corrected and forgiven, who would want others browsing through the pages of her life, thinking about the foolish mistakes she had made? This is essentially what a person endures when others mention her unflattering past.

The words our mouths reveal should be those that cast light on other people's good qualities, their potential and their achievements. Anything that casts a shadow on their image should be kept in the spot Hashem provided us all—locked away behind closed lips.

Reality Check:

Do I know information about others that could cause them to be seen in an unflattering light? Even if I don't think it's so serious, I will be careful not to remind them of anything at all that reflects negatively on them.

What If...

Devorah had spoken freely to Chana about her past? Would there be any harm in Chana bringing it up?

---

5 Cheshvan — לזכות אברהם אליעזר בן נעמי ברריינדל וחי' שרה בת יוכבד':
ילדינו היו, שמואל לוי יצחק, יוסף חיים, אלימלך משה ונחמה גיטל שיחיו

5 Adar — In memory of Paul Jacobowitz z"l לע"נ פסח יוסף בן צבי חיים ז"ל
Dedicated by his children

5 Tammuz — לע"נ חיים מאיר בן ר' מנחם מנדל ז"ל
לע"נ חי' זיסל בת ר' שמואל יעקב ע"ה נלב"ע ה' ניסן

My Interesting Past ~ Revealing past sins

DAY 36

Not Normal
~ Causing others to feel self-conscious

וְחֶשְׁוָן
6 Cheshvan/Cycle 1

וַאֲדָר*
*6 Adar/Cycle 2

וְתַמּוּז
6 Tammuz/Cycle 3

* During Hebrew leap years, a thirteenth month called Adar Sheini is added to the calendar. During those years, the lessons for the days of Adar should be studied during each of the Adars.

וַאֲדָר ב
6 Adar Sheini

The girls arrived at the Shabbaton in high spirits. It was the big school event of the year: a weekend at a beautiful country resort, a program packed with inspiration and fun, a time to bond with teachers and friends. Even the bus ride was fun for everyone—except Etty. No one could understand why their normally lively classmate seemed so morose. It was as if she were going to jail instead of a hotel.

Throughout the four-hour ride to the resort, Etty's best friend and seat-mate, Lonny, kept asking her what was wrong. Etty claimed to be tired. When they got settled into their room, Lonny suggested Etty take a nap. Rivky, the third girl in the room, concurred. "We'll leave and shut the blinds and you can rest up."

"I'm not tired!" Etty retorted with irritation. "Just leave me alone!"

"What's the big problem?" Lonny asked, annoyed at her friend's outburst.

"O.K., O.K., here's the problem," Etty confessed. "I hate sleeping away from home. You know I never went to sleepovers, and I still don't. I only came because my mother insisted that it's time I get over it."

"What? You're scared of sleepovers?" Rivky laughed. "Come on, you don't mean it! You're 15 already!"

"Really, Etty?" Lonny chimed teasingly. "You're really not normal! You should get help! Well, we're going to check out the pool. You'd better nap now before it gets dark and spooky!" she said. The two girls breezed out of the room, leaving Etty feeling like a strange specimen on display at the science museum.

84   Chapter Three: Insults of Character and Reputation

The word "normal" is a brick wall against which many people's self-esteem has been thoughtlessly dashed. **We all want to be considered normal**: not too tall or short, not unusually smart or simple, not so nice that people take advantage of us, and not too selfish. But **even the most average people have doubts about themselves**. They cringe at the idea that others might find out about their odd habits, fears, ideas, family members, weaknesses or even unusual interests and hobbies. When people label them as "not normal," it confirms their doubts.

This is a message that can come in many forms. "You should speak to someone about that [habit, fear, problem, etc.]." "What are you *doing*?" "What's wrong with you?" "How could you even think such a thing?" These are all phrases that deliver the same message: "You're weird."

If the "average" person feels this insecurity, we can only imagine how vulnerable a person is when she really does have some seemingly abnormal traits. There are, of course, times when we are obligated to encourage another person to seek help. In that case, however, we still have to choose our words very carefully and avoid causing unnecessary pain to the other person.

Children are especially prone to teasing those who are different from them. "Retarded" and "crazy" are childish insults that, unfortunately, can even sometimes be heard coming from adults.

Unless you are a doctor or therapist, there is rarely a useful purpose in labeling someone as "not normal." For the rest of us, **it's important to keep in mind that Hashem made us all, and He does not make mistakes**. Our job is to appreciate, not deride, the uniqueness of the people in our lives.

Reality Check:

Do I use the term "not normal" or some other similar term when people act in a way that I find out of the ordinary? I will try to replace that reaction with a more positive one.

What If...

Lonny and Rivky had taken Etty's problem seriously? What, if anything, could they have done to help? Is it possible that they thought they *were* helping? How?

---

6 Cheshvan — לע"נ מלכה יענטא בת יהושע זובער ע"ה
Dedicated by Izzy Zuber and family

6 Adar — לע"נ עוזר בן ישראל ז"ל
Dedicated by his family

6 Tammuz — לע"נ בינה מחלה בת יהודה ברוך ע"ה
Dedicated by the Bina Machla Tzedakah Fund

DAY 37

Who Do You Think You Are?
~ Insulting family background

ז חשון
7 Cheshvan/Cycle 1

ז אדר*
*7 Adar/Cycle 2

ז תמוז
7 Tammuz/Cycle 3

* During Hebrew leap years, a thirteenth month called Adar Sheini is added to the calendar. During those years, the lessons for the days of Adar should be studied during each of the Adars.

ז אדר ב
7 Adar Sheini

Lizzy's father had once been a professional actor, and her mother had been a ballet dancer. Both ended up learning Torah in Yerushalayim, getting married and raising a religious family. Lizzy knew that some people thought her family was odd, but she was proud of them.

Rochel's family, on the other hand, was descended from a long line of Chassidim, many of them quite prominent back in Europe. Unfortunately, Rochel's parents had a difficult time supporting their large family. Rochel knew some girls looked at her as a "nebach case," but she was proud of her large, loving family.

One day in class, Rochel asked to borrow a pen from Lizzy. Later, just as Rochel finished her notes, the bell rang. Instinctively, she stashed the pen inside her book-bag and headed off to the next class. Afterwards, at lunch, Lizzy asked for the pen back.

"Oh, I'm sorry! I forgot!" Rochel apologized. She dug around in her threadbare book-bag. "Uh-oh," she told Lizzy. "There's a hole in the bottom. It must have fallen out. But don't worry, if I can't find it I'll replace it."

Lizzy was exasperated. The pen was a birthday present from her grandparents. It was silver-plated and set with little rhinestones. Why had she ever trusted Rochel with it?

"Really, Rochel, look hard for it, because you're never going to have the money to replace it. I guess in your family you don't learn much about how to take care of nice things," Lizzy said bluntly.

The comment stung Rochel. Did everyone in the school look down on her? She felt that she had to go to war for her family's name.

86　Chapter Three: Insults of Character and Reputation

> *"Well, maybe that's because my family is religious and they're not movie stars,"* Rochel countered. *"They taught me a lot more than how to take care of a pen!"*

Lizzy and Rochel were having a dispute. Perhaps the least relevant factor in that dispute was their families' backgrounds. People might be able to change how they think, what they say or what they do, but they can never change their lineage, native language and cultural background. Those are factors that are in Hashem's control alone. When we criticize these aspects of someone's personality, we are wasting our effort, for there is nothing the other person can do to change it.

Not only is such an insult completely useless, it is also especially hurtful. That is because we are not just criticizing what someone did or said, but what she *is*. She may feel that she is seen as an inferior product, raised by faulty people in a faulty manner.

Such an attack also causes the listener to feel embarrassment for her family's sake. A child naturally feels shame when someone brings up unflattering information about her parent or sibling. **No one wants to hear the people she loves being insulted or made to look ridiculous.**

Professional boxers and wrestlers have strict rules about how and where they are allowed to attack each other. That is because the consequences of some moves are far too serious to risk. In real life, the consequences of an unfair attack are far more serious, and so it is all the more important to stop ourselves before we say something whose only purpose is to cause pain. Even in the midst of conflict, that is a purpose we can never justify.

Reality Check:

Do I see some people's cultural background or family in a negative light? If so, I will try to remember, when those factors arise in my mind, that Hashem placed them in exactly the right location and family to achieve their greatness in life.

What If...

Lizzy had not mentioned Rochel's family's poverty? How might the dispute have developed and been resolved?

---

7 Cheshvan — In honor of the birthday of לזכות יהודה אריה בן חנוך אלעזר נ"י
7 Adar — לע"נ מרת גאלדא בת ר' ברוך שמחה ע"ה נלב"ע ז' אדר תשנ"ד
Dedicated by Yisroel and Freyda Berger
7 Tammuz — In honor of my wife Mindy Amsel on our anniversary
Dedicated by her husband

DAY 38

Photoshop
~ Damaging others' self-image

ח חשון
8 Cheshvan/Cycle 1

ח אדר*
*8 Adar/Cycle 2

ח תמוז
8 Tammuz/Cycle 3

* During Hebrew leap years, a thirteenth month called Adar Sheini is added to the calendar. During those years, the lessons for the days of Adar should be studied during each of the Adars.

ח אדר ב
8 Adar Sheini

Zahava saw herself as a good girl with a bright future. Despite the fact that she was a mediocre student, she participated in all the school's extracurricular activities, she played piano beautifully and she had a wide circle of friends. Her teachers sometimes reprimanded her about being too "laid back" about her schoolwork, but Zahava just could not get herself to sit for long hours over her books.

In Zahava's picture of her future self, she owned a children's clothing store, where she could use her creativity and friendly nature to become successful. Or, perhaps she would start a girls' choir in her community, where she could use her musical talent. Or perhaps something else altogether—the possibilities were limitless!

One day, Zahava's second-term 11th-grade report card arrived at her house. An "A" in gym, a few B's, a lot of C's and two D's. "Great news! I didn't flunk anything!" she told her friend Ruthie on the phone that night.

"That's great news?" Ruthie replied. "Zahava, you'd better start getting serious. You've gotta grow up and start thinking about seminary and marriage and all that. If you'd study once in a while, you wouldn't get such loser marks!"

The word "loser" immediately cast a cloud over Zahava's sunny picture of herself. Maybe, with nothing but eleven years of bad grades to show for herself, she never would amount to anything.

We each carry around a mental picture of ourselves. It's not just a picture of how we look, but also of who we are: personality, strengths,

88 Chapter Three: Insults of Character and Reputation

weaknesses, priorities and so forth. But we are not the sole creators of this picture. Everyone we meet helps to create it. If they compliment us, the image is enhanced by the compliment. If they insult or criticize us, the image is altered by the insult.

A healthy self-image is strong enough to resist a certain amount of negative input. For instance, if a girl gets straight A's in all her classes, someone telling her that she is not very intelligent will have little or no impact. She knows she's smart, and the other person's words cannot alter that. But what if she is a struggling student? What if her image is weak in that area? Then, the comment can make a large impact, and repeated comments, especially if they come from someone the girl respects, can completely destroy her sense of her own intellectual ability.

Negative assessments of someone else's personal traits, looks, abilities or any other aspect integral to her are like a Photoshop alteration of the person's self-image. That means that people making such comments bear a huge responsibility. They are changing, sometimes permanently, another person's level of confidence and self-esteem.

As any psychologist can confirm, low self-esteem is a devastating problem. People who believe that they are not worthy of respect, that their efforts do not amount to anything, are people in despair. They are without hope, for hope comes from the belief that things can get better.

On the positive side of the situation, however, is our vast power to enhance other people's self-image. **Every time we sincerely praise another person, whether it's for her taste or her kindness or the good question she asked in class, we are beautifying that picture she carries around in her head.** Our words help build in her the sense that she is a person worthy of respect and admiration. And from there, everything is possible.

> **Reality Check:**
>
> Do I have an impulse to "tell it like it is" to others, even when my words might harm their self-image? If so, I will carefully consider whether there is any benefit to my words, and whether I can achieve the same benefit in a positive way, before saying something that might negatively "Photoshop" someone's self-image.

> **What If...**
>
> Ruthie were really concerned about Zahava's future? Are there things she could do or say to help? Is her concern justified?

---

8 Cheshvan — לזכות יצחק בן רונית נ״י לתורה, לחופה ולמעשים טובים
Dedicated by his parents

8 Adar — Dedicated as a *z'chus* for our family
By Mr. and Mrs. Jack Blumenkopf

8 Tammuz — לע״נ פינחס מרדכי בן יהודה ואשתו בילא נעכא בת יעקב ז״ל
Dedicated by Nachum and Tzippy Shaum and family

DAY 39

Ulterior Motives
~ Doubting sincerity

ט חשון
9 Cheshvan/Cycle 1

ט אדר*
*9 Adar/Cycle 2

ט תמוז
9 Tammuz/Cycle 3

* During Hebrew leap years, a thirteenth month called Adar Sheini is added to the calendar. During those years, the lessons for the days of Adar should be studied during each of the Adars.

ט אדר ב
9 Adar Sheini

Peri loved her grandmother and her heart broke to think of her all alone in the hospital over Shabbos. But with a newborn baby to take care of, Peri's mother couldn't camp out in a hospital room.

"I'll stay with Bubbi for Shabbos," Peri volunteered.

"Oh, you don't have to do that," her mother said. "Bubbi's feeling much better and she'll probably be coming home on Sunday. Besides, you'd have to sleep in a chair in her room."

"I don't care," Peri said. "I don't want her to be alone. It will be fine."

And so it was agreed that Peri would be her Bubbi's companion. When she arrived back home after Shabbos, she was glowing with satisfaction.

"It was so lucky that I was there," she told her mother. "They forgot to bring her grape juice, so I found someone from Bikur Cholim and got it for her. Then at night she couldn't sleep, so I read to her until she dropped off. I was able to take her for a walk down the hall on Shabbos morning, and she said she felt alive again!"

Penina, Peri's twin sister, listened to the story with narrowed eyes, her head shaking back and forth in disdain. "Wow, Peri, are you applying for the Granddaughter of the Year award? Want a medal?"

Peri's pride and satisfaction in her good deed quickly drained away. Maybe she was just seeking approval. Maybe it wasn't such a chesed after all.

The twin sister's words were clearly *ona'as devarim*, possibly coming from a feeling of rivalry with her sister, or a sense of guilt for not volunteering for the

90 Chapter Three: Insults of Character and Reputation

job herself. **Many times, when we doubt other people's motives for doing a good deed, it is a way of soothing our own guilt for not having done such a deed ourselves.** For instance, if a person donates a large sum of money, others might say, "He just loves the honor." If someone becomes stricter in her Torah observance, others might say, "She just wants everyone to think she's so righteous."

Casting doubt on a person's motives makes her feel hurt and humiliated, "caught in the act" of doing something good with less than perfect intentions. As a result, she might even give up the good deed, which brings no benefit to anyone.

Sometimes it is appropriate to ask another person to examine his or her motives, but this only occurs in the course of a loving relationship like that between parent and child, teacher and student, spouses or close friends. Even then, whatever is said must be worded carefully so as not to discourage the other person's efforts.

A final danger in assessing other people's motives is that we can be completely wrong. The person who gives a lot of money might accept an honor so that his children will be encouraged to follow their father's giving ways. A girl who adopts stricter religious observance, even if she is not yet a *tzadekes,* might sincerely hope that these stringencies will help her grow.

A good way to avoid critiquing other people's motivations is to ask ourselves, "Why do I care?" We will discover that there are very few reasons why someone's positive actions should be attacked. On the other hand, recognizing their efforts and encouraging them to keep moving forward can only lead to good.

Reality Check:

Do I tend to analyze other people's motives for doing good things? If I find myself thinking of others' positive deeds in a negative light, I will focus instead on the good they've accomplished and, if the opportunity arises, praise them for it.

What If...

Penina were truly concerned that her sister's "goodness" was just a way of getting adult praise and approval? Is that really something to criticize? Why or why not? If it is worthy of criticism, what should Penina say?

---

9 Cheshvan — As a *z'chus* for our children and grandchildren to be close to Hashem with *simchah* • Dedicated by Ralph and Brenda Pindek

9 Adar — As a *z'chus* for our family
Dedicated by Mr. and Mrs. Jay Levine

9 Tammuz — In loving memory of Imre Lefkovits *z"l* לע״נ יצחק בן יהושע ז״ל
By his wife Rachel Lefkovits and children Susan & Moshe Wiesel

Chapter 4

Offensive, Disrespectful Speech

Harsh or crude words hit a person with the force of a physical blow. Someone who develops the habit of using these words spreads more pain, shame and embarrassment than she may ever realize. We protect the dignity of others in our lives—and we protect ourselves—by identifying these words and banning them from our vocabulary.

DAY 40

Bursting With Blessing!
~ The urge to shout

י׳ חשון
10 Cheshvan/Cycle 1

י׳ אדר*
*10 Adar/Cycle 2

י׳ תמוז
10 Tammuz/Cycle 3

*During Hebrew leap years, a thirteenth month called Adar Sheini is added to the calendar. During those years, the lessons for the days of Adar should be studied during each of the Adars.

י׳ אדר ב
10 Adar Sheini

> *Chani's Zeidy and Bubbi loved each other and gave to their children and grandchildren with no limit of energy and devotion. When they disagreed, they did it with the same all-out energy. Yet there was something special in the way they argued.*
>
> *"Chaim, you should be gebentched (blessed); what on earth did you do at the grocery store? Half the things on my list are missing! Hashem should give you wisdom. How are we going to make Shabbos?" Bubbi exclaimed one Erev Shabbos while Chani was visiting.*
>
> *"Reva, you should stay healthy and strong… your handwriting is getting worse by the day. Whatever I could read, I got," Zeidy replied.*
>
> *"Zei gezunt (be healthy), Chaim. But why should I have to do everything myself? Hashem should give us long years to argue with each other."*

Complaints and blessings, irritation and blessings, a little Yiddish, a little English, minor frustrations running over the surface of rock-solid love and affection—that was Zeidy and Bubbi's way. They had their frustrations, which made them feel like bursting, but what they burst out with was a stream of blessings.

Contrast that method of communication with the way people react to frustration today, when nearly everything is instant and patience seems to have disappeared. When someone cuts another person in line, or takes the last slice of pizza, or causes any discomfort whatsoever, people feel justified in letting loose with anger and curses far out of proportion to the situation.

But it is not only the secular world that lives in this state. **Our technology has trained everyone to think of a two-**

94   Chapter Four: Offensive, Disrespectful Speech

minute wait as an eternity. We are all prone to becoming irritated. Tension mounts up inside us and then, inevitably, we want to burst.

The question is, what comes out when we burst? Bubbi and Zeidy had the right idea: Burst out with blessings. To burst out with a curse or a wish for harm to another person is not only *ona'as devarim*, it is also a Torah prohibition when Hashem's Name is used in the curse (*Vayikra* 19:14), and a rabbinical prohibition even without Hashem's Name.

On the other hand, **blessings are real, even when they are driven out of our mouths by frustration**. Previous generations of Jews would sometimes burst out with *"Zei gezunt!"* in a moment of frustration. They relieved their need to shout something without shouting something hurtful. Their blessings brought blessing into their own lives as well, as Hashem promises that He will bless those who bless His children (*Bereishis* 12:3).

How can this apply in our own generation, with the types of words and expressions that are natural to us? Imagine that a girl named Yocheved once again forgets to return class notes that she borrowed from her friend Rachel. Rachel's first, frustrated thought is to say, "Don't you have a brain?" Instead, she blesses Yocheved, saying, "Hashem should give you an incredible memory!" She might say it with the annoyance she feels, but it is still a blessing.

Wishing good and happiness on others, especially those who cause us frustration, can only help them and us. It pumps new supplies of blessing into circulation in our world, and everyone reaps the benefits.

> *10 Cheshvan* — לזכות אהרן מרדכי בן חיי נ"י
> *10 Adar* — לזכות לנו ולכל ישראל לבוב"ב עוסקים בתוי"ש ומקדשים שם שמים
> *10 Tammuz* — As a *z'chus* for the Kahn and Schon Families
> Dedicated by Shloimie and Malkie Kahn

Reality Check:

Do frustration and impatience sometimes make me lose my temper and say something harsh? If so, I will prepare a short list of blessings to use when I feel that I'm going to burst.

What If...

the person you are blessing is still hurt or insulted because she perceives your frustrated tone of voice? What are the right situations for using this "bursting with blessing" strategy?

DAY 41

Use Only as Directed
~ Making others feel inferior

י"א חשון
11 Cheshvan/Cycle 1

י"א אדר*
*11 Adar/Cycle 2

י"א תמוז
11 Tammuz/Cycle 3

* During Hebrew leap years, a thirteenth month called Adar Sheini is added to the calendar. During those years, the lessons for the days of Adar should be studied during each of the Adars.

י"א אדר ב
11 Adar Sheini

Rivka was out shopping with her friend Batya when she noticed a plastic baseball bat and ball for sale.

"This is just what Dovi is dreaming of," she told her friend. "He's turning 4 tomorrow... I'm going to get him this as a present!"

Rivka went home and wrapped the large item in bright paper. The next night, when her mother brought out a birthday cake in honor of Dovi's big day, Rivka proudly presented him with his gift. He ripped it open and, with a delighted grin, ran to hug his sister. Then he raced off to the playroom to practice his swing.

Seconds later, 2-year-old Nechama came running into the kitchen crying. "Dovi hit me with the bat!" she wept.

Dovi slithered into the room, a perfect picture of guilt.

"Dovi!" Rivka reprimanded. "I gave you a gift to enjoy, not to hurt people with!"

When Hashem gives a person an extra dose of intelligence, strength, good looks, money or any other sought-after asset, it is a gift. Hashem provides these gifts to enable a person to accomplish her purposes in life. There are thousands of positive purposes for which Hashem's gifts can be used, and as we live our lives, we discover what these purposes are.

Sometimes, however, like Dovi in the story, we use these gifts to "bang someone else over the head." We forget that if it were not for Hashem's kindness to us, we would be as clumsy or unattractive or bad at math or disorganized as the person we are demeaning. On top of that, we forget that there is always

96 Chapter Four: Offensive, Disrespectful Speech

someone out there whose gifts are greater than ours. Therefore, our superiority is not really so superior.

When someone flaunts her gifts and puts down those who are lacking, she demonstrates that she does not understand what greatness really is. **A person who is smart or pretty or rich is not necessarily good and righteous.** If she does not develop these vital spiritual traits, she might be great in the eyes of her friends, but she will not be great in the ways that really count in the long run.

Even if we take a strictly practical view, we see that many happy, successful people are not particularly gifted, and some very gifted people are unhappy or unsuccessful. **Therefore, when we see someone as "lacking," we may be evaluating that person's value in a completely inaccurate way.** In the most important ways, they may be the truly superior ones.

Obviously, teasing someone because she seems to lack intelligence or some other gift is a classic case of *ona'as devarim*. If the person is aware of her deficit, teasing her about it is like hitting her right where it hurts. If she does not think of herself as lacking, another person's negative comment can shake her confidence.

So why do people do it? Commenting on someone else's deficiency sometimes helps the speaker feel more powerful and superior. However, in the process of making the other person feel foolish, the speaker is only proving her own foolishness. She is taking credit for something that is not even hers, because all our gifts and assets are on loan to us from Hashem.

There is only one appropriate response to the realization that we possess a special asset or talent: to thank Hashem for giving it to us, and try every day to use what we've been given for the best possible purposes.

Reality Check:
How much do I take credit for the gifts and talents Hashem has given me? How much do I fault those who do not have those gifts?

What If...
someone who is tone-deaf wants a singing part in the school play? Do we have to pretend she can sing? How can we address this situation without *ona'as devarim*?

---

11 Cheshvan — As a *z'chus* for our family
Dedicated by Ben and Penina Mokhtar

11 Adar — לע"נ אסתר לאה בת אבּיגדור ע"ה
Dedicated by her children and grandchildren

11 Tammuz — As a *z'chus* for our משפחה
Dedicated by Mr. and Mrs. Eli and Roizy Kaufman

Use Only as Directed ~ Making others feel inferior 97

DAY 42

Talking Funny
~ Ridiculing accents, pronunciation

י"ב חשון
12 Cheshvan/Cycle 1

י"ב אדר*
*12 Adar/Cycle 2

י"ב תמוז
12 Tammuz/Cycle 3

* During Hebrew leap years, a thirteenth month called Adar Sheini is added to the calendar. During those years, the lessons for the days of Adar should be studied during each of the Adars.

י"ב אדר ב
12 Adar Sheini

Ahuva raised her hand shyly. Rabbi Rosen, the 10th-grade halachah teacher, called on her.

"Um… Rabbi, what's the halakah for cuttin' up veggies on Sha-BAT?" she inquired.

Ahuva had been religious for only a couple of years. Her parents had agreed to allow her to attend a Bais Yaakov school in New York, where she boarded with a religious family. She grew up in North Carolina, and with her thick southern accent, she sounded as though her tongue might crack from the strain as she tried to pronounce the sounds of Hebrew letters.

At recess, Temmi strolled over to Ahuva and said, "Repeat after me. Ch-ch-ch-ch-Chanukah. Boruch-ch-ch-ch. Ch-ch-ch-Chumash. Come on, Ahuva, let's hear you give it a try!"

Ahuva's face turned red. "I can't. Go 'way, Temmi." But instead of Temmi going away, Racheli joined the group.

"I'm trying to teach Ahuva how to pronounce a 'chaf' and a 'ches,'" Temmi told Racheli.

Racheli laughed. "She never heard Hebrew before, Temmi. It's like Mr. McNeil, the custodian. He says 'boruk Hashem' when you ask him how he is."

If a person is afraid to make mistakes, she cannot learn. If a person is ridiculed when she makes mistakes, she will be afraid to try anything new. We all know that we are likely to make mistakes as we tackle unfamiliar tasks, but those mistakes are essential to the process of learning and growing. To create roadblocks for others by teasing, mimicking or otherwise ridiculing their efforts holds them back from striving for their goals in life.

This is a situation that comes up much more often than we think. For instance, if a person has a young brother who mispronounces words, laughing at his errors can actually make him reluctant to speak. If someone has a lisp or stutter, ridicule may force her into silence.

People who emigrate to a new country may also experience this type of *ona'as devarim* if others make fun of their accent. We may not hear the intelligence and thoughtfulness in the person's words as we focus on her mixed-up tenses and odd ways of phrasing things. Nevertheless, behind the accent, there may be a keen intelligence. If we would imagine ourselves trying to speak to the other person in her language, we would quickly come to respect her effort and her achievement.

None of this means that we cannot try to help others learn the correct way to pronounce words. That is enabling them to sound like everyone else, which ultimately is what they want. For instance, in the scenario above, Temmi could have made a sincere effort to help Ahuva by befriending her and becoming a trusted guide in the new world of Bais Yaakov. In that role, she would have the opportunity to gently, respectfully work with her on her pronunciation.

The issue is not correction itself, but the spirit in which a correction is offered. Does it make the other person feel ignorant, or does it make her feel that others care about her progress? Everyone wants to feel competent and respected. While it is true, as many people say, that "If I don't correct her, she'll never learn," it is also true that shame has never motivated anyone to strive for success. With a little patience, sensitivity and good will, we will see the gaps in people's abilities not as an opportunity to make a joke at their expense, but an opportunity for us to really help.

Reality Check:

Do I see other people's foreign accents or unusual pronunciations of Hebrew as great "material" for mimicry? Is it possible that I may be hurting others with my sense of humor?

What If...

Temmi sincerely wanted to help Ahuva improve her Hebrew pronunciation? What might she have said to Ahuva to bring up the subject without insulting her?

---

12 Cheshvan — For הצלחה in עבודת ה' for our children and all of כלל ישראל
Dedicated by Yechiel and Gitty Benari

12 Adar — As a *z'chus* for our family
Dedicated by Mr. and Mrs. Ephraim Bassen

12 Tammuz — לע"נ רב אברהם חנוך בן רב אלעזר ז"ל

DAY 43

Looking Good
~ Insulting physical appearance

י"ג חשון
13 Cheshvan/Cycle 1

י"ג אדר*
*13 Adar/Cycle 2

י"ג תמוז
13 Tammuz/Cycle 3

* During Hebrew leap years, a thirteenth month called Adar Sheini is added to the calendar. During those years, the lessons for the days of Adar should be studied during each of the Adars.

י"ג אדר ב
13 Adar Sheini

Browsing the evening-wear collection in the department store was one of Rena's great pleasures in life. Her cousin's wedding was coming up and she wanted to look special, so she set out to buy a new dress and the perfect accessories. Fortunately, she had brought along a fat pile of baby-sitting money to finance her mission.

It was a summer wedding, which meant that dresses in all Rena's favorite, airy, silky fabrics abounded on the racks. A saleslady, spying a serious customer, helped her select five different dresses that fit Rena's criteria. She tried each one on in turn and finally settled on a navy satin dress with beautiful rhinestone trim.

The clerk rang up the purchase and placed an elegant garment bag over the dress and its hanger. Rena felt like a princess standing there among the designer dresses, taking the chic bag from the clerk. She moved onto the shoe department, where she found a pair that exactly matched her dress. Finally, she found a pair of rhinestone earrings to finish the outfit. The cost of her new outfit was $350 altogether—35 hours of baby-sitting. But to Rena, it was worth every penny!

Why was she willing to spend the money? The reason was that Rena wanted to feel pretty at her cousin's wedding. She is not unusual. Take a walk down the "health and beauty" aisle of a department store and you will see thousands of types of shampoo, conditioner, bath soap, deodorant and make-up, because everybody, not just Rena, wants to look, feel and smell nice.

Because the desire to feel good about ourselves is so universal, some people tend to feel particularly sensitive about

100 Chapter Four: Offensive, Disrespectful Speech

what they perceive as their flaws. For instance, they may be very self-conscious about a certain trait, such as a large nose or thin hair, which may in reality not be remarkable at all. However, when such a person looks in the mirror, her flaws are all she sees.

The fact that people are so sensitive in the area of their looks means that there is tremendous potential to cause insult and injury by making a negative statement about someone's appearance. When we criticize a facial feature, such as a large nose, or a person's shape or size, we are criticizing something the person cannot change. If she had managed to overcome some of her sensitivity about her "flaw," she is now pushed back into a state of insecurity, having proven to herself that people really *do* think her nose is huge or that she is ridiculously tall.

Even if we insult something that can be changed—for instance, someone's outfit—the comment still constitutes *ona'as devarim*. The clothes may not be a part of the person, but the taste she exercised in choosing the clothes is indeed a part of her self-image.

An insult about someone's looks is also an insult of the One Who designed the person. This is what the Gemara (*Taanis* 20b) tells us in explaining why we are not permitted to call another person "ugly." While some features are more pleasing to our personal tastes, and some are more accepted as "beautiful" by our culture, no features deserve ridicule, because Hashem created them all.

There is an old saying: "She has a face that only a mother could love." It is the love a mother feels for her child that focuses her eyes on the beauty Hashem invested in the child. When we connect to our friends, family and fellow Jews in a spirit of love, their physical flaws often seem to disappear as their true beauty shines through.

---

13 Cheshvan — M. Zylberberg לע״נ מרדכי מנחם מענדל בן ר׳ יעקב יצחק ז״ל כ״ז חשון
Chaya Zylberberg לע״נ חיה שפרינצא בת ר׳ יעקב ע״ה י״ג חשון

13 Adar — In memory of Florence Aronowitz *a"h* לע״נ פייגע בת ישראל ע״ה
Dedicated by Gilbert Aronowitz

13 Tammuz — לע״נ לייב הירש בן ישראל נתן ז״ל
ואשתו פרומא בת יעקב פרמט ע״ה

Reality Check:

Do I ever tease people about their looks? If so, I will switch gears and find something attractive about them to compliment.

What If...

a person has a flaw in her appearance that can be fixed? For instance, what if someone does not keep her hair well groomed or her clothes neat and clean? Is there a way to suggest improvement without speaking *ona'as devarim*?

DAY 44

Nothing Left to Lose
~ Humiliating criticism

י"ד חשון
14 Cheshvan/Cycle 1

י"ד אדר*
*14 Adar/Cycle 2

י"ד תמוז
14 Tammuz/Cycle 3

* During Hebrew leap years, a thirteenth month called Adar Sheini is added to the calendar. During those years, the lessons for the days of Adar should be studied during each of the Adars.

י"ד אדר ב
14 Adar Sheini

In elementary school, Mindy's group of friends had been very good girls. But what had happened to Zahava? All of a sudden, in the middle of ninth grade, she started to change. She began dressing differently, acting differently and talking differently. Soon, Zahava was splitting her time between her "boring but nice" old friends and a small group of new friends who shared her interests.

Mindy felt that something needed to be said, something strong that would let Zahava know how far she had fallen. One day, finding Zahava alone during recess, Mindy approached her.

"Zahava, I don't think you consider me a friend anymore, but I still care about you and I need to tell you something," Mindy began. "Zahava, you're turning into a bum! What's going to be? Before you know it, you'll be kicked out of school and you'll probably end up not even being religious. You'll end up on drugs! You'll end up marrying a bum, or never getting married at all! We're all so disgusted with what you're doing."

That sealed the deal for Zahava. If she had thought for a moment that her old friends still liked her, she knew now that it was not true. She realized that she had been heading off course; schoolwork was very difficult and boring, and there was so much else that seemed more exciting to her. Her old friends, all good students, didn't understand what it was like to struggle every day to keep up. Now, they considered her "gone," and Zahava, seeing herself now through their eyes, believed they were right. She threw herself into her new life, and indeed was soon asked to find a new school.

102 Chapter Four: Offensive, Disrespectful Speech

Mindy meant well, but her effort to help Zahava failed. She thought that if she spoke straight and painted in dramatic terms the likely outcome of the course Zahava was taking, she would be shocked into changing. Instead, Zahava let go of her last connection to the "good girls" and dropped into a free fall.

Why did Mindy's reprimand backfire? The reason is that a reprimand can never accomplish something positive if it does not leave the other person with her dignity intact. When a person falls into a deep ditch, she cannot climb out without a foothold—a ladder or some rocks or branches along the sides of the ditch, upon which she can boost herself and eventually pull herself over the top. **When we destroy someone's self-respect, we take away her only foothold for rising out of their situation.**

If the real motivation of a reprimand is to awaken a friend to her error and inspire her to improve, then the only effective method is to build her sense of dignity. That is what Aaron HaKohen would do when he encountered a sinner. He would befriend the person, causing him to think, "If Aaron HaKohen thinks so much of me, how can I keep committing this sin?" The sin no longer befitted the person, once he viewed himself as someone of importance.

We have the opportunity to benefit others immensely by learning how to correct and criticize effectively. Like a gardener tending a rosebush, we must use pruning shears, not a chain saw. The goal is not to cut the person down, but to cut back the unproductive branches in order to channel all of the person's energy into healthy, long-lasting growth.

Reality Check:

When I criticize, is it to express my dislike for the person or her actions, or is it sincerely meant to encourage improvement? I will make sure that when I criticize, my motives are positive and my comments focus on the person's potential and value, rather than her faults.

What If...

Mindy had approached the situation differently? Was there anything she could have said or done to keep Zahava from falling further, and perhaps help her reverse course?

---

14 Cheshvan — לע"נ פישל בן דוד ז"ל
Dedicated by Mr. Martin and Marilynne Vogel

14 Adar — In memory of Marilyn Dickman Pass *a"h* לע"נ מרים בת ניסן ע"ה
Dedicated by Alan and Tzila Pass

14 Tammuz — In honor of Aryeh Ben-Zion *ben* Lenoa

DAY 45

The Speaker
~ Embarrassing a speaker/performer

ט"ו חשון
15 Cheshvan/Cycle 1

ט"ו אדר*
*15 Adar/Cycle 2

ט"ו תמוז
15 Tammuz/Cycle 3

* During Hebrew leap years, a thirteenth month called Adar Sheini is added to the calendar. During those years, the lessons for the days of Adar should be studied during each of the Adars.

ט"ו אדר ב
15 Adar Sheini

The seudah in honor of Ezzie Stein's bar mitzvah was attended by the Stein family's Uncle Yaakov, a highly accomplished talmid chacham who had come from Israel for the event. Of course, Ezzie's father had invited Uncle Yaakov to speak. Uncle Yaakov had spent several days before the simchah researching commentaries on Ezzie's bar mitzvah parashah and getting to know the bar mitzvah boy a little better, all so he could offer just the right words of inspiration and blessing.

The time came for Uncle Yaakov to take the podium. He began his speech, and soon, he was plunging into a certain concept, presenting a variety of points of view in depth. Between the detailed nature of his material and his somewhat monotonous voice, some of the guests began to lose interest and resumed their conversations. The murmuring soon became a rumble of chatter that made the speech impossible to hear.

"Sh-sh-sh!" some guests hissed. Uncle Yaakov paused for a moment like a schoolteacher waiting for the class to calm down. The chattering got a little quieter and he resumed. Then, so did the talking.

Uncle Yaakov soldiered on, determined to deliver the words he had carefully chosen for his nephew. In his heart, however, he felt foolish. He realized that his speech was too deep for this crowd, that they were bored and annoyed. Finally, he abandoned his notes, turned to his nephew, offered him a warm blessing and sat down.

Whether or not we enjoy a lecturer, performer or even a teacher's regular class, we can certainly understand that much thought and effort go

104 Chapter Four: Offensive, Disrespectful Speech

into every public appearance. No one wants to be a failure in front of a crowd of people. Those who appear in public, whether regularly, as part of their livelihood, or occasionally, may seem unafraid to put themselves "out there," and yet, ignoring or ridiculing them is certainly a source of *onaas devarim*.

If we take a closer look, we see that demeaning a performer or speaker is nothing less than holding that person up to embarrassment of a most public kind. All the strong prohibitions against embarrassing a person in public apply to this situation, multiplied by the number of people who witness the insult.

Furthermore, the detractors ruin the lecture for those who could and would enjoy it. In the above story, there may well have been many who would have learned something valuable from Uncle Yaakov's words, had they been able to hear them. Even those who were listening were surely distracted by the noise and the speaker's occasional pauses as he waited for order. By treating the speaker disrespectfully, a small group managed to undo the speaker's preparations and hopes for delivering a meaningful speech.

This would be bad enough if the person performing were merely entertaining the crowd. However, when the person is delivering a Torah lecture, the harm is more pronounced, because by showing disregard for the lecturer's words, the detractors are making light of a message that could be relevant to many people and benefit them greatly.

No one is obligated to enjoy a speaker or performer. However, no one has the right to take away from someone the opportunity to give his best to those he hopes to reach.

Reality Check:

Do I tune out when a performance or lecture is not to my liking? If so, do I disrupt it for others? The next time I am in that situation, I will imagine that I am the one on stage, noticing the audience's displeasure.

What If...

a performance is so unbearably bad that it is embarrassing to watch? What are appropriate options for people in the audience?

---

15 Cheshvan — Eleanor Broyde *a"h* לע״נ עלקא יהודית בת רפאל גרשון ע״ה
נלב״ע ג׳ שבט • Dedicated by Rabbi and Mrs. Berel Broyde
15 Adar — לע״נ ישראל בן יצחק דוב ז״ל
Dedicated by Shoshana Lefkowitz
15 Tammuz — לזכות חיים צבי בן דבורה ואשתו חנה מלכה בת אלישבע עמו״ש,
לזכות אלישבע שרה אליענה בת חנה מלכה שתחי׳

DAY 46

What's in a Name?
~ Unwanted/negative nicknames

ט"ז חשון
16 Cheshvan/Cycle 1

ט"ז אדר*
*16 Adar/Cycle 2

ט"ז תמוז
16 Tammuz/Cycle 3

* During Hebrew leap years, a thirteenth month called Adar Sheini is added to the calendar. During those years, the lessons for the days of Adar should be studied during each of the Adars.

ט"ז אדר ב
16 Adar Sheini

> "Blimpie's on the phone," the girl tells her older sister. "She wants to talk to you."
> "'Blimpie'?" asks the girls' mother, overhearing the conversation. "You call your friend Blimpie?"
> "She's Blima Penina," the older girl tells her mother. "And she's kind of, you know, on the heavy side, but she's awesome. She totally doesn't care. She even makes jokes about her weight. Blimpie's been her nickname since sixth grade."
> "Doesn't she mind?" the mother asks.
> "She doesn't say she minds," the girl responds. "She uses it too. She thinks it's funny."
> "That doesn't mean she likes it," the mother replies.

If you've ever studied the way a cartoonist makes a caricature of someone, you will notice that he manages to reduce the person's many, varied features into a few overexaggerated lines, which often capture his least flattering features. A nickname does the same thing. It takes all a person's strengths and weaknesses, likes and dislikes, talents and goals, and boils them down to the one trait brought out by the nickname. **In using someone's nickname, we can easily stumble into *ona'as devarim*.**

Sometimes, a person gets a nickname as a child and wants to get rid of it as she gets older. When people keep calling her by that nickname, she feels "stuck" in a childish identity. "Chanala" has the right to be called Chana if she prefers, and those around her must take her preference seriously. It often takes a long time for people to get used to calling her the name she prefers, even when they are willing and cooperative. However, we are obligated to make that effort, because everyone is entitled to hear themselves called by the name they prefer.

A nickname can be a friendly, harmless name that causes no pain at all. In that case, it is not considered *ona'as devarim*. However, if the person does not like the name (for instance, a girl named Yehudis may not want to be called Hudy, even though many people are called by that name) the Sages (*Taanis* 20b with *Tosafos*) teach that one should not call her by that name. Even though the name might not have any negative meaning, the fact that the person does not like it makes the name painful to her ears. It might be a slight pain, but it is an unnecessary and preventable one, and therefore, using the name is prohibited.

Certainly if the name does have a negative meaning, such as "Blimpie" in the story above, we are prohibited from using it. The damage done by such a name can be a lot more than the annoyance of hearing it. It can become a label by which the other person may come to identify herself, thereby limiting her potential and growth in life.

Besides nicknames, there are other names that people call each other, often on the spur of the moment, out of frustration or anger. While such names might not be an outright curse, they, too, have the potential to take root in the other person's identity and cause damage for many years to come.

Even if we justify ourselves, saying that a particular name is "not so bad" and that the other person "doesn't take it seriously," we often know that our words are out of bounds. In fact, there is a way to test the appropriateness of what we are saying: Imagine our words being overheard by a teacher or a rav. If we would be embarrassed in that situation, we can be sure that what we are saying is something that should not be said.

> **Reality Check:**
> Do I have unflattering or unwanted nicknames for friends or family members? I will drop those nicknames and focus on remembering to call them by their real or preferred names.

> **What If...**
> the girl in the above story thinks about her mother's comment and decides that "Blimpie" is indeed not an appropriate name for her classmate? How can the girl go about changing the situation? Should she get others involved? Should she get "Blimpie" involved?

---

16 Cheshvan — Dedicated as a *z'chus* for Rabbi Abba Bronspigel, *shlita*

16 Adar — לע״נ גרשון בן יצחק הלוי ז״ל נלב״ע י״ג אדר
Dedicated by Mr. and Mrs. Ken Stern

16 Tammuz — As a *z'chus* for our family
Dedicated by Dr. and Mrs. Daniel Mishaan

Chapter 5

Statements that Damage Self-Image

People base their evaluation of themselves at least partly on the messages they receive from others. That means that through the words we use to characterize others, each of us has the power either to strengthen or to damage their self-esteem, and in doing so, either to encourage or to cripple their ability to reach their goals in life.

DAY 47

The Absentminded Professor
~ Criticizing forgetfulness

י"ז חשון
17 Cheshvan/Cycle 1

י"ז אדר*
*17 Adar/Cycle 2

י"ז תמוז
17 Tammuz/Cycle 3

* During Hebrew leap years, a thirteenth month called Adar Sheini is added to the calendar. During those years, the lessons for the days of Adar should be studied during each of the Adars.

י"ז אדר ב
17 Adar Sheini

Meira felt the tension building up inside her. How could she tell Chavi that she forgot the money for their teacher's Chanukah gift yet again? Chavi was such an organized, serious girl. Of course she would be the one to collect for the class gift and choose just the right thing and wrap it up perfectly.

"I'm sorry, Meira," Chavi had warned her, "but I can't lay out the money for you again. You always forget to pay me back and I don't want to have to keep asking you. So if you don't bring the money by Thursday, you're not going to be part of the class gift."

Well, it was Thursday. Chavi would be going shopping after school for the gift and Meira, who commuted an hour to school, would not have a chance to go home and bring back the money in time. Her only hope was to try to get some sympathy out of Chavi.

"Oh, give me a break, Meira," Chavi said with annoyance. "You're like a little kid! I'm surprised they don't pin notes to your coat to give to the teacher!"

It was true that Meira had a poor memory. It wasn't because she lacked intelligence or that she did not care, it was just the way her brain worked. She earned top grades, was a genius at mathematics and could play piano, guitar and flute. But it seemed as if her brain was so overcrowded with the "big stuff" that she could not find a place to store the details of life.

Like Meira, many people find that the long list of obligations, activities and stresses of life overpowers their ability to stay focused. There are other people who, although not overwhelmed, simply were not blessed with a good memory. Also, some people suffer from Attention

Deficit Disorder, which makes focus and organization a challenge. Then, as people enter their elder years, they often find their memory becoming weaker. There are many reasons for people's forgetfulness.

And like Chavi, there are many people who are impatient with other people's memory lapses. They fume when someone loses something, saying things like, "You'd lose your head if it weren't attached!" Or they jump into the middle of an elderly person's sentence to supply the word she can't seem to come up with. While memory lapses can cause loss or inconvenience, insulting the person who has forgotten does nothing to reduce the damage.

In fact, the opposite is true. Insulting a forgetful person is guaranteed to make her feel unintelligent, irresponsible and childish. In the case of elderly people, an annoyed response sometimes discourages them from socializing at all. They would rather sit quietly than be embarrassed. For a child, **a harsh response to poor memory can create nervousness that makes the situation even worse**. The child might freeze when called on in class or panic during tests, proving to herself over and over again that she cannot remember things.

However, because poor memory is a real problem with negative results for the person who suffers from it, there is a constructive purpose in trying to help someone with this problem. Rather than showing annoyance, a person can suggest some of the many strategies and tools that really are useful, such as electronic organizers, file folders, notebooks, checklists and so forth. For an elderly person, the best way to help might be by taking care of certain chores or errands. In all cases, it's important to remember that forgetfulness is not an evil to uproot, but rather a deficit to accept, and if possible, help to alleviate.

> *17 Cheshvan* — לע״נ יצחק בן אברהם שפרן ז״ל ואשתו בתי׳ בת מאיר יהודה ע״ה
> Dedicated by their children; Safran, Persoff and Fogel families
> *17 Adar* — In memory of our Bubby לע״נ מרים בת מנחם מנדל ע״ה
> Dedicated by her grandchildren, Dr. Reuven & Mrs. Rochel Shanik
> *17 Tammuz* — Dedicated as a *z'chus* for the Neiburg family
> to grow in Torah, *middos* and *maissim tovim*

Reality Check:

How do I react when I am inconvenienced by people's forgetfulness? If I find that this makes me angry, I will try to change my response to one of empathy and suggest, if possible, a way to avoid similar problems in the future.

What If...

Chavi had not said anything insulting, but still refused to include Meira on the class list? Would this be a legitimate way for her to get Meira to be a more responsible member of the class? What other strategies might Chavi have tried?

DAY 48

Creating an Undertow
~ Deflating confidence

י"ח חשון
18 Cheshvan/Cycle 1

י"ח אדר*
*18 Adar/Cycle 2

י"ח תמוז
18 Tammuz/Cycle 3

> "Before I accept this award, I would like to say that even though I am the one standing up here, this award belongs to many other people. First of all there are my parents, who always encouraged me and had faith in my abilities, even when I felt like quitting. Then there are my teachers, who not only taught me the skills to succeed but gave me the confidence to try. And finally, I want to thank my friends. They never looked at me and said, 'You're nuts!' They always showed that they were proud of me and hoped for my success. If not for all of you, I could never have dreamed about starting this organization, through which we have been privileged to help thousands of people."

* During Hebrew leap years, a thirteenth month called Adar Sheini is added to the calendar. During those years, the lessons for the days of Adar should be studied during each of the Adars.

י"ח אדר ב
18 Adar Sheini

The typical acceptance speech, whether the awardee is standing at the podium of a fundraising dinner or giving the valedictory address, illustrates a basic concept in human psychology: people absorb messages about themselves from those around them. **Successful people often credit the confidence others showed in them as a main ingredient in their success**. However, the mirror image of this incredible potential is also true. Just as we can powerfully motivate people with positive input, we can deflate them with negative input.

Take, for instance, the case of Esti, who plans to apply to a particular seminary she has always dreamed of attending. She tells her friend Gittie about her idea, and Gittie says, "Even if you could get in, I don't think you could keep up with the classes there." Gittie believes that she is simply offering wise advice that will prevent Esti from suffering frustration or failure. However, in Esti's ears the message is, "You can't do

112   Chapter Five: Statements that Damage Self-Image

it." The immediate effect is to deflate Esti's self-confidence and slap a lid on her hopes.

Words that damage a person's confidence are subtle but dangerous. They can take up residence inside her mind and direct her choices throughout life, causing her to shy away from opportunities that would bring her fulfillment. This type of *ona'as devarim* pulls on its victim like a powerful undertow far beneath the ocean's surface, working against her progress as she tries to make her way through life.

It would be wonderful if everyone could always support everyone else's ideas, but sometimes an idea is truly impractical, dangerous or wasteful. Even so, we are obligated to think carefully before speaking out against it; we must be sure that in our effort to protect the other person from a mistake, we are not crippling her in a way that will keep her from trying anything new or challenging. For instance, in the example of Esti and Gittie, Gittie might have said, "Wow! It would be amazing if you could go there! My sister has a friend who went there last year. You could ask her what you need to get in and what it's like. I don't know about you, but I'm going to apply to a few places in case my first choice doesn't work out."

The more our opinions mean to others, the more potential we have to undermine or boost their confidence. Parents, siblings, teachers and close friends are the ones we count on to tell us the truth. Therefore, when we give our opinions to friends, or later in our lives, to our children or students, we must be sure to deliver the *real* truth: that limitations can be overcome and that each person comes into the world equipped with the assets meant to bring her fulfillment in life.

18 Cheshvan — Leon Lief z"l לע"נ אריה בן יעקב שלום הלוי ז"ל
נלב"ע כ"א חשון • Dedicated by the Lief and Dienstag families
18 Adar — לע"נ העניא בת יצחק אייזיק ע"ה
Dedicated by her children Mr. and Mrs. Irwin Cohen
18 Tammuz — In memory of Edith Coven *a"h*
Dedicated by Albert and Amy Coven

Reality Check:

Am I the type that likes to give others the "downside" of their ideas? If so, I will ask myself two questions: Do they need to hear this from me? And is there a more encouraging, less deflating way to express my doubts?

What If...

you feel certain that a person's plans will lead her to trouble or damage? How do we balance the idea in today's lesson with the Torah's prohibition of "*lo saamod al dam rei'acha*," standing idly by while a fellow Jew is being harmed?

Creating an Undertow ~ Deflating confidence 113

DAY 49

Threads of Brilliance
~ Coloring others' self-image

י"ט חשון
19 Cheshvan/Cycle 1

י"ט אדר*
*19 Adar/Cycle 2

י"ט תמוז
19 Tammuz/Cycle 3

> *"Akiva, are you crazy? You're 40 years old and you've never learned a word of Torah in your life. What on earth makes you think you can start now? You don't even have the skills of a second grader!"*
>
> Had that been the attitude of Rabbi Akiva's wife, the Jewish people would be missing one of their most important links in the chain of the Oral Torah.
>
> Fortunately, however, Rabbi Akiva's wife believed in him with all her heart. As a result, he was able to throw himself into his mission and use the intellectual and spiritual gifts that had until then remained hidden inside him.

* During Hebrew leap years, a thirteenth month called Adar Sheini is added to the calendar. During those years, the lessons for the days of Adar should be studied during each of the Adars.

י"ט אדר ב
19 Adar Sheini

Rabbi Akiva's accomplishments were not a miracle. They were the natural outgrowth of an environment that nurtured his confidence and self-esteem. Just as a tree will naturally grow strong and healthy where there is suitable soil and light, a person will naturally rise to her full potential if she is rooted in a nurturing environment. She may not become a giant of the ages, but she will become all that her own allotment of talents and abilities permit her to be.

When a person lacks faith in her own potential, she can feel like a failure even in the face of success. No matter how high she climbs, she does not feel a sense of accomplishment; instead she worries that her "luck" will run out and she will fall, or fail to get to the next level. On the other hand, someone who believes in herself can find success even in the midst of failure. One of the most successful business people in the world today says his first business venture ended in bankruptcy court. Nevertheless, he did not see himself as a failure. Rather than viewing bankruptcy as the end of his brief career, he used it as an opportunity to learn how to avoid mistakes the next time.

114   Chapter Five: Statements that Damage Self-Image

Calling someone a failure is one of the cruelest expressions of *ona'as devarim*. **A person's self-image is a fabric woven of thousands of threads, and each of those threads is an impression created by someone's words.** If the threads are mostly light and bright, reflecting encouraging, warm, kind words, the person's self-image is light and bright as well. However, some people are covered by a heavy fabric made of dark, somber tones of criticism and insult. It hangs over their lives like a shroud, blocking out all of life's possibilities.

Even without using blunt, negative labels, if a person's efforts are constantly met with criticism she perceives the overall message that "You can't do anything right." A critical person might believe she is actually doing others a great service by pointing out their flaws and pushing them to achieve a higher standard; but in reality, the secret to bringing out the best in others is just the opposite of the critic's methods. Great leaders are masters of encouragement. They seek out the smallest shred of talent in others and nurture it. Around such people, we feel free to come up with our most creative ideas and put forth our most idealistic plans. We have the confidence to try because we know we will never be knocked down for failing.

This power to build up another person is a fantastic gift that is given to every one of us. Our words can be the brilliant threads that make up the fabric of our friends' lives. In fact, this is one of the key purposes for which Hashem granted us the power of speech.

Reality Check:

Do I consider my critical eye to be a great benefit to those who I feel need improvement? If so, I will consider that perhaps I am giving them the "threads" to weave a negative self-image, and I will try to focus on their positive traits instead.

What If...

it seems impossible to find the "brilliant threads" in a certain person in your life? How can you avoid *ona'as devarim*?

---

19 Cheshvan — לזכות ליהודה ליב ודבורה שיחיו׳
19 Adar — לזכות ס״ד ושדרוכים לכל המשפחה
19 Tammuz — As a *z'chus* for a *refuah shleimah* for all חולי ישראל
Dedicated by Ezra and Miriam Ogorek

Threads of Brilliance ~ Coloring others' self-image   115

DAY 50

Their Pride and Joy
~ Finding the negative

כ חשון
20 Cheshvan/Cycle 1

כ אדר
*20 Adar/Cycle 2

כ תמוז
20 Tammuz/Cycle 3

* During Hebrew leap years, a thirteenth month called Adar Sheini is added to the calendar. During those years, the lessons for the days of Adar should be studied during each of the Adars.

כ אדר ב
20 Adar Sheini

> *Gila Rubenstein paid top dollar for a front-row seat at the high school play. It was worth the expense, because this year her daughter Tova had a major role! Gila sat through the first act completely enthralled, marveling at her daughter's perfect delivery of her lines and at her wonderful singing voice.*
>
> *In Gila's eyes, no one else on stage came close to having Tova's talent. Of course she would applaud and congratulate the girl who got the lead and all the other performers. They were all wonderful. But Tova, she had to say, was something special. She had always had such a presence!*
>
> *At intermission, Gila strolled out to the lobby and there she met Leah Glick, the mother of another student in her daughter's class.*
>
> *"Was that your Tova on stage?" Leah asked Gila.*
>
> *"Yes, it was," Gila answered proudly. "She almost got the lead, but this part has nearly as many lines and it actually has more singing."*
>
> *"Well, you can see why Rochel Goldstein got the lead," Leah replied. "She's got a real stage presence. But I'm sure that by next year, Tova will be up to it."*

We can imagine the shadow that immediately passed over Gila's glowing face when she found out that the entire world did not share her conviction that Tova was the most talented performer ever to set foot on stage. **Clearly, demeaning someone or something that another person holds dear is a type of *ona'as devarim*.** In fact, it is a form of insult that is easy to stumble into, because the "insult" may seem like a perfectly innocent statement. Its power to wound comes from the fact that it is directed at a particularly sensitive area of the other person's heart.

For instance, a person who thinks of herself as a good pianist and loves to play might feel hurt by a comment such as "You play really well, I just don't like that style of music." The speaker might think she is just being honest, and she is careful not to criticize the musician, only the type of music she plays. However, since the pianist identifies herself closely with her music, when she hears that it displeases someone she feels hurt.

This is also true of people's prized possessions. Telling someone that the treasured pearl earrings that she got from her grandmother are probably not valuable antiques but are just plain old, or that her new computer got a low rating in Consumer Reports, serves no purpose other than to reduce the joy the owner takes in her possession.

One area in which we must tread very carefully is in commenting on other people's family members. Your friend's little brother might be a world-class brat—your friend might even complain about him all the time—but if you make a negative remark about his behavior, you are guaranteed to cause your friend pain. That is because no matter how difficult a child he might be, your friend, his sister, loves him. Therefore she wants others to see him as lovable too.

If we want to play the role of enhancing other people's lives, there is no sense in telling them about the negatives we see in the people, places, activities and things they love. Doing so cannot enhance their happiness or pleasure in life; it can only cause damage. Rather than laying a coat of tarnish on someone's treasure, we can admire it with them. After all, the wonder and beauty they see in the thing they love may well be the truer view.

---

20 Cheshvan — In memory of Freida Breiner *a"h* לע״נ פריידא בת בנימן ע״ה
Dedicated by the Lipson family

20 Adar — Harold Palokoff *z"l* לע״נ הירשל בן ר׳ מאטל הכהן ז״ל נלב״ע כ״ח טבת
Molly Palokoff *a"h* לע״נ מאשא בת אברהם יצחק ע״ה נלב״ע כ׳ אדר

20 Tammuz — As a *z'chus* for more לימוד תורה and less לשון הרע
Dedicated by Mr. & Mrs. Gary & Loren Puterman and family

Reality Check:

Do I feel free to offer my opinion on my friends' belongings, talents, or other things or people meaningful to them? If so, I will think carefully about whether my comments are useful; if they are not, I will refrain from saying them or I will say something positive instead.

What If...

Leah Glick had taken more notice of the obvious pleasure and excitement on Gila Rubenstein's face? Do you think she would have made the same comment? Was there any constructive purpose to her assessment of who deserved the lead role?

DAY 51

The Career Critic
~ Belittling someone's profession

כ"א חשון
21 Cheshvan/Cycle 1

כ"א אדר*
21 Adar/Cycle 2

כ"א תמוז
21 Tammuz/Cycle 3

* During Hebrew leap years, a thirteenth month called Adar Sheini is added to the calendar. During those years, the lessons for the days of Adar should be studied during each of the Adars.

כ"א אדר ב
21 Adar Sheini

Bais Yaakov of Middleville was having a class reunion. Matti Gelb stood at the buffet table piling her plate with pasta and salad when someone tapped her shoulder.

"Matti!" the girl exclaimed. "You look amazing! It's so nice to see you!"

"Hi, Nechama. It's great to see you too!" Matti responded. She noted with surprise the enthusiasm of Nechama's greeting. They hadn't exactly been friends in school, but maybe Nechama's personality had softened up over time.

"So tell me, what are you up to?" Nechama asked. "Are you working? Are you in school?"

"Actually, I'm studying for my CPA," Matti said. "It's a lot of work, but it's really interesting. I'm probably going to work in auditing with my uncle's firm once I pass all the CPA tests."

"An accountant?" Nechama responded. "You really want to do that? My father's friend is an accountant and he says they're the dullest people in the world. Himself included!" Nechama laughed at her own joke, expecting Matti to laugh with her. After all, everyone knew that accountants were nerdy guys with thick glasses. In Nechama's mind, being a CPA was simply not a normal job.

However, Matti did not laugh. With a weak smile, she gave Nechama a nod and said, "I better get back to my table and eat this pasta before it gets cold."

"See you later," Nechama said, suddenly feeling that it was not just the pasta that was getting cold. She turned her attention to the buffet, shaking her head and wondering, "What's her problem?"

118　Chapter Five: Statements that Damage Self-Image

Matti's "problem" was that with one thoughtless joke, Nechama had completely put down her chosen career. Her hard work to get into a good program, her long hours of study, her high level of intelligence and her commitment to preparing for the expenses of family life were all discounted by someone who hadn't even spoken to her in three years.

For most people, their choice of profession and their competence at their profession form an important part of their self-image. It is *ona'as devarim* to belittle their profession, for instance by saying that teachers are ignorant and just stay "one chapter ahead of the class," or that businessmen are ruthless, or that doctors are "quacks." **Expressing doubt about a person's abilities in her profession is also *ona'as devarim*.**

There are, however, occasions when discussing the negative side of someone's career is legitimate. For instance, if the person is not making enough money and her friend has a good idea about changing careers or advancing in her field, this is not *ona'as devarim*. Rather, it is a *chesed*.

Likewise, a person might see that someone is not as efficient or competent as she might be. It is a *chesed* to offer helpful advice, but only in the most tactful way. For instance, a friend might say: "I saw an ad for a course that might interest you." Or, "Would you like to speak to my uncle about real estate? He has a lot of experience and might have some good advice."

Generally, however, most people are not involved in their friends' career choices, training, performance or other practical aspects of their work. Therefore, their negative offhand remarks serve no purpose. By avoiding such comments, we can avoid insulting someone who is simply doing her best to earn a living.

Reality Check:

Do I weigh in on my friends' or relatives' choice of careers, training or jobs? If so, I will try to think, before making a comment, about whether my remark might undermine someone's satisfaction with her work, job or career plans.

What If...

Nechama had a closer relationship with Matti? Would she have made the same comment? If so, would Matti have responded the same way?

---

21 Cheshvan — לע"נ ר' משה יוסף בן ר' שמעיהו ז"ל
21 Adar — *L'zchus* our dear children Adina, Shira, Yehudah and Yaakov
Dedicated by Ricky and Kalman Groner
21 Tammuz — לע"נ אברהם ציון בן נאוה ז"ל
Dedicated by Natalie & Max Mizrachi

DAY 52

Recipe for Disaster
~ Criticizing the cook

כ"ב חשון
22 Cheshvan/Cycle 1

כ"ב אדר*
*22 Adar/Cycle 2

כ"ב תמוז
22 Tammuz/Cycle 3

> *Tehilla came home from school famished. However, the second she walked through the front door she caught a whiff of bad news: her mother's greasy, batter-falling-off-the-cutlet schnitzel. In her mind, she thought of it as "bald schnitzel," a thought that made the dish even less appetizing.*
>
> *Soon she and her sisters were seated at the table with a platter of schnitzel there for the taking. There were side dishes too: boiled cabbage, slimy canned string beans, and instant mashed potatoes that, to Tehilla, seemed like the flour-and-water paste she used to make in kindergarten. "This is one of Mommy's dinner-in-a-minute meals," Tehilla thought.*
>
> *"Eat up, everybody," her mother said brightly. "I made the schnitzel a new way."*
>
> *"Looks a lot like the old way," said Tehilla. "Why doesn't the breading ever stay on?"*

* During Hebrew leap years, a thirteenth month called Adar Sheini is added to the calendar. During those years, the lessons for the days of Adar should be studied during each of the Adars.

כ"ב אדר ב
22 Adar Sheini

Cooking is a personal gift of love from one person to another. Seeing others enthusiastically eat what she has cooked, hearing them praise its taste and perhaps even take a second helping is all the payment the cook wants from her "customers." **When a mother prepares a meal for her family, she is performing the most basic act of giving.**

On the other hand, the husband and children of the family can expect to eat their wife's/mother's cooking every day for years to come. Therefore, they have a strong interest in somehow making sure that the food is to their liking. The key is in the word "somehow."

A remark like Tehilla's is obviously not the way. In fact, Tehilla would most likely feel guilty the second the remark

120 Chapter Five: Statements that Damage Self-Image

escaped her lips, realizing that it was hurtful, and disrespectful as well. An alternative might be to suggest a different way of preparing the dish without claiming it as a better way. For instance: "I know another chicken recipe, too. I'd love to try it next time we have schnitzel."

Another way to avoid insult is to express the criticism in terms of our own personal taste, rather than the quality of the cooking. For instance, Tehilla might say, "Mommy, the part I like best of the schnitzel is the crunchy breading. Is there a way to make it so it has more breading on it?" This tells the mother that her daughter has a taste for a certain texture, rather than telling her that what she has prepared is unappetizing.

At school or camp, there is also a cook busy in the kitchen, working hard and aiming to please a lot of people with various tastes. The cook is also usually working with a limited budget and ingredients. She might not be investing as much of her heart in her food as a mother does, but comments like "you could play Ping-Pong with these meatballs" are sure to sting.

Another area with great potential for *ona'as devarim* is in comparing one cook's food to another. It's one thing for a girl to tell her mother, "I love Mrs. Weissman's cheesecake!" It's quite another to bite into her mother's cheesecake and say, "Mrs. Weissman's is much creamier."

The exact words we say when we are faced with food we don't wish to eat will vary from situation to situation. However, if before we speak we acknowledge that the food before us represents the cook's personal gift, prepared with love and anticipation, we will naturally have the correct tone and attitude when and if we speak. Appreciation is the key.

Reality Check:

Do I voice complaints about my mother's cooking or that of anyone else who cooks for me? If so, I will make sure that the words I use do not insult the cook.

What If...

Tehilla's mother just does not care much about cooking? Perhaps she is overwhelmed with work or family responsibilities and must prepare everything in a rush. How can Tehilla handle this situation without insulting her mother?

---

22 *Cheshvan* — לע"נ ישראל ליב בן מרדכי ז"ל נלב"ע כ"ד טבת
22 *Adar* — לע"נ חיים בן אברהם הלוי ז"ל
Dedicated by Alvin Segal and family
22 *Tammuz* — לע"נ יחיאל משה בן ישראל חיים ז"ל
ואשתו רוחמה לאה בת יקותיאל חנני' יום טוב ליפא ע"ה

DAY 53

To Each Her Own
~ Ridiculing others' taste

כ"ג חשון
23 Cheshvan/Cycle 1

כ"ג אדר*
*23 Adar/Cycle 2

כ"ג תמוז
23 Tammuz/Cycle 3

* During Hebrew leap years, a thirteenth month called Adar Sheini is added to the calendar. During those years, the lessons for the days of Adar should be studied during each of the Adars.

כ"ג אדר ב
23 Adar Sheini

Kayla's shopping trips with her big sister, Simi, always ended with Kayla feeling depressed. Now she was getting ready for the Yamim Tovim and she needed a whole new wardrobe to accommodate the three inches she had grown since last Rosh Hashanah.

"What do you think of this sweater?" Kayla asked her sister, pulling her selection off the rack.

"Nice—if you're joining the circus," her sister replied wittily.

"I guess you're right," Kayla said. "It's kind of dumb looking."

Kayla's lack of taste was well known to her family members. In fact, her sisters joked that if Kayla liked something they brought home from shopping, that was a sure sign that they should return it.

Simi, on the other hand, seemed to have perfect taste in clothing and everything else. Her comments such as "Don't you have a mirror in your room?" made Kayla feel like a silly child compared to Simi. What was wrong with her, she wondered, that she had such poor taste?

Clearly, Kayla suffered from her sister's comments regarding her taste. Simi, on the other hand, thought she was being tactful, guiding her color- and style-blind sister with criticism coated in a thick layer of humor. She thought she was being a responsible older sibling, protecting Kayla from the stares and comments she would surely get if she were to go out of the house wearing the clothing she chose on her own.

In some ways, Simi was right. Kayla did need some help with her clothing choices. It was also true that if Simi didn't

122 Chapter Five: Statements that Damage Self-Image

mention that Kayla's skirt didn't match her shirt or her sweater was two sizes too big, Kayla's friends certainly would. **But to prevent the necessary corrections from becoming *ona'as devarim*, tact and regard for Kayla's dignity are the essential ingredients.**

Rather than saying, "Nice—if you're joining the circus," when asked for her opinion on the sweater, Simi could have answered without using sarcasm. For instance she might have said, "It's cute, but do you think that maybe the colors are too bright?"

Before we say anything at all about another person's taste, we should ask ourselves if there is any real purpose. If the person would really look ridiculous to others, then there is something to be gained by trying to guide her to a better choice. However, we also have to realize that people's tastes differ. One person cannot set herself up as the judge of good taste and put down anyone whose style is different. **Learning to appreciate the differences among people goes a long way toward reducing our temptation to criticize or insult someone's taste.**

The worst time to criticize someone's taste is when she is in public, for instance, at *shul* or a *simchah*. At that point, she has no choice but to wear what she has on. All the critic accomplishes is to make the other girl feel conspicuous and foolish, when she probably walked out of her house feeling well dressed and confident.

Reality Check:

Do I consider my own definition of style the one and only? Do I look down on people whose clothing I don't consider stylish? I will consider that maybe others have a different definition of style than I do. If I give clothing advice, I will make sure it is gentle and helpful.

What If...

Kayla would not have responded to more subtle suggestions? What if she would have just shrugged it off and gone ahead with her unattractive choice of clothing?

---

23 Cheshvan — לע"נ ר' שרגא פייבל בן חיים יהודה ז"ל
23 Adar — Aaron Rosenbaum z"l לע"נ אהרן דוב בן דוד ז"ל נלב"ע כ"ג אדר א'
Dedicated by Eliyahu & Yehudis Zidele and family
23 Tammuz — In honor of our children; Meir, Yossi, Nechama and Chayala
Dedicated by Chaim and Leora Grinspan

DAY 54

Nothing to Celebrate
~ Pleasure in others' misfortune

כ"ד חשון
24 Cheshvan/Cycle 1

כ"ד אדר*
*24 Adar/Cycle 2

כ"ד תמוז
24 Tammuz/Cycle 3

* During Hebrew leap years, a thirteenth month called Adar Sheini is added to the calendar. During those years, the lessons for the days of Adar should be studied during each of the Adars.

כ"ד אדר ב
24 Adar Sheini

For years, Simone had listened to her friend Naomi boast about her excellent study habits and fabulous grades. "I'm just very self-disciplined," Naomi would explain with supreme confidence. "You have to take yourself seriously if you want to get somewhere."

And indeed, Naomi was at the top of every class. She won every award and seemed to head every organizing committee for school events. No one ever heard her say she had forgotten her homework or needed an extra day to study. Even when she had a bout of mononucleosis, she arrived in school on her first day back with her research paper finished and ready to hand in. She was always neat, alert and energetic; her ponytail never even came loose.

To Simone, a disorganized student who never seemed to go to bed early enough to display much sparkle in school, Naomi's perfection was like a constant reminder of her own flaws. Therefore, when she discovered that Naomi was being treated for depression and an eating disorder, she felt a strange sense of satisfaction. "I knew it!" she thought silently. "I knew all that perfectionism couldn't be healthy!" Simone felt guilty rejoicing in her classmate's difficulties. She knew it was wrong, and yet the feeling was there; she couldn't deny it.

Simone's thoughts were shameful, even to Simone. She knew that Naomi was not a cruel or evil person who deserved no sympathy. However, her years of envy over Naomi's stellar success as a student created the perfect environment for her to feel satisfaction, rather than empathy,

124   Chapter Five: Statements that Damage Self-Image

at the news of Naomi's troubles. The situation would have been far worse had Simone spoken her feelings or somehow let Naomi get a sense of them.

If a person feels a sense of satisfaction over someone else's troubles, her first action must be to try to overcome those feelings by empathizing with the other person. Even if her troubles were as predictable as the end of a poorly written novel—even if her misfortune was the only logical outcome of her attitudes and habits—once the troubles arise, a Jew's first response is to feel the other person's pain and if possible, try to lighten her burden.

In some situations, it might take a lot of time and effort to arrive at this level. For instance, if there is a history of ill will between two people, empathy might be too difficult to arouse right away. If a person cannot find the strength to shake off feelings of satisfaction at someone else's distress, her best strategy is to stay away from the other person. In this way, she can make sure that hints of the negative feelings do not leak out into her conversation. Perceiving those negative feelings would cause the other person the additional, terrible pain of knowing that others are happy at her misfortune.

Of course, this strategy is only an emergency measure meant to prevent someone from stumbling into *ona'as devarim.* **The long-term solution for anyone who finds herself greeting other people's bad news with a secret smile is to strengthen the *ahavas Yisrael* in her life.** In doing so, she will revive the trait of compassion that is within the heart of every child of Avraham.

Reality Check:

Do I ever feel a little less sympathetic than I should when a person I dislike or envy runs into trouble? If so, I will try to improve my level of *ahavas Yisrael*, perhaps by learning this topic or making an effort to greet that person in a friendly way.

What If...

Simone realized that she was jealous of Naomi even before Naomi's bad news came to her attention? How could she handle those feelings?

---

24 Cheshvan — In memory of Al Bernstein z"l — לע"נ יעקב יוסף בן שלמה ז"ל

24 Adar — לע"נ רחל בת אליהו יצחק ע"ה
Dedicated by Ira and Chava Berkowitz

24 Tammuz — לע"נ שמואל בן חננא-ל ז"ל
Dedicated by Kaenan & Dafna Hertz and family

Nothing to Celebrate ~ Pleasure in others' misfortune

DAY 55

"I Told You So"
~ Unhelpful reminders

כ"ה חשון
25 Cheshvan/Cycle 1

כ"ה אדר*
*25 Adar/Cycle 2

כ"ה תמוז
25 Tammuz/Cycle 3

* During Hebrew leap years, a thirteenth month called Adar Sheini is added to the calendar. During those years, the lessons for the days of Adar should be studied during each of the Adars.

כ"ה אדר ב
25 Adar Sheini

"I want to buy a good camera for my trip to Israel, but I spent all my money on that suede coat!" Gitti complained to her cousin Leah.

"I told you not to buy it!" Leah responded. "You see, now there's something you want and you're all out of money! You already had a winter coat. I don't know why you didn't listen to me!"

. . .

"Uh-oh, I forgot the money for the Shabbaton," Penina told her friend Sara. "Mrs. Steinberg said anyone who doesn't have it in by today can't go! And no one's home at my house to bring it in for me. Why am I so dumb?"

"I told you last night to stick it in your book-bag so you wouldn't forget it," Sara replied. "Why don't you ever listen to me? You see what happens? It's all your own fault!"

If there are four words in the English language that achieve nothing but *ona'as devarim*, they are "I told you so." They are usually the response of someone whose good advice has been ignored and as a result, the person who ignored the advice is suffering. The words have no positive purpose. The person who is suffering does not need anyone to add to her suffering.

These words, or similar ones, are the classic example of "rubbing salt in the wound," making something that is already hurting hurt more. Why, then, do people so often say things like, "You should have listened to me," or "I told you this would happen"?

People sometimes express these thoughts because they hope that by doing so, they will "teach" the other person to

126 Chapter Five: Statements that Damage Self-Image

pay attention to their advice in the future. Does this strategy work?

Showing a lack of empathy toward people very rarely inspires them to improve. Instead, it gradually shrinks the list of people from whom the person feels she can find support in her times of need. The people who respond with "I told you so" appear to lack love or sincere concern for the person. Eventually, that feeling causes honest communication between the two to fade away; **no one trusts her honest emotions to someone who doesn't really care about her.**

Among friends and siblings, there is little that can do more damage than breaking lines of communication. When that happens, we lose our opportunity to influence those close to us in a positive way when they face difficult choices and challenges. This is a very high price to pay as we reach adulthood and raise our own children.

On the other hand, there is great value in learning to listen to good advice. It is something we would want our friends, siblings and eventually our children to learn. However, a poorly timed "I told you so" is not the way to build the trait of seeking and listening to advice. There are other ways to do it. For instance, after the crisis has passed, a person can ask, "Do you think this problem could have been avoided?" Or, when a similar situation comes up, she might suggest that her friend try a different strategy this time, as the last time, things did not work out well.

The right point will come across if the right feelings are behind our words. If we are speaking out of a desire to help the other person avoid costly errors, and not out of our desire to show our superior judgment, the words will most likely come out right.

> *25 Cheshvan* — לע"נ ברוך יצחק ז"ל בן ישרא-ל בן מרדכי יבלח"ט
> נלב"ע כ"ה חשון תשס"ג • Dedicated by his parents Yisroel and Freyda Berger
> *25 Adar* — לע"נ הרה"ג ר' יהודא ארי' בן ר' משה מנחם זצ"ל
> Dedicated in loving memory of Rabbi Leib Potashnik zt"l, by his daughters
> *25 Tammuz* — לע"נ י-הודית משא בת נח ע"ה
> Dedicated in loving memory of our mother and grandmother by the Panish family

Reality Check:

Do I ever say "I told you so" or a similar phrase? I will stop myself, knowing that these words serve no positive purpose.

What If...

someone repeatedly refuses to listen to your advice and gets herself into difficulty as a result? Are you obligated to try to stop her? Under what circumstances? What might be an effective approach?

DAY 56

Loaded Questions
~ Insults hidden in questions

כ"ו חשון
26 Cheshvan/Cycle 1

כ"ו אדר*
26 Adar/Cycle 2

כ"ו תמוז
26 Tammuz/Cycle 3

* During Hebrew leap years, a thirteenth month called Adar Sheini is added to the calendar. During those years, the lessons for the days of Adar should be studied during each of the Adars.

כ"ו אדר ב
26 Adar Sheini

The first few months of ninth grade had been overwhelming for Raizy. Most of her elementary school friends had gone to a different high school, and most of the girls in her high school already knew each other. Breaking into a new social circle did not come easily to Raizy, who was by nature a bit shy. But she tried her best, and took all the advice her mother and her guidance counselor gave her.

Now it was February, and the school was having its annual Melaveh Malkah. "Get involved! Volunteer for activities!" all her advisers had advised, and so she did. Because she had some artistic talent, she joined the decorating committee headed by Mirel Golden, a popular and stylish young lady whose mother was a professional event planner.

Raizy's first assignment was to fold the napkin at each place setting into the form of a flower and put it into the cup. Mirel showed her the technique and then went off to do something involving tulle and a glue gun. Raizy had finished napkin-flowers for five tables when Mirel returned, stared at her procedure and said, "What are you DOING?"

It was just a question. But it was an accusation. Raizy felt tears pushing their way into her eyes. She looked away from Mirel.

Often, "innocent" questions are *ona'as devarim* in disguise. There is no doubt that these questions will hurt the other person, yet the one who asks the question excuses herself by thinking, *What's the problem? It's just a question!* By examining the message contained in these

128   Chapter Five: Statements that Damage Self-Image

questions, we can develop a sharper sense of where the *ona'as devarim* is hidden.

In the story above, Mirel is not really wondering what Raizy is doing. Rather, through her question, she is telling Raizy that she disapproves of the way she is folding the napkins. Perhaps the project really is coming out a mess.

If that is the case, Mirel does need to say something, but not something sarcastic. Her first thought should be that Raizy is trying to help; she does not deserve to suffer for that. If Mirel thinks a little about Raizy's feelings before she speaks, her words will come out differently. She might say something like, "Raizy, thanks so much, you're working so hard. The only thing is, I should have spent more time showing you how to do the flowers. It's just not quite right. Let me help you fix up the ones that are already done and then I'm sure the rest will be great."

There are other questions that come under the category of *ona'as devarim* as well. For instance, a girl tells her friend that she found the perfect birthday present for her sister. "Doesn't she always return your presents?" the friend asks. The question instantly deflates the girl's pride and confidence in the gift she selected. The "question" is a statement: "You don't give good gifts."

Other "loaded questions" point out to a person a certain area of weakness or ignorance. "What do *you* think this sentence means?" a girl asks a weak student who has difficulty translating Hebrew. The girl is not expecting an answer; she is highlighting the other girl's deficiency.

Sometimes a question is just a search for information. Other times, as in the examples above, it is a weapon. If we ask ourselves why we are posing a certain question, and answer ourselves honestly, we will not fall for our own deception.

> **Reality Check:**
> Do I ask things like "What do you think you're doing?" or other "loaded questions"? If so, I will choose a more direct, respectful way to make my point, if it actually needs to be made.

> **What If...**
> Mirel had corrected Raizy respectfully, but Raizy was still embarrassed to be told that she was not doing a good job? Would Mirel's statement still be *ona'as devarim*?

---

26 Cheshvan — לע"נ הרה"ג רב ציון רחמים בן הרב יעקב לוי זצ"ל
By his grandchildren: Esti, Kelly, Avi, and Noam Levy
26 Adar — לזכות אביבה בת לאה הינדא שתחי'
26 Tammuz — לע"נ בנימין בן שרה ז"ל
Dedicated by his family

Loaded Questions ~ Insults hidden in questions

Day 57

Don't Ask
~ Nosy questions

כ"ז חשון
27 Cheshvan/Cycle 1

כ"ז אדר*
*27 Adar/Cycle 2

כ"ז תמוז
27 Tammuz/Cycle 3

* During Hebrew leap years, a thirteenth month called Adar Sheini is added to the calendar. During those years, the lessons for the days of Adar should be studied during each of the Adars.

כ"ז אדר ב
27 Adar Sheini

"Wow, your overnight bag is a Coach!" Mindy commented in a tone of awe. Mindy had a taste for brand names, but a budget that lent itself more to discount-store shopping. Nevertheless, sitting side-by-side with Leora on the bus to the school Shabbaton gave Mindy a chance to engage in her passion. She admired the smooth, sturdy leather, the styling, the clasp and golden-tan color of the bag. She reached out and ran her hand over it appreciatively.

"What did you pay for this?" Mindy asked Leora. But Leora didn't answer the question. "I've had it for a couple of years already," she said. Where Leora came from in New England, people did not ask such questions. She realized that Mindy did not mean to be rude, but she still felt uncomfortable. She changed the subject.

"I can't wait to hear Rebbetzin Klinger speak tonight," Leora said. "I heard her once before and she's amazing."

"Yeah, it'll be great," said Mindy. "Hey, what did you say you paid for that bag? Because my cousin got one on sale for about $350."

"I'd really rather not say," Leora finally answered.

"Oh, did you overpay?" Mindy ventured. "Or maybe you don't want anyone to know what a bargain you got!"

Leora calculated that she would be sitting next to Mindy on the bus for another three hours. It was going to be a long ride.

Different people have different ideas about what they consider to be personal information. Most people do not like to publicize details about health, family troubles, money and uncertain future plans. For instance, if a

130   Chapter Five: Statements that Damage Self-Image

girl's parents are considering moving to another city but the decision is not yet final, they may instruct their children not to reveal the plans to their friends. Similarly, if a sibling is getting near to her engagement but is not yet engaged, the information is usually kept quiet until it is official.

Our right to ask about these areas of another person's life depends on several factors. They include how close we are with the other person, how open or private the other person tends to be, and the normal standards of the family and community.

When a person is asked a question that seems too personal, she feels uncomfortable. Sometimes she feels resentful as well, because she sees the question as "nosy" or she imagines that we are simply searching for items of gossip. **Even if we are asking out of real concern for the other person, we still need to be sensitive to the fact that our question may not be welcome.**

One way to approach asking a personal question is to start with a general question on that topic, giving the other person the option of taking up the subject or letting it slide. Sometimes, it helps to acknowledge to the other person that we may be overstepping boundaries: "Don't feel you have to answer this…" or "If you'd rather not discuss this, I understand…" Caution is especially important if we do not know the other person well enough to know what areas of life she considers off-limits.

Even with close friends, questions that delve into painful areas of their lives should not be asked unless we have concrete help to offer. Rather, we should leave those discussions up to the other person if she wishes to open the subject. Often, the greatest level of caring is shown not by asking probing questions, but by just being there in whatever way the other person requires.

---

27 Cheshvan — לזכות שלמה בן לאה נ"י
As a *z'chus* for Rosana bas Clementina

27 Adar — Rochelle Berkowitz *a"h* לע"נ רחל בת אליהו יצחק ע"ה נלב"ע כ"ד אדר
Dedicated by Mr. & Mrs. Tuvia Berkowitz

27 Tammuz — Dedicated as a *z'chus* for the Rosenwald משפחה

Reality Check:

Am I someone who likes or even needs to get the firsthand news on other people's lives? Before I ask a personal question, I will think about whether it may be improper or unnecessary to ask.

What If…

Mindy was considering buying a similar bag and wanted price information so she could find the best deal? Would her question still be *ona'as devarim*? Could she get the information from Leora in a way that would not make Leora uncomfortable?

DAY 58

Boasting or Sharing?
~ Relating good news

כ"ח חשון
28 Cheshvan/Cycle 1

כ"ח אדר*
*28 Adar/Cycle 2

כ"ח תמוז
28 Tammuz/Cycle 3

* During Hebrew leap years, a thirteenth month called Adar Sheini is added to the calendar. During those years, the lessons for the days of Adar should be studied during each of the Adars.

כ"ח אדר ב
28 Adar Sheini

Visiting day was coming to a close at Camp Ahavas Olam. The counselors had worked hard running the day's special activities. Then they worked even harder as some of the more homesick campers plunged into post-visiting-day tearfulness. Shuli was sitting on a bench taking a break when Mr. and Mrs. Gelbstein found her.

"So here you are!" said Mrs. Gelbstein to Shuli. "We've been looking for you all afternoon. First of all, we want you to have this…"

Mrs. Gelbstein handed Shuli an envelope that contained a tip.

"But most of all, we wanted you to know what you have done for our Devorah. We've had so much trouble with her all year in school," Mrs. Gelbstein explained. "She was not getting along with the girls. Her teachers didn't know what to do with her, and to tell you the truth, we were fully expecting a call from camp asking us to come get her.

"But she's been happy with everything in camp, and she says it's all because she finally has a best friend. And that best friend is Shuli. You've literally given her a new life, and we really cannot thank you enough!"

Shuli told the Gelbsteins how cooperative Devorah had been, wished them well, and walked them toward the parking lot. When she got back to her bunk she opened her envelope and found $200, a tip beyond all expectations. "Devorah's parents said I actually turned her around," Shuli told her co-counselor. "They said I gave her back her life. Unbelievable."

Was Shuli boasting? If the co-counselor had a frustrating summer and felt ineffective in her job, Shuli's words would be *ona'as devarim* because the co-counselor would feel more like a failure next to Shuli's soaring success. If, on the other hand, the co-counselor would be happy for Shuli, then sharing the information would not cause pain; it would add to the co-counselor's own happiness.

There are people in our lives who we can safely assume will share our joys. First and foremost are our parents. In addition, teachers almost always appreciate news of their students' achievements. After that, the effect our tales of triumph will have cannot be assumed. Unfortunately, sibling relationships often include a certain amount of rivalry, and therefore brothers and sisters may not be as eager to applaud our success as we would hope. Friends may also have sensitivities that make our accomplishments difficult to hear.

Some examples of "sharing good news" that might be seen as boasting include talking about your A+ to someone who struggles to learn; talking about your big, happy family to an only child; relating your plans for a lavish vacation to someone from a family that can't afford one; or talking about your three seminary acceptances to someone who has not been accepted to even one seminary.

Ideally, we would hope that people in our lives would be happy for us even when they are suffering from something they lack. **Being happy with one's lot is an important concept in the Jewish outlook on life, but it is a concept we each must work on within ourselves, not demand from other people**. People should indeed be happy for us, but we should not be the ones to force-feed them the information. Rather, we should share what we must in the most humble way possible, so that our joy does not become someone else's pain.

Reality Check:
Do I love to burst out with my good news? If so, I will now try to hold back until I think about how my news might be taken by the people I am telling it to.

What If...
Shuli can't tell whether or not her co-counselor will be happy or jealous? What, if anything, could she say in that case?

---

28 Cheshvan — לע"נ אברהם טובי׳ יהונתן בן ר' צבי באום ז"ל
נלב"ע כ"ח מרחשון • Dedicated by Feivy & Leah Weinberger and family
28 Adar — In memory of Yaakov Lampner *z"l* לע"נ יעקב יוסף בן זונדל חנוך ז"ל
In memory of Rochel Leah Newman *a"h* לע"נ רחל לאה בת שמואל ע"ה
28 Tammuz — In memory of my beloved friend לע"נ עטיל בת אשר ע"ה
Dedicated by Golda Rivka

DAY 59

The Happy Buyer
~ Too-late shopping advice

כ"ט חשון
29 Cheshvan/Cycle 1

כ"ט אדר
29 Adar/Cycle 2

כ"ט תמוז
29 Tammuz/Cycle 3

• When this month has only 29 days the lesson for the 30th day should also be studied today.

* During Hebrew leap years, a thirteenth month called Adar Sheini is added to the calendar. During those years, the lessons for the days of Adar should be studied during each of the Adars.

כ"ט אדר ב
29 Adar Sheini

It wasn't easy for 5'10" Michal to find clothes that fit her well. Her lanky frame always looked even lankier in the store's three-way mirror. With Pesach coming and nothing nice to wear, she spent days checking out the selections in the local dress shops and department stores. Finally she found an outfit that suited her and now, on the first day of Pesach, she walked to shul with that special feeling of wearing something brand new.

"Good Yom Tov, Michal. Nice outfit," said Avigail as she caught up with her neighbor. "It's new, isn't it?"

"Yes," Michal said proudly. "I got it at The Dress Spot on sale."

"The Dress Spot? Really?" Avigail said. "Didn't you know that Value Palace has the same brands, and even without a sale they're always a lot cheaper than The Dress Spot? And now they're having a sale! You probably paid twice what you had to. You know, why don't you bring it back and go to Value Palace?"

"I can't return it," said Michal. "I already had the skirt lengthened."

Michal's royal "new dress" posture was a little more slumped as she went on her way to shul. She hadn't considered traveling a half-hour out of town to Value Palace.

When someone buys a new item, we are obligated to be careful not to rob her of her satisfaction with her purchase. Unless there is a constructive purpose in criticizing the purchase, we should take note of the item and find something about it to praise (*Kesubos* 17a). The more expensive the item, the more careful we must be to hold back any negative comments.

134   Chapter Five: Statements that Damage Self-Image

Even if the item does not meet our own standards of quality or value, we can assume that the person who bought it was satisfied. Otherwise she would not have made the purchase. If we cannot find something to praise, we can at least acknowledge that the item is bringing the other person satisfaction: "It must feel great to walk into your bedroom and see the zebra rug you always wanted."

Sometimes, however, there is a constructive purpose to telling someone about a better price, better quality or a defect in the item they bought. The key question is whether the item can be returned. If it can, then the person has the option of acting on the advice and saving money or buying a better product. However, the *Pele Yoetz* (*Derech Eretz*) says that if the purchaser cannot return the item, we should not tell her that she overpaid.

How do we know whether the item can be returned? Sometimes this is easy to determine; perhaps the tags are still on the garment, or we know that this particular store accepts returns. However, there may not be any subtle way to find out. What we are certainly not permitted to do is to ask, "Can you return this? Because if you can, I want to tell you something, but if not there's no point." By asking that question, we tell the other person that we have information that would motivate her to return the item if she could. That alone will reduce her satisfaction with her purchase. Therefore we may, in many instances, have no option but to keep our advice to ourselves.

Most of the time, all someone wants is for us to admire her purchase and share her enjoyment of it. It's one of the simplest ways in the world to make another person happy; it requires no expertise, no great advice—just a generous heart and a kind word.

---

29 *Cheshvan* — In memory of Alferd I. Sutton z"l לע"נ יהושע בן שרה ז"ל
Dedicated by Abe and Barbra Chehebar

29 *Adar* — May today's learning be a זכות for הצלחה ברכה for our children: Tehila Ahava, Yaacov Moshe and Shumel Yitzchak.

29 *Tammuz* — Anonymous

Reality Check:

Do I weigh in on the value, quality or style of other people's purchases? From now on, I will make sure that my comments increase rather than reduce the person's satisfaction with her new item.

What If...

Avigail wanted Michal to know about Value Palace so that the next time she shopped, she could take advantage of that store's better prices? Could she relate that information without lessening Michal's happiness with her new outfit? How?

DAY 60

Helpful Hints
~ Killing with kindness

ל חשון*
30 Cheshvan/Cycle 1

ל אדר*
30 Adar/Cycle 2

א אב
1 Av/Cycle 3

* When this month has only 29 days, the lessons for the 30th day should be learned together with that of the 29th.

> *When Yehudis came home from work, her 12-year-old sister Dina was on baby-sitting duty, taking care of little Eli until their mother got home. Dina was locked in what looked like a life-or-death struggle with the baby as she tried to get his diaper on. Eli kicked and flailed and waved his arms, screaming with all the power he could muster.*
>
> *"Move over a second and I'll show you the right way to do this," Yehudis told her sister. "He's too hard for you to handle."*
>
> . . .
>
> *Bubbie Cohen stood at her daughter's kitchen sink wearing an apron and rubber gloves. She hummed a Shabbos song as she slowly and carefully soaped and rinsed the pile of dishes.*
>
> *"Bubbie, let me do that," Bluma said to her grandmother. "Your back will start hurting if you stand there too long."*
>
> *"Don't be silly," Bubbie said. "You go study for your final and I'll finish up in here."*
>
> *"Really, Bubbie, let me do it," Bluma repeated. "I can get the whole thing done in a few minutes."*

On the surface, each of these scenarios presents someone who is trying to help. Yehudis is trying to help Dina handle the baby. Bluma is trying to relieve her grandmother of the job of washing the dishes.

Beneath the surface, however, there is another message: "You can't handle this."

When we offer help using words that express our impression that the other person is helpless or incompetent, our kind offer turns into an insult. In the above scenarios, Dina, the younger sister, gets the message that her sister does not see her as capable of taking care of the baby. Bubbie, who is happily washing the dishes, discovers that her granddaughter thinks that she is frail and that she works too slowly.

Helping someone is a *chesed* and certainly not to be avoided. However, **the words we use when we offer to help are an important factor in whether our offer causes the other person to feel grateful or to feel resentful.**

The best way to keep help helpful is to concentrate on positive instructions rather than criticism of the other person's performance and abilities. For instance, Yehudis could have told her sister who was struggling to diaper the baby, "It helps if you distract him," rather than demanding to take over the job. In the case of Bubbie and Bluma, the granddaughter could have simply said, "Tell me if you need help."

When a person wants to help, she wants to perform an act of kindness. Her deed can and should be a great source of merit for her. However, if her words cause pain to the person she is trying to help, then the merit she should be receiving shrinks dramatically. To protect the priceless value of helping others, it pays to carefully measure the words that are spoken in the process.

> **Reality Check:**
>
> Do my offers of help ever deflate the people I'm trying to help? If so, I will make sure that I phrase my offer in a positive way without making even subtle reference to any weaknesses I see in the other person.

> **What If...**
>
> someone refuses your help but you know that it is just out of pride? For instance, what if Bubbie really had a bad back and should stay off her feet? Are we then justified in pointing out the flaw that makes our help necessary? Are there other ways to solve the problem?

---

30 Cheshvan — In memory of Abbe Lederberger *z"l*
לע"נ אברהם שלמה בן ישראל ז"ל
30 Adar — לזכות הצלחה רבה לגדליה שמואל בן יהודית נ"י ומשפחתו
1 Av — In loving memory of my grandmother Chaya Sara *bas* Heshel *a"h*
Dedicated by her granddaughter Liane Pritkin

Helpful Hints ~ Killing with kindness

Kislev

לע"נ מסעודה שושנה בת אברהם ע"ה נלב"ע י"ט כסלו

In memory of Shoshana Lieberman a"h

*Dedicated by the Lieberman
and Baumgarten families*

לע"נ אברהם צבי בן ברוך ז"ל נלב"ע כ"ז ניסן
In memory of Horace A Bier z"l
לע"נ יהודה צבי בן אלחנן יצחק נלב"ע א' כסלו
In memory of Dr. Leon Hirschfus z"l
לע"נ רחל אסתר בת משה ע"ה ו' ניסן
In memory of Reyetta Hirschfus a"h
Dedicated by Bryan and Andrea Bier

לע"נ מיידא הודיא בת משה ע"ה נלב"ע כ"ב כסלו

In memory of Helen Polonsky a"h

Dedicated by Alex & Amy Polonsky

Nissan

As a z'chus for our family

Dedicated by Mr. and Mrs. Albert David

לע"נ בת שבע רחל בת שמואל ע"ה נלב"ע ד' ניסן

In memory of Susan Ruth Fastow a"h

Dedicated by Melvin Fastow

לע"נ ישכר דוב בן אלעזר ז"ל
ואשתו קלערעל בת בנימין ע"ה
לע"נ שלמה חיים בן יוסף דוב הכהן ז"ל
ואשתו פריידא יענטא בת ישראל ע"ה

Dedicated by their children Moshe and Mindi Gewirtz

Av

In honor of our children, Faigy, Yocheved, Esty,
Avi and Chaya Shira

Love,

Mommy & Daddy

As a z'chus for
Rina Sarah bat Tanya Adina
David Yisroel ben Tanya Adina
Yitzchok Moshe ben Tanya Adina
Yehuda Levi ben Tanya Adina
Zahava Ziva bat Tanya Adina
שיחיו

Dedicated in the memory of our beloved and dear mother and grandmother

לע"נ אמי מורתי האשה החשובה והצנועה המפורסמת במידותיה
מרת חיה גיטל וואלצער בת הרה"ח ר' צבי שלום מיללער ע"ה
נפטר ט"ו מנחם אב תשע"א לפ"ק
נדבת ע"י בנה ר' יעקב שלמה וואלצער נ"י ומשפחתו שיחי'

Chapter 6

Manipulative, Defensive Tactics

What are we willing to do to get our own way in an argument or situation? Sometimes we use words as our secret weapon, saying things that frighten or demoralize the other person into dropping her opposition, or that manipulate her into doing what we want. We may win the battle, but we lose the valuable perspectives the other person may have offered if we had only given her the chance.

DAY 61

The Dark Side
~ Spreading pessimism

א כסלו
1 Kislev/Cycle 1

א ניסן
1 Nissan/Cycle 2

ב אב
2 Av/Cycle 3

Adina's course ended at 9 p.m. As she drove home she thought about her friend Ita's vort, which was going on at that very moment. "I'll run into the house, change my clothes, pick up Pearl and we'll be there by 10 o'clock," she thought.

Then the traffic slowed down. She spied some flashing lights in the distance. "Oh, no. An accident. This could take forever."

By the time she got home it was well after 10. The phone rang.

"Adina? It's Pearl. What's doing? It's getting late," her friend said.

"I know, I'm sorry. There was an accident on the highway and it took me forever to get home from school. But I'm almost ready."

"Maybe we should forget it," Pearl said. "It's starting to pour outside and it's going to be 11 by the time we get there. And that's if we're lucky, because if the accident hasn't been cleared up yet, we'll be in the same traffic you were in and miss the whole thing."

"I know. But I told Ita I was coming," Adina replied.

"Ita knows you have school. She'll understand. And besides that, you just got over bronchitis. Do you think you should go out in the rain and then go to work tomorrow on four hours' sleep? You'll get sick again."

Adina began to feel less committed to her plan to be at Ita's vort. She imagined the pleasure of crawling into her nice warm bed and getting a good night's sleep. The hammering of the rain against her window provided another argument against going.

"Never mind all that," Adina finally told Pearl. "I said I was going and I'm going. Should I pick you up?"

144 Chapter Six: Manipulative, Defensive Tactics

> *Pearl agreed to go along, but as Adina drove through the rain to her house she felt unsettled inside. She should never have told Ita she would be there.*

Reading the scenario above, we get instant insight into the workings of pessimism. It is highly contagious. A person who sees all the negatives quickly throws the proverbial wet blanket on other people's enthusiasm. Challenges they might have take in stride suddenly appear to be obstacles large enough to stop progress altogether.

A pessimist creates a reality out of negative possibilities that may never actually happen. She pulls other people into her grim view, causing them to dwell on suffering or disappointment that might never occur. Even if the pessimist's predictions really do come true, there is usually no benefit in having worried about them in advance.

Of course, wise people do consider the consequences of their actions. That is not the same, however, as dragging someone down with a dose of pessimism.

A common pessimistic statement is the one that sometimes greets girls just home from seminary: "You know, after the inspiration wears off you'll see reality setting in again." Rather than casting a cloud over a girl's newfound idealism, a person could suggest a class or a mentor that could help her keep growing.

But unless someone is personally involved in another person's life, even these suggestions are usually uncalled for. The best response to someone else's bright ideas and high hopes is just plain *"Hatzlachah!"* because it's very possible that, despite other people's wise warnings and dark predictions, she will actually succeed.

---

1 Kislev — לע"נ יהושע בן חיים יצחק ז"ל נלב"ע ב' כסלו
Dedicated by Moshe and Malky Feldman

1 Nissan — בזכות זה ירבו שמחות בישראל
Dedicated by משפחת קוויאט

2 Av — לע"נ ראובן בן אהרן הכהן ז"ל
לע"נ שמעון בן ראובן הכהן ז"ל

Reality Check:

Do I feel obligated to point out all the potential problems of other people's plans? If so, I will review in my mind the last few times I offered the downside and ask myself, "Did any of my predictions come true? Even if some of them did come true, was there any benefit in my negative input?"

What If...

Pearl had said, "Let's just do our best to get there. Even if we catch Ita on the way out, at least she'll see we tried"? Would Adina still have felt unsettled as she set out for the *vort*? What would the mood of the trip have been?

DAY 62

Enough Said
~ Overly long rebuke

ב כסלו
2 Kislev/Cycle 1

ב ניסן
2 Nissan/Cycle 2

ג אב
3 Av/Cycle 3

Every Shabbos afternoon Rikki led activities at her shul for a group of 15 pre-school girls. Her neighbor Batya was her assistant. One Shabbos, Batya was sick and Rikki was left without help.

"I'll do it," offered Miri, Rikki's younger sister.

"Thanks, Miri, but you're too young. It's a big group and they're little kids. You have to really be on top of them," Rikki replied.

"I'm only six months younger than Batya!" Miri insisted. "I can do it. Let me try!"

With no other option, Rikki agreed.

That afternoon, Rikki and Miri met their group in the shul's Kiddush room where the program took place. After a few games, some songs and a talk about the parshah, the Shabbos party began.

"You watch them while I go get the candy and chips," Rikki instructed Miri. Rikki disappeared into the kitchen. Meanwhile, an adorable little girl began telling Miri a story about her trip to the bakery with her mother. Unnoticed by Miri, another girl began walking along the chairs aligned at the table, leaping from seat to seat. A chair slid and she crashed to the floor.

Rikki came running from the kitchen to find Miri hovering over the crying girl, trying to help her. "I told you to watch them!" Rikki exploded. Fortunately the child was not hurt, but Rikki spent the entire 20-minute walk home from shul scolding Miri. "She could have cracked her head open! And whose fault would that have been?" Little by little, Miri's remorse for her carelessness turned into resentment of her older sister, who just couldn't stop verbally pounding her.

146 Chapter Six: Manipulative, Defensive Tactics

A long, drawn-out lecture or an angry tongue-lashing can sometimes be more painful than a physical blow. At times, however, a strong rebuke is needed. Where does rebuke end and *ona'as devarim* begin? We have already learned two elements that distinguish between the two. One is the emotion behind the words: Are they coming from a desire to help someone improve, or from anger and frustration? The other is the choice of words: Do they show respect for the other person's dignity?

Another less obvious factor is the length of the rebuke. How much needs to be said to get the point across? **If a simple sentence like "I'm very disappointed in what you did" will deliver the message, then anything more is *ona'as devarim*.** More words only increase the other person's pain and embarrassment at having done wrong. Also, a long harangue can backfire and anger the other person to the point where she rebels rather than reforms.

All a rebuke is supposed to accomplish is an awakening. We are trying to bring the other person to recognize her mistake and make a commitment to improve. But if we do not stop long enough to let the other person speak, we will not even be able to tell if she is in fact being awakened.

How do we know that our message got through? Sometimes we have to wait and see if the other person acts differently in the future. Some people find it difficult to admit when they are wrong, but through their actions we see that they have accepted the rebuke.

The final proof of whether a person has gone too far with rebuke is in the consequences of her words. If they drive the other person further away, they have failed. If they motivate her to improve, they have succeeded. It is always better to say too little, for if necessary we can find a new opportunity to say more.

> **Reality Check:**
> When I feel that I am justified or even obligated to rebuke someone, do I try to limit my words to the absolute fewest necessary? If not, I will train myself to think, *Do I need to say anything more?*

> **What If...**
> Rikki had kept anger out of the situation? What might she have said to Miri that would have gotten her point across? Did she need to give any rebuke at all?

---

2 Kislev — Mr. Harry Bohrer z"l לע"נ צבי הרש בן שמעון ז"ל נלב"ע כ' כסלו
Dedicated by Steven & Marjorie Kellner and family

2 Nissan — ברכה והצלחה to our children and grandchildren on our anniversary
Dedicated by Sam and Esther Gross

3 Av — In memory of Cecil Solomon Herbert z"l לע"נ שלום בן בנימין ז"ל
Dedicated by Joseph & Bette Herbert and family

DAY 63

"I Can't Say"
~ Anonymous rumors

ג כסלו
3 Kislev/Cycle 1

ג ניסן
3 Nissan/Cycle 2

ד אב
4 Av/Cycle 3

Suddenly one day, the rug was pulled out from under Penina's social life. She was a happy girl with a nice circle of friends, but now her best friend Ruthie was no longer allowed to come to her house.

"But WHY?" Penina asked urgently as she spoke to her friend on the phone. "What did I do?"

"I wish I could tell you, but I can't," her friend answered quietly. "Someone said something to my mother and me, something about your family, and I'm not allowed to say who it was and I don't even think it's true. But my mother said it's better if we get together at my house or at school, and I can't come to you anymore."

Penina hung up the phone and told her mother the news. Both of them sat silently, thinking about the possible scenarios that could have led to this. Who was this informant? What was the information?

"It's horrible!" Penina cried out. "Someone out there is saying things about us and I don't know who it is. It could be anyone! It could be someone we think is our friend!"

Returning to school the next morning, Penina's view of her entire class had changed. Was it Yaelle who started the rumor? Was it Chavi, or Tehilla? What were people saying? What was there even to be said? Was her family somehow different from other people's families?

I n the situation above, Ruthie is committing one sin in an effort to avoid a different one. **Knowing that naming the source of her information would be** *rechilus* **(words that stir up hatred between two people)**, she

148 Chapter Six: Manipulative, Defensive Tactics

instead speaks *ona'as devarim*, conveying information that shatters Penina's image of herself and her place in the community. Penina loses some of her trust in just about everyone, because she cannot know who has spoken about her. She loses pride in her family, realizing that her home has become off-limits to one friend and perhaps will be banned by others too, as the mysterious information spreads.

While this situation raises many problems and questions, there are ways that it could have been handled which would have at least reduced the pain for Penina. The first issue, of course, is Ruthie's and her mother's acceptance of the negative information as fact. The laws of *lashon hara* and *rechilus* forbid a person from accepting as true the negative words said about another person. We are allowed only to take the information as a warning that we should look into a situation.

If it happened that for some reason Ruthie's mother was right to keep her daughter out of Penina's house, that fact should have been conveyed without alarming Penina. No mention should have been made of a rumor or an informant. The unknown—the sense that someone out there is drawing conclusions and spreading rumors about a person—creates far more tension and unhappiness than the known. In such a situation the victim is being accused, but has no way of confronting the accuser.

In a case where there seems to be no winning solution, a *rav* should be consulted to determine what information may or may not be believed, what may be repeated, and what may be acted upon. It is a situation that has to be approached with the utmost seriousness, because the person who is the subject of the rumor stands to lose her most precious possession: her good name.

> **Reality Check:**
> What is my response when I hear a negative rumor about someone that requires a response from me? I will ask a *rav* or a teacher how to deal with this rumor in a way that does the least harm to the person involved.

> **What If...**
> Penina's parents permitted some activities in their home that other parents in the community did not? How could that situation be handled without the shattering results of the above scenario?

---

3 Kislev — In memory of Rozita Safia ט"יבלחט ניסן בת צפניה ע"ה רוזיטא נ"לע
Dedicated by her parents and siblings, the Mahpari family

3 Nissan — As a *z'chus* for our family
Dedicated by Rabbi and Mrs. Yehuda Abrams

4 Av — Mr. Selig Wolf ל"ז אביגדור 'ר בן זעליג אשר 'ר מורינו אבינו נ"לע
Dedicated by his children

DAY 64

"Boo!"
~ Frightening others

ד כסלו
4 Kislev/Cycle 1

ד ניסן
4 Nissan/Cycle 2

ה אב
5 Av/Cycle 3

"So you're going on a 747?" Avigail asked her friend Dassi. "I don't know… it seems that lately every airplane that crashed has been a 747."

Dassi's face went pale. "That's not funny, Avigail. Cut it out!"

"Oh, don't worry. I think they give out parachutes nowadays. You know, just in case," Avigail giggled at her witticism. She was really getting a reaction out of Dassi.

"You know I hate flying," Dassi said pleadingly. "Why do you want to drive me crazy? I'm serious, just cut it out!"

"Oh, stop it, Dassi. Millions of people fly every day and they get where they're going," Avigail scoffed. "You're not going to tell me that you lose sleep over an airplane flight. Maybe you should get hypnotized or something." She laughed again and then finally changed the subject.

After the conversation, Dassi began researching current airplane-crash statistics for 747s. Her flight was in two days, and she was pretty sure that she would not sleep again until she had arrived in Israel. She imagined the massive, swelling waves of the Atlantic Ocean underneath the flimsy little plane as it skidded along on thin air. Even if she survived the crash, she'd probably die of hypothermia or a shark attack. What a terrible end! Dassi kept trying to shake the morbid thoughts out of her head, but her heart was pounding and her stomach churning with fear.

150   Chapter Six: Manipulative, Defensive Tactics

When a person frightens someone, she thrusts her into one of the most emotionally painful states that exist. Fear is a paralyzing, overpowering emotion that quickly floods out any other thoughts or feelings. There would seem to be no motivation to impose it on someone else.

However, some people enjoy the attention they get when they "sound the alarm." They take pleasure in spreading the latest scary news reports: nuclear threats by maniacal dictators, killer hurricanes heading up from South America, a supervirus epidemic that has no cure. The news is filled with frightening possibilities, many of which are completely out of the average person's control. For some people, these topics are nothing more than interesting material for conversation. Others, however, may take these reports to heart. If a person hears of a threat of war against Israel, for instance, she might become obsessed with worry about the welfare of her relatives who are living there. That sense of foreboding might last just a few minutes, or she might carry it around with her for days.

Doing or saying things to scare others is forbidden by Jewish law (*Choshen Mishpat* 420:32). That rule even prohibits jokingly arousing someone's fears with the intention of telling her the truth right afterward. Shouting "Boo!" or making a loud sudden noise in order to startle someone is also forbidden, especially if it is done in a dark, deserted area where the victim already feels on edge.

Sometimes other people's fears seem groundless and therefore silly. Avigail cannot imagine how frightened of flying Dassi is since Avigail does not have that fear. If we find ourselves downplaying another person's fears, we can arouse our empathy by thinking of something that really does scare us, and imagine causing that feeling in someone else.

Reality Check:

Do I enjoy being the bearer of dramatic news that gets everyone agitated? Do I sometimes tease people about things they fear? If so I will remember how unpleasant a feeling fear is and refrain from inflicting it on others.

What If...

you had to warn a sensitive person about a real danger, for instance, a tornado that has been forecast to hit your town? How would you word your warning?

---

4 Kislev — In memory of Silvia *bas* Ruby *a"h* Yahrtzeit 14 Kislev
Dedicated by Abraham and Sandra Getzel

4 Nissan — In memory of my sister Ruth Novellas *a"h* לע"נ רות בת משה ע"ה
Dedicated by Marcia Brumberg

5 Av — Rebbetzin Etta Rivka Zucker *a"h* יבלחט"א לע"נ עטא רבקה ע"ה בת שמעון
A beloved friend and eternal inspiration צבי-ה, י-הודה לייב וא-ליהו זוסע

"Boo!" ~ Frightening others

DAY 65

Who's Laughing?
~ Practical jokes

ה כסלו
5 Kislev/Cycle 1

ה ניסן
5 Nissan/Cycle 2

ו אב
6 Av/Cycle 3

Nava, Serach and Menucha were bored out of their minds one Sunday afternoon. The three friends had spent the day together at Nava's house. They had studied for a test, played Monopoly, baked sugar cookies, styled each other's hair—and it was only 3:30 p.m. The dull December sky and cold drizzle outside made them even more glum.

"I've got an idea," said Nava. "Let's play a joke on Shira. Let's get her to come over."

"That's mean," said Serach.

"No, not a mean joke, a funny joke," Nava said. "You know how she is always so, so, so helpful? How she can't say no to anyone? Well, I'll bet that I can get her to come over here if I ask her to help me, even if it's the dumbest problem in the world."

"O.K.," Menucha agreed. "Let's see if she comes. I'll bet you an ice-cream sundae that she doesn't."

"I still think it's mean," said Serach. "But whatever. I bet she'll come."

Shira lived four blocks away. She hadn't joined her friends at Nava's house that afternoon because she studied better on her own. As she sat at her kitchen table trying to memorize the kings of Yehudah, her phone rang.

"Shira, listen, I really need your help. I'm baby-sitting for Tzippy and she wrote all over herself with marker so I put her in the bath and now her toe is stuck in the faucet! I can't get it out! Can you come over and help me?"

"Me?" Shira asked. "I probably can't do anything more than you can do. Maybe call Hatzolah."

"Oh, please!" Nava begged. "I'd feel so much better if you were here!"

Shira closed her book, pulled on her coat and rain-boots, and trudged four long, chilly blocks to Nava's *house. When she arrived, she was shocked to find Nava and her two other friends peering out the living-room window laughing wildly at the sight of her as she tramped up to the door.*

"I told you she'd come," Nava said victoriously. "Shira Tzivia Rosenberg cannot say no to anyone. If we called her at 3 a.m. to kill a spider, she'd be here!"

Shira was not amused. In fact, she was humiliated. She felt that her helpful nature was an object of ridicule, a sign of gullibility that everyone could see. The group of friends had put time and creativity into devising their "joke," but sadly, all their effort achieved was *ona'as devarim*. The same talent and energy could easily have gone into achieving a positive goal, but these girls felt that the laugh was worth the price.

While the Torah pays tribute to the virtue of *simchah*, it denounces in the strongest terms any kind of mockery. Practical jokes, false alarms, and other such pranks are aimed at arousing alarm in someone for other people's amusement. They clearly fall within the definition of mockery, and *ona'as devarim* as well.

Even though the victim quickly finds out that the emergency was not real, the harm comes from the humiliation the person feels when she realizes that she has been manipulated and set up for ridicule. That hurt does not go away when the prank is revealed.

How can a person be sure not to fall into causing this type of *ona'as devarim*? She can ask herself, as she imagines how funny a certain prank will be, *Who will be laughing?*

5 Kislev — לע"נ הבחור יעקב ז"ל בן ר' ברוך יהודה יבלח"ט
הונצח על ידי משפחתו

5 Nissan — Dedicated as a *z'chus* for our daughter

6 Av — לע"נ יכט בת רבקה ע"ה
Dedicated by the whole family

Reality Check:

Do I sometimes participate in practical jokes? If so, I will use the advice above and think about whether the object of the joke will truly find it funny.

What If...

the girls had played their prank just to get Shira to join them because they wanted her company? Would Shira have been less hurt? Why or why not?

DAY 66

Really Pushing It
~ Nagging

ו כסלו
6 Kislev/Cycle 1

ו ניסן
6 Nissan/Cycle 2

ז אב
7 Av/Cycle 3

"Clean this thing out!" Daniel commanded Moshe. "You were supposed to clean out the filter after the last car we vacuumed. Now it doesn't pick up anything!"

For the past three years, Daniel and Moshe had been making a small fortune in the weeks before Pesach. From the minute they arrived home from yeshivah, they were busy 12 hours a day with their car-cleaning service. Moshe had hatched the idea, but Daniel was the one with the business and organizational skills to make it happen. After three years of working together, Moshe did not seem to have learned anything about responsibility. Daniel had to remind him and remind him and remind him again to tend to the details of the job.

"But I told you a zillion times that the filter has to be cleaned out after every car!" Daniel reminded his partner. "How are we ever going to run this business if you forget everything you're supposed to do?"

"All right, all right, I'll take care of it as soon as I come back," Moshe responded. "My mother needs me to go to the store for her."

"But you forgot after Levy's car and you forgot after Rosenbaum's car and you forgot after Hirschberg's car. You can't forget about it when you come back," Daniel added for good measure.

"Look, I've got to go now. My mother needs some stuff for supper."

"Fine, but make sure you clean out the filter right after that. It's got to be cleaned out after every car. I really mean it!"

In this story, one fact is certain: Daniel's nagging has not improved Moshe's sense of responsibility. The fact that Daniel is still so frustrated proves that his nagging hasn't worked. In fact, nagging almost never works under any circumstances; it just irritates people, causing them to become less and less sensitive to the message. *There goes Daniel again, with something else I didn't do right,* is a much more likely thought in Moshe's head than *I really should be more responsible. Daniel is right.* Eventually, the nag's message becomes nothing more than annoying background noise, like the rumble of a lawn mower on a summer day.

Besides the fact that it doesn't work, nagging also damages relationships. People avoid nags.

Sadly, the damage is often done over a fairly trivial issue. If the issue were serious, the person would most likely take a more serious approach. For Daniel and Moshe, for example, that might mean sitting down together, discussing the problem and working out a real solution.

Annoying and harassing someone rarely gains his cooperation. People believe that "the squeaky wheel gets the oil," but even if that were true, who wants to spend his life as a squeaky wheel?

> **Reality Check:**
> Do I try to manage some other people in my life by nagging? If so, I will first decide whether the issue is truly worthwhile, and if I still think it is I will develop a more effective strategy to deal with the problem.

> **What If...**
> Daniel realized that his nagging had not accomplished anything? How else could he handle the situation?

---

6 Kislev — לע"נ מרת גאלדא חנה בת ר' חיים אלטר ע"ה
Dedicated by her family

6 Nissan — In memory of Rachel Mograby *a"h* לע"נ רחל בת מרגלית ע"ה
Dedicated by her loving family

7 Av — Jack Fogel לע"נ ר' יעקב זאב בן ר' יהודה ארי-ה ז"ל
Dedicated by Shalom & Ettie Fogel

Really Pushing It ~ Nagging 155

DAY 67

"Don't Ask Me"
~ Harsh refusal to help

ז כסלו
7 Kislev/Cycle 1

ז ניסן
7 Nissan/Cycle 2

ח אב
8 Av/Cycle 3

"Hi Tali, it's Bella Goldstein. You remember me from tenth grade?" Tali hadn't seen or heard from Bella since the latter moved from their hometown to Los Angeles.

"I haven't heard from you in years. What's the occasion?" Tali asked, already tensing up for the request for money that she was sure would follow. With her family's prominence and wealth, she was on everyone's list.

"Well, I have a list of all my old classmates and I'm calling everyone trying to raise money for a family here that's in a desperate situation," Bella answered, oblivious to the simmering pot of frustration bubbling on the other end of the phone.

The timing of the unexpected phone call could not have been worse. Tali had come home from a year of seminary in Israel and had spent the past three months trying to figure out her life. The morning mail had brought her a rejection letter from the study program she had chosen, and a few hours later her new car broke down, forcing her to wait in the heat for her mother to rescue her. She was stuck at home and bored. She just wanted to be left alone.

"Bella, you know lots of people are in desperate situations," said Tali sharply. "I can't believe a normal family can't find some relatives to help them. Everyone's got a scam these days. I'm sorry, but try the next girl on your list."

Bella said a quick good-bye and shook her head. "What did I do?" she wondered. Shell shocked, she dialed the next number.

156   Chapter Six: Manipulative, Defensive Tactics

Tali was in a state of depression. She had no patience for a hard-luck story, but she did not want to admit this to Bella. Instead, she belittled Bella's *chesed*.

This is a common form of *ona'as devarim*, which people use to exempt themselves from helping a person or a cause. It may arise as high-school and post-seminary girls begin to earn money and find themselves pressured to donate their *maaser* money to a certain *tzedakah*. But even donating time can raise this issue.

For example, a Chesed Program coordinator asks a student to spend an hour a week as a homework tutor for a child whose mother is very ill. The high-school girl is afraid that the home will be depressing and she won't know how to act or what to say to the child. But instead of admitting those feelings, she berates the coordinator. "Why did you volunteer us to do that? Bikur Cholim has girls who do tutoring. You really should look into these things before you get our school involved."

This does not mean that every person must help everyone who asks. However, if we feel we must refuse a request for *chesed* we are obligated to do it with words that show respect for the person who is asking for our help.

If someone is asking for help on her own behalf—a favor, a loan of an object or money, assistance with a task, etc.—tact is all the more important. A straightforward but gentle refusal is all that is needed. "I'm really sorry, but I have to say no."

A harsh refusal is often the result of a guilty conscience. The person does not want to give; to justify the feeling, she thinks of a reason why the would-be recipient is unworthy. Then she treats the request itself as unworthy. The result is a completely unjustified attack on someone who is doing nothing more evil than asking for another person's help.

Reality Check:

Do I become annoyed when people ask me for help or *tzedakah*? If so, I will remind myself that the person requesting my help is doing something good, and even if I refuse I will be careful to speak with respect.

What If...

Tali, due to her parents' wealth, was constantly being harassed for donations? How could she handle the overload without insulting those coming to her for help?

---

7 Kislev — Sam Nussbaum — לע"נ שמואל בן שמעון ז"ל נלב"ע ט"ו כסלו
Dedicated by Jack and Renee Nussbaum

7 Nissan — לע"נ הרב משה דוד בן דוב ז"ל ואשתו חנה בת יוסף ע"ה
Dedicated by their daughters Sarah and Leah Berkovits

8 Av — Dedicated as a *z'chus* for *Moshiach* to come quickly

DAY 68

Or Else
~ Threats

ח כסלו
8 Kislev/Cycle 1

ח ניסן
8 Nissan/Cycle 2

ט אב
9 Av/Cycle 3

> "If you don't buckle down and start studying you'll be sorry," Toby told her classmate. "What are you going to do two years from now when you get rejected from every seminary you apply to?"
>
> • • •
>
> "If you keep drinking diet soda, you'll end up getting cancer, chas v'shalom," Shaina told her cousin. "Do you know what kind of poison they put in that stuff? Every drop of it is messing with your whole system!"
>
> • • •
>
> "If you don't help me with the dishes," Shulamis told her younger sister, "I won't take you shopping, and that outfit you wanted to buy will probably be gone."
>
> • • •
>
> "If you don't put your stuff away," Yaffa told her roommate, "I'm tossing it all in a box and stuffing it into your closet. You won't be able to find anything and it will be your own fault. I told you a million times that I can't stand living in a mess."

There are people whose favorite way to motivate others is by threat. They think that if they paint a negative-enough picture of the consequences of doing things the wrong way, the other person will see no alternative but to change. They hope to raise such an alarm in the other person that she will think, *Oh, no! I better shape up or that terrible thing will happen to me!* Threats can become a habitual way of dealing with certain people or certain relationships. Sometimes they become a way of dealing with life.

Using threats to get your way generates many negative results. First of all, it is often ineffective. Once someone becomes accustomed to another person's constant threats, the threats stop having any meaning. When, time after time, the threatened result does not happen, or does not seem so awful when it does happen, the threats lose their power.

It may also be that the other person doesn't care if the threatened result happens. For instance, the younger sister in the above example may not care about going shopping with her sister. The message of the threat might be interpreted by the recipient as "if you're willing to accept this consequence, then you don't have to do what I say."

In that case, the threat doesn't motivate the person hearing it. It simply calls upon her to weigh the two options and choose the one that is less distasteful. The older sister's threat invites the younger sister to decide which option she finds less bothersome, washing the dishes or forgoing a shopping trip. She feels free to choose either one.

On the other hand, believable threats can be a constant source of *ona'as devarim*. People who are "motivated" in this manner live in a state of fear, continually aware of all the terrible things that will happen if they do not perform as others demand.

The better way of gaining cooperation is to turn the threat around and create an incentive instead. "If you help me with the dishes, we'll have some time to go out shopping." "If you put in more time studying in 10th grade, you'll have a lot more options for seminary when you get to 12th grade." "If you drink water instead of diet soda, you'll feel much more energy." Rather than giving another person something to worry about, give her something toward which to strive.

---

8 Kislev — In memory of Herman Lazar *z"l* לע״נ חיים בן יהודה ז״ל
8 Nissan — In honor of our dear grandchildren
Dedicated by Rabbi and Mrs. Uri and Bracha Mandelbaum
9 Av — Dedicated as a *z'chus* for *shidduchim* for *Klal Yisrael*.

Reality Check: How often do I use threats to get my way? In what circumstances and with which people do I tend to use them? From now on, I will try whenever possible to motivate through an incentive instead of a threat.

What If... a particular behavior really does have a dire consequence about which others should be warned? Does that warning amount to a threat? If the warning frightens the other person, could it be *ona'as devarim*?

DAY
69

ט כסלו
9 Kislev/Cycle 1

ט ניסן
9 Nissan/Cycle 2

י אב
10 Av/Cycle 3

The Last Word
~ Adding insult to injury

When Temima won a spot on the yearbook photography committee, she was thrilled. She was an avid photographer whose photos had already appeared in the local Jewish newspaper. She could barely wait to get started documenting the memorable moments of senior year with her new Nikon camera.

At the first meeting of the photography committee the photo editor, Hindy, introduced herself with her trademark confidence. She had plans to vastly improve the photography in the yearbook and to ensure that as many girls as possible would see themselves in the candid shots.

"The best way to get lots of girls in the candids is to use a wide-angle lens," she told her staff. "So I want everyone to take all their pictures with a wide-angle lens, and let's aim for a minimum of five faces in each picture."

Temima knew that Hindy's plan would not turn out well. "Hindy, I'm sure the wide-angle shots will be great and everyone will get their faces in there, just like you said. But I do much better with close-ups and regular shots, you know, catching a certain funny situation or an expression. So how about everyone else doing wide angle and I'll take the pictures that need a regular or a close-up lens."

"I'm sorry you don't like the idea, Temima, but I'm the editor and I've thought a lot about how to do this. Everyone else is doing it this way," Hindy replied with forced sweetness. "And you're such a great photographer. I'm sure you can do it too."

Temima's heart sank. She realized that Hindy was worried about losing her leadership role to "famous photographer" Temima Hershberg. Temima knew that

160   Chapter Six: Manipulative, Defensive Tactics

> *if she wanted to be part of the committee she would have to let Hindy run the show. She held back what she really wanted to say and gave in.*
>
> *"Well, maybe you're right," she said. "I'll try it."*
>
> *"Don't try it, do it!" Hindy asserted. "And don't get too artsy. Make sure your first batch of pictures is done by the deadline."*

I f Hindy's first hostile comments disturbed and disappointed Temima, the last, extra comments were just salt in the wound. Temima had said she was willing to follow Hindy's instructions, even though it was clear that this was not what she really wanted to do. Why did Hindy feel it necessary to have the last word, when there was nothing more that needed to be said?

In this case, it is clear that those last few words were meant to show Temima who was in charge. Their only real accomplishment, however, was to irritate a sore spot. **Saying more than is necessary, especially after someone has given in on a disagreement or is already doing that which they were not eager to do, is simple *ona'as devarim*.** No new information is added by those extra words.

Any time we must say something that will be unwelcome to someone else's ears, the rule is to say the least possible that will get the message across. If a person adds unnecessary extras to his unwanted message, it appears that she's enjoying her moment of victory. By keeping her words to a minimum, she shows that her real interest is not in stroking her ego but in getting the job done.

> **9 Kislev** — לע"נ חביב יונס בן לונה ז"ל נלב"ע ט"ז כסלו
> Dedicated by his loving children
> **9 Nissan** — לזכות בריאות, הצלחה, פרנסה, נחת והרחות הדעת וכל טוב סלה,
> ללאה יהודית בת שיינדל שתחי' ויצחק מרדכי בן רבקה פיגא נ"י ומשפחתם
> **10 Av** — לע"נ אליהו בן צבי הרשל גרשון ז"ל

Reality Check:

How do I deal with winning an argument or getting my way? Am I sensitive to my adversary's feelings? If not, I will watch my words to make sure that they do not add to the other person's feelings of defeat.

What If...

Hindy had not added the extra "Don't try it, do it" after Temima had already given in? Would her earlier words insisting that Temima follow her instructions also be considered *ona'as devarim*? Why or why not?

The Last Word ~ Adding insult to injury 161

Chapter 7

Counterproductive Comments

When others wrong us or anger us, it can be difficult to steer clear of *ona'as devarim*. However, we can start with a much easier task: to avoid making thoughtless, unnecessary comments that hurt people who have not even offended us. Often, it is a matter of being more aware of others' sensitivities.

DAY 70

How Dare You!
~ Dramatizing

י כסלו
10 Kislev/Cycle 1

י ניסן
10 Nissan/Cycle 2

י"א אב
11 Av/Cycle 3

It was 11 p.m. and Mr. and Mrs. Kahan were exhausted from a long, busy day.

"Where's Reva already?" Mrs. Kahan asked.

"Didn't we tell her to be in by 11?" Mr. Kahan asked his wife. "But on the other hand, does she ever come in at 11?"

"My sister said we should lock the door and let her figure it out," Mrs. Kahan commented. "But how can we do that? She has to know that this is her home."

The worried mother dialed her daughter's cell phone number, but no one picked up. By midnight, Mrs. Kahan was asleep on the sofa and her husband was out cold on the recliner. Reva walked in and her parents stirred.

"Reva?" Mrs. Kahan said sleepily. "Where were you?"

"Oh, I'm sorry. Ella had to pick up her sister from her babysitting job so she couldn't bring me home until now. And my cell phone died, so I couldn't call you."

"Well, couldn't you have borrowed someone else's phone? You have to let us know where you are. We spent the past hour worrying," Reva's father said.

"Why? What do you think I'm doing? No matter how nice you try to be, the bottom line is that you don't trust me! You can't stand me! You wish I wasn't here because I make everything so hard for you!" Tears formed in her eyes as she railed about her loveless life.

"Where are you getting all this?" Mrs. Kahan tried to cut in. "We're just talking about consideration, you shouldn't leave us to worry about you."

But by now Mrs. Kahan was talking to herself. Reva had stomped up the stairs and slammed her door shut. Moments later, her parents heard her voice, calm and happy, chatting with her friend on the phone.

164 Chapter Seven: Counterproductive Comments

Reva had learned a lesson in life: the more dramatic her reaction, the quicker everyone backed off. She knew her parents dreaded the idea of wounding her already weak self-esteem or pushing her even further out of the mainstream than she had already gone. So she used her sensitivity to criticism to manipulate everyone in her household. No one dared to insult Reva.

Reva truly was sensitive, but not nearly as sensitive as she would have everyone believe. Her overreactions were meant to arouse guilt in her family members as they berated themselves for hurting her yet again.

People who use this kind of overreaction know that it enables them to control others. However, it then becomes their habitual way of dealing with adversity. They react to all criticism as if they've been misunderstood and emotionally crushed. They are the cause of much *ona'as devarim* as they pull the strings of guilt and pain in other people's hearts.

To avoid making this kind of *ona'as devarim* a way of life, we must find the strength to face criticism and disappointment head-on, without resorting to drama. Not only will this prevent us from inflicting pain on others, but ultimately it will enable us to gain the benefit of honest give-and-take with the people in our lives.

Reality Check:

Do I ever dramatize my pain or disappointment? If so, I will think about what I am trying to gain by this and try to achieve my goal in a more forthright way.

What If...

Reva's dramatic accusations reflected her true feelings? Could she express these feelings in a way that did not make her parents feel guilty? Would it be as effective?

---

10 Kislev — לע״נ אליעור צבי בנימין בן יעקב ז״ל
ואשתו שרה פעסיל בת אברהם אלי-הו ע״ה

10 Nissan — As a *z'chus* for our family
Dedicated by Mr. and Mrs. Avraham Aufrichtig

11 Av — In memory of Mr. Etan Savir *z'l* לע״נ איתן בן דוד ז״ל נלב״ע י״ד אב
Dedicated by his wife Stephanie Savir and family

How Dare You! ~ Dramatizing

DAY 71

Seeing the Future
~ Lashing out

י"א כסלו
11 Kislev/Cycle 1

י"א ניסן
11 Nissan/Cycle 2

י"ב אב
12 Av/Cycle 3

Shira usually avoided speaking on the phone when she was baby-sitting. But today she had no choice. She had already arranged a telephone-admissions interview with the principal of a seminary in Israel when her mother asked her to watch her 5-year-old sister Ahuva for the day.

"I'm sorry, sweetie, I know it's not a good time," her mother had said, "but Bubbie needs me right away."

It wasn't going to be easy to concentrate with Ahuva's attention-getting antics in the background. However, Shira was eager to attend this seminary and today was the only time the principal was available to speak to her.

"Ahuva, I'm going to be on the phone with a very important lady," Shira explained to her sister. "Here's a new coloring book. You can make a pretty picture while I talk to the lady. And you have to be very quiet, O.K.?"

"'Kay," Ahuva agreed, and she began to color. Seeing her sister happily absorbed, Shira called the the principal.

A few minutes into the conversation, Shira felt a tug on her skirt. There stood Ahuva, grasping the coloring book in her chubby little hand.

"Shira! Look! Look!" Ahuva insisted. Shira tried every hand-signal and facial expression she knew to get Ahuva to see that this was not a good time. But Ahuva soon added a chorus of whining to her campaign. Finally Shira hung up.

"Now you wanna see my picture?" Ahuva asked.

"No, I don't want to see your picture now. You behaved like a baby! And stop pulling my skirt!"

If Shira could have done an on-the-spot CAT scan of Ahuva's heart at that moment, she would have seen that the little girl's bubbling enthusiasm had gone

166 Chapter Seven: Counterproductive Comments

instantly flat. Her anticipation of her sister's "Wow! Beautiful!" had been met with harsh rejection. She felt that her sister wanted her to go away.

Twenty minutes later Shira was absorbed in a book, while Ahuva sat on her bed playing with her dolls and trying to ignore the heavy feeling inside. That taste of sadness lasted into the next day, surfacing whenever there was a lull in activity. Only that night, when Shira gave Ahuva her usual bear hug, did the pain finally wash away, leaving just a trace.

Reality Check:

Do I tend to speak harshly when I've been irritated? The next time I am about to do so, I will imagine the expression on the other person's face. What will she think? How will she feel?

If Shira would have known beforehand that her irritable outburst would pack such firepower, she never would have pulled the trigger. Her sister would have gone to bed that night feeling secure and loved.

Foresight—the ability to look ahead to the consequences of our actions—is a key to avoiding *ona'as devarim.* If we take a second to consider the impact of what we are going to say before we say it, infinite damage can be avoided. Will our words discourage the other person or leave her feeling anxious, depressed or hurt? Will they plant a troubling idea in her mind? If one of these results seems possible, then the words we are about to speak are probably *ona'as devarim.*

Even so, we are still sometimes required to communicate unwelcome information to another person. Shira was not wrong to let Ahuva know that interrupting someone is incorrect behavior. However, she could have done so in a way that would not have damaged her little sister's trust in her love.

What If...

Shira really wanted Ahuva to understand that it is wrong to interrupt someone on the phone? How might she have expressed this idea to a 5-year-old without conveying anger and irritation?

---

11 Kislev — In memory of my loving wife, Marilyn *a"h* -Yahrtzeit 11 Kislev
Dedicated by Robert Bressler

11 Nissan — Dedicated as a *z'chus* for the Baars family

12 Av — לע"נ ישראל בן ר' יעקב יוסף וויינבערגער נלב"ע י"ב אב
Dedicated by Feivy and Leah Weinberger and family

Seeing the Future ~ Lashing out 167

DAY 72

Just Trying to Help
~ Dealing with unwanted help

י"ב כסלו
12 Kislev/Cycle 1

י"ב ניסן
12 Nissan/Cycle 2

י"ג אב
13 Av/Cycle 3

On a lazy Sunday afternoon, Miriam decided to hem the skirt that had been hanging in her closet since the beginning of the winter, waiting for a trip to the seamstress. "I know how to sew," Miriam thought. "Why pay a seamstress just to make a hem? I'll do it myself."

She set out the skirt, thread and scissors. She measured four inches from the existing hem and began pinning the new hem in place. As she worked, there was a knock on the door. Rivky, her next-door neighbor and best friend who considered herself quite handy, offered to help.

"What are you doing, Miri?" Rivky asked as she watched her friend pinning up the hem.

"I think you need to first cut off about two inches and then make the hem."

"I don't think so," Miri said. "That's such a bother. I'll just turn it up like this and it will be fine."

"It gets all bunched up if the hem is too big," Rivky countered.

"I can handle this myself, Rivky," Miriam said irritably. "It's not brain surgery."

"I'm just trying to help!" Rivky insisted,

"All right, stop helping! You're driving me nuts!" Miriam exploded. "Go home and cut up your own skirt."

Rivky shook her head. "I was only trying to help," she repeated as she turned and walked out.

People have varied tolerance for letting others into their lives. Some seek advice and help, some accept it when it comes along, and others become confused and distracted by the input, or feel that it shows a lack of confidence in their abilities. Those who dislike suggestions may find themselves acting like Miriam in the story, hurling hurtful, insulting statements at people who are simply trying to help.

The helper might really know what she's doing, as in the scenario above, or she might actually lack competence and be more of a hindrance. We may find ourselves slowed down by the well-meaning help of younger siblings who are eager to get involved in tasks like washing the dishes or baking a cake. Elderly grandparents, too, want to be useful and may insist on helping out, even though their slower motion and their forgetfulness can test the patience of someone who is just trying to get the job done. In these and so many other cases, we must avoid showing impatience and speaking words that can only hurt.

It would not seem possible that someone can be "too nice," but there is in fact such a personality. These are people who insist on involving themselves in situations even when they are not wanted. Some people fail to pick up the social signals coming from the other person. Some know they are being a bother, but they think, *She'll thank me in the end.*

Most often, when people insist on offering their help or advice, their motive is love for the person they are trying to help. They feel they are offering a gift. A harsh response is like throwing the gift back in the giver's face. This is a response we cannot justify. Even when someone is "killing us with kindness," there is no need for self-defense.

Reality Check:

What is my mode of dealing with help or advice I did not request and may not want? I will make sure to keep in mind that the person giving the advice is doing so mostly out of concern for me, and try to respond accordingly.

What If...

Miriam had recognized Rivky's desire to help her? Would she still have rejected the advice? Why or why not? If she did reject it, how might she phrase her rejection?

---

12 Kislev — In honor of my אשת חיל, Leah Tatel שתחי׳
Dedicated by R' Chaim Tatel

12 Nissan — לע״נ פיגא בת ר׳ ישראל וויינבערגער ע״ה נלב״ע י״ב ניסן
Dedicated by Feivy and Leah Weinberger and family

13 Av — לזכות לזיווג הגון בקרוב, חי׳ שרה בת פרידא רחל לאה שתחי׳

Just Trying to Help ~ Dealing with unwanted help   169

DAY 73

The Eggshell Skull Rule
~ Causing unforeseen damage

י״ג כסלו
13 Kislev/Cycle 1

י״ג ניסן
13 Nissan/Cycle 2

י״ד אב
14 Av/Cycle 3

> *What happens if Tziona, carelessly handling a sharp chef's knife, accidentally nicks Chaviva, and Chaviva ends up in the hospital with a dangerous infection from the small cut? Is Tziona responsible for the serious consequences Chaviva suffers, even though neither of them could have expected those results?*
>
> *A concept in American law called "the eggshell skull rule" says that a person who wrongfully hurts another is responsible for the full extent of the damage, even if the damage is unusual and unexpected. The rule is named for a hypothetical situation in which a person hits someone on the head and the victim has an unusually thin skull that cracks under the blow. The person who struck the blow is responsible for the broken skull, even though he could not have foreseen that his light blow would cause so much damage. Once a person wrongfully or carelessly harms someone, the results—whatever they are—are that person's responsibility.*

This legal rule illustrates an important concept in *onaas devarim*. We never know where another person's weaknesses and sensitivities might lie. Once someone strikes at another person she is responsible for the damage, even if she did not know the victim would react so strongly. She cannot say, "My words should not have affected her like that."

The person's weak spot might be her intelligence, appearance, family background, economic status or standing in the community. In sensitive areas, even a half-joking comment can hurt. Since it is not always possible to know where another person's sensitivities lie, **the only way to avoid doing**

170 Chapter Seven: Counterproductive Comments

unintentional harm is to avoid doing any harm at all. In the case of Tziona and Chaviva, had Tziona not been careless with the knife, no damage would have been done.

Once the "blow" is delivered, the damage can echo on and on. If the victim takes the painful words to heart, every time she sees the person who said them or she thinks about them she will suffer all over again, and the speaker bears responsibility for this pain.

People sometimes justify their insults as humor, claiming that even the victim thinks it's funny. One fifth grader made this keen observation about a boy in his class who was teased: "If you look in his eyes you see that he wants to cry, even though his mouth is laughing."

Even if someone jokes about her own perceived flaws, she can suffer humiliation when others make similar jokes. For instance, Ella's mother offered to drive a big group of Ella's friends to the roller-skating rink. The family's noisy old 12-passenger van reflected their overstretched budget, and Ella often joked about its clunky performance. The van pulled up to one girl's house and the girl was already waiting at the curb. "Wow, you're right on time!" said Ella's mother. "Sure," said the girl. "I could hear the van coming from down the block!" Ella cringed; even though she joked about her family's car, she was embarrassed to think that it was now a neighborhood joke.

The reality is that no one has a special meter that can measure another person's reaction to a sharp comment. Given the fact that the potential for damage is so immense, and yet so unknowable, there is only one solution. Speak wisely.

> **Reality Check:**
> Do I sometimes "blame the victim," i.e., blame someone who has taken offense at my words for being too sensitive? If so, I will remind myself that it is always my job to avoid hurting others whenever possible.

> **What If...**
> a person says something that she believes is sensitive or completely neutral, and yet the other person is hurt? Is that *ona'as devarim*, and if so, how can it be prevented?

---

13 Kislev — לע"נ נתן יהודה בן יצחק יוסף ז"ל ואשתו פריידה בת יוחנן ע"ה
Dedicated by their children Mr. & Mrs. Alter and Faige Leah Kane

13 Nissan — לע"נ משה נתן בן ראובן פנחס ז"ל ואשתו פערל חי' בת דוד אפרים הכהן ע"ה

14 Av — In memory of Cantor Jack Schartenberg לע"נ החבר יעקב בן חיים ז"ל
Dedicated by his daughter Harriet (Hadassa) Zitter and family

DAY 74

In His Shoes
~ Specific sensitivities

י״ד כסלו
14 Kislev/Cycle 1

י״ד ניסן
14 Nissan/Cycle 2

ט״ו אב
15 Av/Cycle 3

"Oh, wow!" Ayala called out as she walked into the lunch room. "You should see the traffic accident in front of the pizza shop! I was just over there getting a calzone when I heard this loud thud. It sounded like a bomb went off. I ran outside and there were two cars practically wrapped around each other, and the ambulances were coming, and a little kid in one of the cars was crying."

"Was anyone hurt?" asked Lizi, a tremor in her voice.

"I can't imagine that no one was hurt. It's amazing if everyone lived!" Ayala answered. "I was afraid to look too closely because I was sure I'd see some…."

"O.K., enough! Stop!" Lizi interrupted. "We don't need the details. We don't need to hear this."

Ayala was taken aback for a moment by Lizi's sharp reaction. Then she remembered. Lizi's father had been seriously injured in a car accident several years ago. He required surgery to save his life, and he had been in a wheelchair ever since. Why hadn't she thought of that before she started blabbing?

"Oh, Lizi, I'm sorry," Ayala said. "I should have kept my story to myself."

The Midrash (*Pirkei Avos* 2:5) teaches that a person should not judge another until he has stood in his place. That means, in essence, that he has lived the other person's life: he has seen what the other person has seen, known who he has known, experienced what he has experienced. Only with that perspective can one person truly judge what another says and does.

Obviously, this is an impossible standard to meet. No one can understand what it feels like to be someone else. That means

172   Chapter Seven: Counterproductive Comments

we can never know what our words will mean to someone else. **A subject that seems harmless to us may be loaded with emotional meaning to someone else because of her particular experience and personality.** If we discover that someone is sensitive to a specific subject, mentioning it is *ona'as devarim*.

The scenario above is one example. Ayala's story might have been perfectly acceptable to the average listener, but for Lizi, mention of a car accident aroused powerful emotions.

There are many areas of sensitivity that make certain discussions *ona'as devarim* for certain people. We cannot always know what those areas are, but once we do know, we are obligated to avoid those topics. In addition, we must try to avoid words that have a negative association for someone. For instance, if someone experienced a terrible or embarrassing incident in a certain location, we should try not to mention that place. If someone's family member is very ill, we should not bring up the subject even in an impersonal way, saying for instance, "I just read that eating hot dogs causes cancer."

These precautions may seem to demand catering to every individual's peculiarity. **The urge to say or think that the other person should "just get over it" may be strong, but the simple fact is that we are not allowed to cause pain to others.**

If there is a constructive reason to bring up a difficult topic—for instance, if we have useful advice to offer and the other person is open to hearing it—then our words are not *ona'as devarim*. The problem arises when difficult subjects are simply tossed into a conversation for no purpose. Rather than speaking out in such situations, there is nothing to lose and much to gain by standing, just for a moment, in the other person's shoes.

> **14 Kislev** — In memory of Jack Feldman לע״נ יעקב בן שושנה ז״ל
> Dedicated by his daughter
> **14 Nissan** — לע״נ חיה מרים בת אלטר יוסף ע״ה
> Dedicated by Kaenan & Dafna Hertz and family
> **15 Av** — Dedicated as a *z'chus* for Moshe Yehuda and the Gordon family, to grow in Torah, *middos* and *massim tovim*

Reality Check:

Do I ever consider before I speak whether my topic might be difficult for the other person to hear about? I will make an effort to think about the person to whom I am speaking and avoid subjects that I know she might find painful.

What If...

Ayala was disturbed by what she saw and felt the need to talk it out? How could she have done that without awakening Lizi's painful memories of her father's accident?

DAY 75

Spilled Milk
~ Irritation at clumsiness

ט"ו כסלו
15 Kislev/Cycle 1

ט"ו ניסן
15 Nissan/Cycle 2

ט"ז אב
16 Av/Cycle 3

> *In her old age, Bubbi's hands had become shaky. Even so, she insisted on feeding herself, feeling that it was beneath her dignity to be spoon-fed by another member of the family.*
>
> *"Mommy, why don't you tell Bubbi that she has to let someone help her?" Brocha Klein asked her mother. "It's always such a mess and she only gets about half her food into her mouth!"*
>
> *"Because Bubbi is my mother," Mrs. Klein responded. "It makes her feel like a baby when people feed her, and I would never want to hurt her feelings like that. It's no big deal to clean up her place when she's finished and gone home. I'm sure she used to do the same for me when I was little and just learning to eat. I did it for you too."*

In this scenario, no one would expect Mrs. Klein to scold her mother, complaining "There you go again, Mom, spilling everything all over the place." First of all, it would violate the *mitzvah* to honor one's parents. But even if Bubbi were not Mrs. Klein's mother, it is clear that anger would be an inappropriate reaction. The elderly woman cannot control her hands well enough to eat neatly. She is not spilling out of carelessness or spite, but out of simple physical limitations.

Yet when people spill or drop things, a common response for many people is, "Watch what you're doing!" or some other similar rebuke. What we fail to realize is that most people who have such an accident also do so because of a physical limitation, even if it is only momentary. Some people are more confident and others are more uncertain. Some are more coordinated and some are less so. **If a person tends to drop things out of nervousness, blowing up at her will**

only cause more nervousness, making the situation worse.

Some people, especially children, drop items because they are distracted and careless. Even in this case, scolding the person for the accident will serve no purpose. It certainly will not clean up the mess. A better response would be to offer to help clean up the spill and then—if dealing with a child—calmly remind her to be more careful.

The best approach is to speak to the child before an accident occurs, while she is mishandling the item. This teaches her to treat things with care. If we wait for the disaster, the child simply learns that breaking things makes people angry because it creates a mess for them to clean up.

Of course, not all accidents and damage to our possessions is caused by innocent children or physically impaired adults. Sometimes we lend an item to a friend and it comes back scratched, dented, stained or otherwise damaged. We lend our notes to a classmate and she gives them back with a casual "sorry" and a coffee stain spread out across the top of the page. Doesn't she know she must be careful with someone else's belongings?

In fact, it is the frustration when one's belongings are broken or something is spilled that usually causes the lost temper and the insults. By realizing that such an occurrence is almost always an accident, and that the person who did the damage is usually embarrassed and regretful about it, we can approach the situation more calmly. Rather than adding further to the other person's embarrassment, we can ease her mind by showing her, through our words and actions, that we do not value objects and convenience above other people's feelings.

Reality Check:
How do I react when someone accidentally damages or makes a mess of something belonging to me? I will remind myself, before my temper takes over, that the person already regrets what she did.

What If...
someone repeatedly shows disregard for your belongings? What strategies can you use to address this situation? Are words the best tool for handling this problem?

---

15 Kislev — In memory of Irving Missry z"l — לע"נ יצחק בן חנה ז"ל
Dedicated by his children and grandchildren

15 Nissan — לע"נ שמואל בן אהרן יוסף ז"ל נלב"ע י"ג ניסן
As a *z'chus* for the גאולה and a *yeshuah* for all of כלל ישראל

16 Av — לזכות שיינא גיטל, טלי'ה מאירה, תמימה ברכה מנדלסן
שלום, מזל, ברכה, הצלחה, פרנסה ואריכת ימים

Spilled Milk ~ Irritation at clumsiness

DAY 76

Amazing Praise
~ Tainted praise

ט"ז כסלו
16 Kislev/Cycle 1

ט"ז ניסן
16 Nissan/Cycle 2

י"ז אב
17 Av/Cycle 3

Every Tuesday night Shoshana met Fraida, a ninth grader, at Burgers Plus. They ate and talked about the confusing events in Fraida's life as she adapted to her widowed father's recent marriage to a woman who, in Fraida's eyes, was a nutty old maid.

As Fraida's "Big Sister," it was Shoshana's job to give the girl a listening ear and encouragement. Shoshana waited at a table in the restaurant. A few minutes later, Fraida appeared.

"Wow! You look amazing!" Shoshana said. Fraida sent a brief eye-roll in Shoshana's direction. "Amazing" didn't seem like the right word to describe a girl wearing a rumpled school uniform, with oily hair and a pimple on her nose.

"The school sweater is a great color for you," Shoshana added. "So how are things going?"

"Well, my aunt suggested that I do a chesed and I would feel happier," Fraida answered. "So I edited a book report for a French girl in my class who has trouble with English. And it really did make me feel happier."

"That's such an amazing chesed!" Shoshana said. "It's a shame you can't feel as giving toward your stepmother."

"Well, I'm trying. She's just so clueless. How am I supposed to respect her?" Fraida said. "This Shabbos I spent the whole day at my friend's house, just to be out of there."

"Well, at least you got through the day without making her cry," Shoshana joked.

After a while the two parted. Shoshana went home satisfied with a job well done. The next day the "Big Sister" coordinator called Shoshana to inform her that

Chapter Seven: Counterproductive Comments

> *"Fraida says she doesn't need a Big Sister any more. Thanks a million. Tizku l'mitzvos!"*

There is nothing as potent as sincere praise to raise a person's spirits. No one is too old, too smart or too accomplished to appreciate positive feedback. The mother who has cooked a thousand meals needs a "This is delicious!" for Meal 1001. The beloved child still needs a hug and an "I love you" every day. The brilliant student still needs to hear "Great question!" from her teacher.

However, praise can become a vehicle for *ona'as devarim*. If we analyze Shoshana's interactions with Fraida, we can see why the Big Sister's effort to encourage her troubled little sister may have had the opposite effect.

Insincere praise can hurt. When Shoshana lavished praise on Fraida's appearance, Fraida knew the words were hollow. People often feel babied or patronized when they are given overblown, insincere praise. Praise can also hurt when it is needlessly hitched to an insult. When Shoshana praised Fraida for helping her classmate, she should have left it at that rather than pointing out Fraida's lack of support for her stepmother. Furthermore, praise can be an insult in disguise, as was Shoshana's praise for Fraida getting through a day without making her stepmother cry.

The best defense against falling into any of these types of hurtful "praise" is to practice recognizing others' good deeds and qualities. Once we make praising others a part of our daily conversation and see how it lights up the other person's face, we will have no desire to ruin the praise with hidden negative messages.

Reality Check:
When I notice something positive in someone, do I say it? I will try to make a habit of giving verbal praise and avoiding the temptation to "spice" those comments with negative jokes and "tag lines."

What If…
Shoshana had been more skillful and sincere in her praise? How could that have enabled her to help Fraida work through her issues with her stepmother?

---

16 Kislev — Leslie Zukor *z"l* — לע״נ יצחק חיים בן יוסף ז״ל נלב״ע י״ז כסלו
Dedicated by his children and grandchildren

16 Nissan — Harvey Felson *z"l* — לע״נ צבי גרשון בן יואל ז״ל נלב״ע ט״ז ניסן
Dedicated in loving memory by his wife Esther

17 Av — לע״נ ר׳ חיים ברוך בן בנימין ז״ל ואשתו אסתר הינדא בת מיכאל ע״ה
By their grandchildren: Carolyn, Barry, Rachel, Noam and Binyamin Stein

DAY 77

Get Over It
~ Belittling others' problems

י"ז כסלו
17 Kislev/Cycle 1

י"ז ניסן
17 Nissan/Cycle 2

י"ח אב
18 Av/Cycle 3

Ita held a Chumash test in her hand. The worst grade she ever got, a 72, was scrawled across the top in red ink, and next to it was what looked like an entire commentary from the teacher.

"I can't believe how unfair Mrs. Berkowitz is," Ita complained bitterly to Simi, her best friend. "I work so hard on Chumash and she picks on every little mistake I make. She thinks I'm not trying. She even said so to my parents at Parent-Teacher Night."

"Don't take it personally," Simi said. "She obviously sees that you're smart, so she thinks you could do better. She's not trying to pick on you. She just has high standards."

"I'm so upset! Does she see me sitting at my dining-room table at 11:30 at night trying to make heads or tails out of this? Does she hear you and me on the phone drilling each other for her tests? I can't believe she thinks I don't try. I've had it with that class!"

"All right, enough," Simi replied. "If you decide you've had it, you're never going to do any better in Chumash this year. Just do the best you can and try to work with her. Don't be a crybaby!"

Ita walked away from Simi feeling more miserable than before. Not only did her teacher misunderstand her, but her best friend seemed to think that she was an immature complainer. It was only lunchtime and there were four more hours of school before she would finally head home. She had no idea how she would get through the day with the knot of tension inside her.

178 Chapter Seven: Counterproductive Comments

If we take a few steps back from this scenario, we might agree with Simi that Ita's attitude was not going to help her situation. In a few days or weeks, Ita might agree as well. But right now, Simi has lost an opportunity to soothe another person's wounded feelings and instead has made the pain worse.

Sometimes when people vent their frustration into our ears, we see what they do not see. For instance, we may realize clearly they are at least in part responsible for their own problem, or we might at least partly agree with the other side of the argument. In such cases, we might think we are doing our frustrated friend a great service by explaining to her why she is wrong or why things happened the way they did. The message is that she should accept what happened and get past it. In our estimation her pain is uncalled for, and we think that if we can convince her of that, her pain will disappear.

Sometimes people do their damage by telling another person that her troubles are "for the best" or that she should appreciate the fact that her situation isn't worse. Regardless of whether a person has a right to complain or not, denying her emotions or criticizing her for feeling them will never help her get over her pain. Instead, the great words of wisdom we think we are offering become simple *ona'as devarim* that make the sufferer feel more alone in her misery.

The first step in dealing with someone in emotional pain is to offer empathy. Show that you care about her suffering, even if you feel it is somewhat justified. Once you have allowed the other person to express her pain, she will usually be calmer and more open to suggestions and perspectives you might be able to offer. But the first order of business is to avoid making matters worse.

> **Reality Check:**
> Do I respond to my friends' tales of troubles with advice on how to get over it? If so, I will make sure that my first response is to hear them out and offer them empathy for as long as they need it.

> **What If...**
> Simi's top priority was to help Ita feel better? What might she have said? How would Ita have realized that her attitude was unproductive if Simi had not told her?

---

17 Kislev — לזכות ברכה, הצלחה, בריאות ואריכת ימים,
יוכבד בת שיפרה שתחי׳

17 Nissan — לע״נ מלך בן יעקב דוד ז״ל נלב״ע י״ז ניסן
לע״נ זלאטא בת יוסף ע״ה נלב״ע ד׳ חשון

18 Av — As a *z'chus* for our children
Dedicated by Dovid and Ruchie Dachs

DAY 78

My Favorite Things
~ Rerouting a conversation

י"ח כסלו
18 Kislev/Cycle 1

י"ח ניסן
18 Nissan/Cycle 2

י"ט אב
19 Av/Cycle 3

Everyone knew that Uncle David had an avid interest in space exploration. He knew the names of stars and galaxies. He knew the dates, missions and astronauts involved in each of America's space launches. And Uncle David loved to share his knowledge.

Unfortunately, not everyone in the family shared his enthusiasm. As his nieces and nephews got older, they began to find his long, detailed lectures boring and sometimes even comical.

One summer evening, when Uncle David was having dinner with his brother's family, he introduced his favorite topic. "Did I tell you about the time they sent up a crew to repair the Hubble telescope?" he asked excitedly. "It was an incredible mission. It was the longest space walk in history. I read that they almost had to…"

The glances among the nieces and nephews silently stated, "Here he goes again." Tzipporah, a 17-year-old niece, had just come home from visiting her cousin in Los Angeles and was bursting with stories to tell. She didn't think she could survive another evening of "Uncle David in Outer Space." As she looked at her siblings, she realized she was not alone in this feeling. She decided to save them all.

"Oh, Uncle David, can't we talk about something else this time?" suggested Tzipporah. "You already told us all about Hubble and astronauts and space dust and all that stuff."

"Tzipporah!" her mother interrupted. "Go ahead, David, we're all listening."

"Never mind," Uncle David said quietly. "Tzipporah's right. I do get carried away."

Many people have "their" topic, whether it's politics, the state of the Jewish community, science, war, health or any of the thousands of other areas that occupy people's minds. Some people can supply very interesting information or offer thought-provoking opinions. Some people, however, seem obsessed with their topic.

To prevent such a person from taking over the conversation whenever he or she is around, it is sometimes necessary to find a way to change the subject. If this is the case, we have to be certain to choose words that get the message across without making the speaker feel like a droning bore. No one wants to think that her conversation, which she thought was interesting, was the cause of silent suffering all around.

Therefore, to say something blunt like "Is that all you ever think about?" is certain to embarrass the speaker. Such a statement is *ona'as devarim*, as are responses like: "What a depressing (boring, unpleasant, etc.) topic!" "Who thinks about things like that?" "Are you just about finished?"

There are times, though, when we really do need to get the speaker to change the subject or stop speaking. One gentle way to do that is to simply bring up an interesting, unrelated subject: "If you don't mind my changing the subject, did you hear anything about (some timely topic)?"

If something must be said directly, the words should be as gentle and polite as possible, taking into account the sting in the underlying message: "you're boring," or "you're inappropriate."

In some cases, the best route is to patiently hear the person out. This is especially so if the speaker is lonely and in need of attention. Once we decide to tune in, we are sometimes surprised to find that we learn something new after all.

Reality Check:

When I find someone's topic of conversation boring, how do I handle the situation? If my response might hurt or embarrass the speaker, I will try to be more patient or, if necessary, find a kind way to change the subject.

What If...

Uncle David's subject was not boring, but rather inappropriate for the family? If you had to get him to stop speaking about it, what would you say to him?

---

18 Kislev — לע"נ משה בן שמואל אלקסנדר ז"ל

18 Nissan — In memory of Nosson Kopolovics לע"נ נתן בן מאיר יוסף הלוי ז"ל
Dedicated by Debbie & Shloimi Kopolovics and family

19 Av — As a *z'chus* for our children to continue to grow happily בדרך ה'
Dedicated by Tuvia and Ahuva Hammer

My Favorite Things ~ Rerouting a conversation

DAY 79

The Nitpicker
~ Correcting small details

י״ט כסלו
19 Kislev/Cycle 1

י״ט ניסן
19 Nissan/Cycle 2

כ אב
20 Av/Cycle 3

Everyone loved it when Hillel told family stories. As the oldest child he had the most complete collection of memories from the Birnbaums' childhood exploits, and as a talented storyteller he could entertain everyone with his true tales. Whenever the children, mostly married or away at yeshivah, got together at their parents' home for Shabbos, Hillel's stories kept them at the table long after the meal ended.

The truth was, though, that the stories were much more fun when he told them out of the hearing of his sister Atara, the next-oldest sibling. That was because Atara's passion for details always ended up stopping her brother's stories in their tracks.

"We were on our way to Rhode Island to visit Bubbi and Zaidy and it was, like, our hundredth rest stop, remember?" Hillel began one Friday night. "And there was this fortune-telling machine. You put in a quarter and this plastic gypsy lady moved her head and..."

"Not her head, her hands," Atara interrupted. "She waved her hands over a crystal ball."

"Well, right. But anyway, after that, the machine spit out a piece of paper with your fortune on it...."

"No, Hillel, it was a card! Don't you remember?" Atara corrected.

"A card. Right. So all I wanted was a quarter to put in the fortune-telling machine, but Mommy and Daddy just wanted to get back on the road..."

"No, no. It was because they didn't have a quarter, and they didn't want to take time to get change," Atara inserted.

Hillel took a deep breath and blew it out, as if he were deflating. "You know what, it's really late, and

182   Chapter Seven: Counterproductive Comments

everyone already knows the story," Hillel concluded. "I'm going up to bed. Good Shabbos, everyone."

Sometimes detail is vital. If we want to perform a *mitzvah* properly, for instance, we have to know the details. When a doctor prescribes medication, the smallest details count.

But some people use their memory for detail to constantly correct and revise meaningless things. Sometimes they want to show their superior memory or knowledge. Sometimes they are driven by the little prickle of discomfort they get from hearing the details inaccurately reported. That feeling is like the distress some people feel when they see a "missed spot" on a cleaned window or blackboard. They claim that "it drives me crazy," and they have an overwhelming urge to fix it.

However, if we were in that situation we would not fix the missed spot if doing so would insult or distress someone. For instance, we would not get out of our seats and erase a smudge on the blackboard while our teacher was in the middle of teaching. Even if it "drove us crazy," we would hold ourselves back in that situation.

Someone who is bothered by the details must weigh the value of the correction against the irritation the interruption might cause. The right balance can only be achieved when we fully respect the feelings of the speaker and consider whether the accuracy of the detail is important enough to be raised at that moment, or at all.

As with most *ona'as devarim*, the key to prevention is to avoid speaking impulsively. The moment of thought we give to the words we are about to say can, and will, save us from this *aveirah* many times every day.

Reality Check:

Do I sometimes interrupt people to correct the details of what they are relating? If I do, I will think before jumping in with my correction, to determine if it is essential or just an unnecessary irritation to the speaker.

What If...

Atara had not spoken up? How might this Friday-night scenario have ended?

---

19 Kislev — לע"נ חיה רבקה בת שלום ע"ה נלב"ע כ"ב כסלו
Claire (Ida) Goldman *a"h* • Dedicated by Rivka Prescott

19 Nissan — In honor of our children
Dedicated by Tova and Dovid Zvi Refua

20 Av — In honor of our wonderful parents Debbie Singer and Earl Nussbaum
Dedicated by Shira, Briana and Levi Yitzchak

The Nitpicker ~ Correcting small details

DAY 80

Just Testing
~ Testing others' limits

כ כסלו
20 Kislev/Cycle 1

כ ניסן
20 Nissan/Cycle 2

כ"א אב
21 Av/Cycle 3

> "What are you going to do this summer?" Elisheva asked her friend Irit.
>
> "I'm going to be a counselor at Camp Sleepaway," Irit responded.
>
> "Ich! A whole month stuck in a bunkhouse with a bunch of little kids!" Elisheva exclaimed. "Why, Irit? Why are you doing this terrible thing to yourself?" she added with mock-tragic drama.
>
> "It's not bad," Irit answered mildly. "I did it last summer and it worked out fine. I kind of liked it."
>
> "Ich," said Elisheva once more.
>
> At that moment another classmate, Rina, walked by. "Oh, there's Rina!" Elisheva said urgently. "She wanted to talk to me about our plans for the summer. She has an awesome idea!"
>
> Elisheva turned her back on Irit and ran after Rina calling, "Rina, Rina, wait up!"
>
> Irit shrugged her shoulders and wondered, "Is Elisheva my friend or isn't she? Sometimes she is the best friend a person could have; sometimes she acts like everyone and anyone is more interesting than I am."

Irit would be less confused if she could read the subtitles running beneath Elisheva's hurtful words and actions. They say, "How do I know Irit really likes me? Maybe she's just my friend when I do what she wants and I flatter her and help her with her math. Or maybe she feels bad for me and I'm just her *chesed* friend. Let's see if she loves me no matter what."

A person who lacks healthy self-esteem is faced with a dilemma when it comes to friendships. How can she believe that others like her when she does not even like herself? How can she trust that others see value in her when she does not see it? She can't imagine what she has to offer that is enough to earn her the friendships she has.

With this point of view, such a person may respond by testing friendships. Each insensitive word she says or act she does is followed by a silent *Now do you like me? Are you still my friend?* Like Elisheva in the scenario, she might make a show of how popular she is and how little she actually needs the "friend" she is testing. She may do knowingly insensitive things, like leaving the friend out of the group's social plans or failing to come through with a promised favor.

This behavior has everything against it. First of all, it will always result in *ona'as devarim*. **The friend who is being tested is being hurt as the other person "experiments" to discover the limits of her friend's affections**. Second of all, the behavior will almost always backfire, for eventually, the victim will tire of the abuse and drop the friendship.

If a person recognizes this behavior in herself, her first goal must be to stop it, even before she does the harder, long-term work of repairing the underlying self-esteem issues that are causing it. *Ahavas Yisrael* is the tool that accomplishes the repair. **No matter what a Jew feels about herself or others, her *mitzvah* is to focus on loving her neighbor**: helping her, encouraging her and treating her with respect.

When we stop gazing inward, constantly thinking about how we feel, and instead turn our focus outward to the needs of others, "testing" friendships becomes a thing of the past. Then real friendship can blossom.

> **Reality Check:**
> How healthy is my self-esteem? Do I ever try to pump it up at the expense of a friend's feelings? If so, I will concentrate on ways to strengthen, rather than test, my friendship.

> **What If...**
> Elisheva had healthy self-esteem and her doubts about Irit's sincere friendship were based on reality? How could she clear the air in an honest, straightforward way? How does that differ from the scenario above?

---

20 Kislev — לע"נ שלום בן אברהם ז"ל נלב"ע ו' טבת
לע"נ חנה בת אהרן שמואל ע"ה נלב"ע כ"א כסלו
20 Nissan — In memory of Mercedes Alegria *bat* Saada *a"h*
21 Av — Leiby Einhorn *z"l* — לע"נ חיים יצחק אייזיק יהודה בן ר' אברהם ז"ל
Dedicated by the Einhorn family, Toronto

Just Testing ~ Testing others' limits

Chapter 8

Mocking

Imitating and exaggerating another person's speech, looks or habits in an effort to ridicule her are just as powerful as cruel words in their ability to cause shame and embarrassment.

DAY 81

The Mimic's Weapon
~ Mocking personal traits

כ"א כסלו
21 Kislev/Cycle 1

כ"א ניסן
21 Nissan/Cycle 2

כ"ב אב
22 Av/Cycle 3

When the Kellerman family moved to New Jersey, they created quite a stir. Born and raised in a small Jewish community in North Carolina, they spoke with a thick Southern accent. Most people found it charming, but their next-door neighbors, the Adlers, found it and everything else about the Kellermans annoying.

The Adlers were a wealthy family with a landscaped garden in front of their grand brick home. The Kellermans had purchased a "fixer-upper," but did not have the money for the fix-up. The Adlers cringed at their neighbor's weedy yard and peeling front door. The Kellerman children were outgoing and casual, while the Adler clan was more reserved. The Kellermans left their windows open, letting the lively music on their CD player waft up and down the block. Behind their backs the Adlers called their neighbors "hillbillies."

One day, 4-year-old Yitzy Kellerman wandered into the Adlers' driveway and hopped on little Shmuely Adler's kiddie bike. Shmuely, standing nearby, began to cry and his big sister Shiffy came to his rescue. "Off that bike, Yitzy!" she scolded. "That belongs to Shmuely."

When Yitzy refused to budge, Shiffy marched next door to her neighbor's yard where Kaila Kellerman stood. "Are you watching your brother?" Shiffy demanded.

"Sure," she said. "He's having fun with your brother."

"Well, maybe in North Carolina, kids are allowed to take other people's toys, but here they're not. You should teach your brother how to be civilized."

"Gosh, Shiffy, we might not be from around here, but we're civilized," Kaila replied, offended.

188 Chapter Eight: Mocking

"Gawwwsh, Shiffy, we're civilaaaazed," Shiffy responded in a thick, mock-Southern accent. And off she went, muttering *"hillbillies"* under her breath.

Reality Check:

Am I the type of person who tunes into other people's unusual traits and habits? Do I enjoy doing impressions of other people as a joke? If so, I will be especially careful never to mimic people in an angry or insulting way.

Hearing her accent mocked in front of her face was a rude shock to Kaila. **Few things are as insulting as mimicking and mocking someone's habits or other personal traits.** People have many unique mannerisms; no one is immune. One person stutters, another has a strange laugh, another speaks with an accent, another has a facial tic, another dresses in an unusual or outdated style.

Some people can barely resist picking up on these characteristics and imitating them. This tendency turns into a weapon when there is a conflict and tempers are rising. In that situation, the mimicry seems to the victim to be the ultimate dose of disdain.

The harm a person does when she gives in to the temptation to mimic cannot be calculated. With children, such treatment can destroy their self-confidence and make them fear social situations. "I'm weird and everyone knows it," is the message they absorb, and it can take decades to shake it.

But even adults, whose self-image should be set on firmer ground, are stung by mockery. It is not only painful; it is humiliating as well. Usually, mimicry is a childish way of expressing our irritation at another person. Much more can be gained by speaking to someone directly, addressing the issues at hand and respectfully trying to resolve them.

What If...

Shiffy wants to find a respectful way to get Kaila to keep her brother away from Shmuely Adler's toys? What might she say to Kaila when she confronts her in the Kellermans' yard?

---

21 Kislev — לע״נ מרים אסתר ע״ה בת הרה״ח ישראל הי״ד
In memory of Esther Amsel • Dedicated by the Scher family, Lakewood, NJ

21 Nissan — In memory of Agnes Lowinger *a"h* לע״נ שרה בת יהודה לייב ע״ה
Dedicated by her sons Robert and Eddie Lowinger

22 Av — לע״נ הרבנית מינדל בת הרב שמעון דוב הכהן ע״ה
Rebbetzin Mindel Potashnik • Dedicated by her children

The Mimic's Weapon ~ Mocking personal traits

Chapter 9

Revealing Private Information

When someone trusts us with her secrets, she puts herself in our hands and allows herself to rely on our good faith. If she discovers that her information has been passed along to others, she feels a devastating sense of betrayal.

DAY 82

Betrayed
~ Violating trust

כ"ב כסלו
22 Kislev/Cycle 1

כ"ב ניסן
22 Nissan/Cycle 2

כ"ג אב
23 Av/Cycle 3

The three roommates were students at a prestigious Jerusalem seminary. One night, long after most of the dorm was fast asleep, they stayed up talking quietly in their room.

"It was the weirdest thing," Bassie told Chavi and Hindy. "I never did anything like this before. But there it was, my older sister's diary, sitting right on the kitchen table. I don't know, maybe I was curious about what she really thought of me or something, but I just couldn't stop thinking about taking a look inside.

"So I opened it. I didn't stop to think that I have my own diary sitting right on my night table, and that I'd be mortified if anyone looked inside it. I knew my sister wouldn't be home for another hour, so I grabbed the diary, brought it to my room and read it cover to cover. Then I put it back where I found it. I never told anyone in the world about this except for you two."

A few weeks later, Bassie borrowed Hindy's notes and left them in the school's library where she had been studying.

"Where are my notes?" Hindy asked her that night.

"I'm sorry, I forgot them in the library. I'll get them back to you tomorrow."

"That's no good! I wanted to study tonight!"

"I'm sorry, but there's nothing I can do now. The library is locked, you know."

"That's so irresponsible of you!" Hindy said angrily. "Those are my notes and tonight I have the time to study and now I can't. It's really not right."

"Well, I don't know what I can do about it now, Hindy. I'm really sorry, but you know, sometimes people do forget things.

192   Chapter Nine: Revealing Private Information

> "Figures," said Hindy, exasperated. "That's what happens when you lend stuff to someone who doesn't respect other people's property. Well, at least it's not my diary."

Nothing stings as much as a betrayal of confidence. Here Bassie had poured out her heart to her friends, believing she could trust them with this story that obviously weighed heavily on her conscience. Both roommates had a responsibility to guard this confidence and never use the information she entrusted to them in order to debase or humiliate her.

By taking this confidential information and turning it against Bassie, Hindy betrayed her friendship and trust in a major way. Bassie had essentially handed a knife to someone she thought would guard it, and instead she used it to stab her. This left Bassie feeling foolish for having trusted the wrong person, and very vulnerable, for who knew what Hindy might do with the information next.

Once a person knows confidential information about another, she is obligated to treat that information with the greatest sensitivity. She must never use it against the person who trusted her, even if she becomes angry or annoyed at that person. It is not the listener's secret to do with as she pleases. It is not an appropriate topic for a joke or even a coded reference that others won't understand.

A trusted friend can, just through listening and acting responsibly with what is told to her, provide others with a priceless benefit. She can be a source of comfort and understanding: the person to go to when there's nowhere else to turn.

22 Kislev — לע״נ Moshe *ben* Shefia *z"l* and his wife Ruth *bas* Esther Rahmey *a"h*
Dedicated by their children and grandchildren
22 Nissan — לע״נ נחמה בת אברהם ע״ה
Dedicated by her grandchildren, Alan & Wendy Gerson and family
23 Av — Dedicated as a *z'chus* by Mr. & Mrs. Yonasan Schwartz

Reality Check:
How careful am I with other people's confidential information? Do I ever pass it along to others with a warning not to tell anyone? Do I ever excuse myself for repeating it by telling myself that "She didn't say it was a secret"? Do I ever use the information against the person who told it?

What If...
Bassie confessed to something dangerous or illegal? Would the other girls then be obligated to keep her confidence? Would they be obligated to tell someone about her deed? At what point does someone's confession have to be revealed for the greater good?

Betrayed ~ Violating trust

DAY 83

The Word's Out
~ Disclosing confidential information

כ"ג כסלו
23 Kislev/Cycle 1

כ"ג ניסן
23 Nissan/Cycle 2

כ"ד אב
24 Av/Cycle 3

Something was up at the Fleischer home. In the past few days, rented chairs and various packages were delivered, and all the members of the family seemed to be in a state of anticipation. Yet no one was talking. It was driving their curious across-the-street neighbor, Gitty Gross, out of her mind.

The cause of the excitement was the oldest girl, Talia, who was about to become engaged. It had taken several years for her to find the right boy, and now that the moment had arrived she insisted on keeping the news under wraps until it was final.

"Until there's a mazel tov, no one but our family and my chassan's family are going to know anything!" she told her siblings.

They obeyed her edict. However, the day before the engagement was to take place Gitty Gross spotted Talia's sisters in a local clothing store. One of the girls was holding out a dress for her older sister to see.

"Tomorrow's only the l'chaim," the older girl said. "Anyway, Talia wants you to wear the navy dress."

Gitty's heart leaped with the pleasure of a solved mystery and a fabulous piece of news. Later she bumped into Talia herself at an accessories store. As Talia sorted through a variety of dressy hair clips, Gitty approached.

"I know what the sparkly clip is for!" she said in a good-natured, way. "I heard the good news!"

Talia's heart plummeted. The word was out! What if something happened and the engagement didn't take place? Then she would have to explain to people. If Gitty knew, she was certain that by tonight the whole neighborhood would know.

194　Chapter Nine: Revealing Private Information

> "Look, Gitty, nothing's official, so please keep this to yourself," Talia said.
> "Really? I heard it's set for tomorrow night."

This might be difficult to believe in our instant media age, but people's lives are their own business. Sometimes it is good news and sometimes it is bad news that a person wants to keep to herself. For instance, she may not want others to know she is ill or that her father lost his job. Some people do not want others to know they are expecting a baby until it's obvious. Most people keep their engagement to themselves until it is just about official.

To people who want to keep their private lives private, it is painful to realize that the word is out. Therefore, if we happen to accidentally find out something we should not repeat it to anyone; in fact, to do so would be to violate the *shmiras haloshon* prohibition against revealing a secret. We should not even discuss it with the person whose secret it is, unless there is some constructive reason for doing so.

Still more painful is for someone to have her private information disclosed to someone else right in front of her. For instance, Talia's sister might have told Gitty right in front of Talia, "I'm sure you've figured out that Talia is getting engaged."

Then Talia would have had to deal with her secret getting out, as well as Gitty's potential hurt at not being told.

The way to avoid these situations is to keep other people's personal information off our agenda, unless there is a constructive purpose for speaking. Then we won't trip on the unseen stumbling block that might be right in front of us.

Reality Check:
Before I talk to someone about her private news, do I first consider whether she wants me or others to know about it? If not, I will consider this before I start such a conversation.

What If...
Gitty had no reason to believe that Talia wanted to keep her news a secret? Are her words still *ona'as devarim*? Why or why not?

---

23 Kislev — As a *z'chus* for our family Daniella, Binyamin and Yehuda
Joseph & Pouneh Hanasabzadeh

23 Nissan — As a *z'chus* for our children to grow in Torah and mitzvos
Dedicated by the Benjamin family

24 Av — לע"נ יונתן בנימין בן יצחק ז"ל
Dedicated by Tzvi & Bella Weinreb

Chapter 10

Misinforming and Misleading People

When we raise another person's hopes, we put her at risk of disappointment. Although there are times in life when disappointment cannot be avoided, we must be careful to avoid causing it unnecessarily.

DAY 84

False Hope
~ Unfulfilled offers of help

כ"ד כסלו
24 Kislev/Cycle 1

כ"ד ניסן
24 Nissan/Cycle 2

כ"ה אב
25 Av/Cycle 3

When Penina arrived home from seminary, she had one desire: to teach. It was a competitive field, as there were only a handful of girls' schools in her town and there were far more applicants than there were openings. But Penina was willing to start at the bottom, working as an assistant for a pre-school class. She would gladly spend her days buttoning coats and preparing arts and crafts.

"You really ought to consider some other options in case a teaching job doesn't come through," Penina's mother advised her. "How about Fashion Oasis? They're looking for a salesgirl and you'd be great at that."

"No way," said Penina. "If I want to teach, I have to start now and get experience."

As the summer rolled along, Penina became despondent. She had sent out as many applications as she possibly could. She had gotten her teachers to call and send letters praising her character and abilities. Still, nothing.

Her friend Avigayil wanted to help. "My aunt is the principal at Bais Zilpah," she said. "I'm sure she can at least get you in somewhere for an interview."

Penina felt hopeful for the first time in a long time. That was just what she needed: someone to help her surface above the mounds of applicants. If she could only get an interview, she felt certain she could get the job.

A week went by and Penina gave Avigayil a call. "Any word from your aunt?"

"Oh, I have to get hold of my cousin to get her cell-phone number. I'll try my cousin again today."

Chapter Ten: Misinforming and Misleading People

> *And so it went. Every few days Penina checked in with Avigayil, whose good intentions were soon lost in a sea of poor excuses. The spark of hope had been an illusion, and as the school year drew closer Penina was more despondent than ever.*

Reality Check:

Do I follow through on my offers to help others? If I tend to lose track of such things, I will write down the commitments I make to ensure that I keep them.

When someone needs a job, an apartment or a *shidduch*, networks and connections are vital. Many people feel that they would love to be the messenger Hashem chooses to make the match, and they may offer to help out of a sincere desire to do so.

However, they may not see that their casual "I'll try" is being taken by the other person as a lifeline of hope. Therefore, they may not realize the hurt they cause when they do not follow through.

Obviously, when someone suggests a seemingly appropriate *shidduch* or a job she cannot guarantee the results. **However, once a person raises hopes, she is obligated to see the matter through in a timely and sensitive way.** If she builds up the other person's hopes and then carelessly lets her down, she has made the situation worse.

To avoid causing this kind of pain, we must be realistic about the help we can offer before we offer it. We must understand how seriously the other person takes our offer; how she trusts that every effort is being made on her behalf and eagerly awaits good news.

Doing less than our best turns the original generous words of concern into *ona'as devarim*. To come through, however, even if we cannot produce the solution, is a precious act of *chesed*. It's the follow-through that makes the difference.

What If...

Avigayil is avoiding telling Penina that her aunt cannot offer any help? Is the bad news worse *ona'as devarim* than no news? Why or why not?

---

24 Kislev — לע"נ אלישבע דינה בת יצחק ע"ה נלב"ע כ"ג כסלו
By her loving daughter and son-in-law, the Golpariani family

24 Nissan — As a *z'chus* for our family
Dedicated by Shelley and Shlomy Berger

25 Av — In honor of my wife Sydney's birthday 25 Av on this special year
Dedicated with love by Andy and the children

DAY 85

Chain Reaction
~ Delayed impact

כ"ה כסלו
25 Kislev/Cycle 1

כ"ה ניסן
25 Nissan/Cycle 2

כ"ו אב
26 Av/Cycle 3

In 11th grade Esti Factor transferred into a new school, a massive institution about four times the size of her old school. Her first acquaintance in her new school was Fraida Feldman, who sat right behind her in their first-period class.

Fraida was unofficially appointed as Esti's guide and adviser by the first-period teacher, but it was a job that did not suit Fraida's personality. She was always in a rush, not particularly outgoing, and impatient with those who were not as quick as she. She tried for a few days to "be nice" and answer Esti's endless questions, but it was getting on her nerves.

One day the teacher reminded the class that the next day would be Rosh Chodesh and they should all dress in something special in honor of the day.

"What are you supposed to wear?" Esti asked Fraida after class. "Oh, gosh, Esti. I guess you should wear your Shabbos clothes," Fraida answered irritably. She turned to her friends and walked off.

The next day Esti missed her bus and her mother drove her to school. Everyone else had already gone into the building, but the bell hadn't rung yet. Esti ran quickly to her homeroom so she wouldn't be marked late.

When she walked into the room dressed in a beautiful deep purple sweater and a matching print skirt, all heads turned. There sat the rest of the class, dressed in their school uniforms, though in honor of Rosh Chodesh each wore a sweater of her choice. She felt as if there were a bright spotlight shining on her face, which instantly turned a deep shade of red.

200   Chapter Ten: Misinforming and Misleading People

The *Shulchan Aruch* (*Choshen Mishpat* 228:4) describes a situation in which someone asks another person where he can purchase a certain item and is sent to a store where this kind of item is not sold. This is forbidden, because one would certainly feel embarrassed when he realized that he had been sent to the wrong place.

But were the words sending him to the wrong store actually *ona'as devarim*? Is there anything hurtful about telling someone, "Go to Dave's Discount Store"? Certainly, at the moment the words are spoken they do not cause any pain. However, the end result of those words is pain. **Therefore, through this example, the *Shulchan Aruch* teaches us that we are responsible not only for the impact of our words when we speak them, but also for the chain reaction they set in motion**.

This idea carries over to many areas of life. If we brush someone off with unclear directions or misleading explanations, we are responsible for the problems the words cause later on. If the person, trying to follow our unclear directions, gets lost and misses an important appointment, her troubles are the fault of the person who gave the directions carelessly. The words are *ona'as devarim*, even if they were spoken days before the actual harm occurred.

The other side of the coin, however, is our ability to cause long-term good with the words we speak. If Fraida would have taken the time to tell Esti about the school and about the Rosh Chodesh program, if she would have shown her around the school and introduced her to other girls, those words would have helped Esti for months or years to come. The point is that once words come out of our mouths, they have a continuing ripple effect in the world. That fact must be taken into account every time we speak.

> **25 Kislev** — May today's learning be a *z'chus* for our parents and our children.
> **25 Nissan** — לע"נ יוסף יעקב לייב בן שלמה ז"ל
> Dedicated by Uri and Riki Sklar and family
> **26 Av** — Anonymous

Reality Check:

Do I sometimes become impatient with questions and give mumbled, unclear or hasty answers? When I answer a question, I will keep in mind that the person may very well end up acting on the basis of what I've said.

What If...

Fraida had no idea that Esti would actually wear Shabbos clothes to school on Rosh Chodesh? Does the fact that Esti could have checked out the information or asked a teacher reduce Fraida's responsibility for her embarrassment?

DAY 86

Just Browsing
~ Asking prices under false pretenses

כ"ו כסלו
26 Kislev/Cycle 1

כ"ו ניסן
26 Nissan/Cycle 2

כ"ז אב
27 Av/Cycle 3

"Wouldn't you love to try on some of those bracelets?" Osnat asked Ariella as the two girls pressed their faces against the glittering window of Levy's Fine Jewelry Shop. It was midwinter vacation and the two girls were on a shopping trip in the city.

"Yeah, but how are we going to do that?" Ariella asked.

"We'll just walk in and ask to see a bracelet," Osnat said confidently. "I'm sure plenty of people try things on and then don't end up buying. Anyway, we're not taking up the salesman's time. I see him standing there dusting the showcase."

"Are you sure it's all right?" Ariella replied doubtfully. "It seems kind of mean."

Ariella was 100 percent correct. According to the *Choshen Mishpat* (228:4), asking for a price when we have no intention of buying is not only mean, it is actually prohibited. The reason is that by asking about the item we raise the salesman's hopes; then, when we walk out empty-handed as planned, the salesman suffers disappointment.

Why is this worse than when a legitimate customer inquires about an item and then decides against buying it? It would seem that the salesman would be disappointed in that case also. The difference is that in a situation like that of Osnat and Ariella, people create his disappointment unnecessarily. If we are truly shopping for an item, asking about prices and comparing what stores have to offer is part of the process. Without it, no business would be done.

Similarly, a salesman would not mind if a person asks about an item that she might reasonably consider buying. Although the person may not think of herself as a customer at that moment, the salesman knows that she might come back one

202 Chapter Ten: Misinforming and Misleading People

day with the intention of buying it. So he is more than willing to answer her questions. **However, the Torah does not allow us to play the shopper when it will not serve any purpose now or in the future.**

We might wonder why someone would ask for a price when she has no intention of buying the item. Curiosity is usually the answer. People are eager to see the inside of a beautiful home that is for sale, or to drive an expensive car they could never afford to buy, or to try on a piece of jewelry that glitters in the showcase. Nothing but a person's conscience stops her from presenting herself as an interested buyer.

Even when someone does not indicate in words that she wants to buy something, she can still stumble on this type of *ona'as devarim*. In the opening story, the girls are not actively pretending to be buyers. They are just curious to see the bracelets and try them on. They do not have to say a word to the salesman about their intentions, because just by asking to see the merchandise, they are signaling their intentions.

In truth, displaying merchandise to a non-customer may not take much time from the salesman's day. He may never even become aware that he was needlessly disappointed. Yet, just because these actions may cause unnecessary pain, the Torah says, "Do not do this to a fellow human being."

A simple way to avoid the problem is for the shopper to tell the salesman outright that she is "just looking." He may still be willing to spend time with her, realizing that a shopper who admires a certain item may someday return to the store to buy it, or might recommend it to someone else who is interested in buying.

> **Reality Check:**
> Do I ever ask about merchandise that I have no intention of buying? If so, I will try to imagine his disappointment when the success and money the salesman is hoping for evaporates.

> **What If...**
> a store is known for its willingness to let people try the merchandise—for instance, a music store that lets people play the instruments? Is it still necessary to tell the salesman that you are not planning to buy anything?

לע״נ בינה לאה בת יוסף ע״ה — **26 Kislev**
In memory of Chana bas Murray a"h

26 Nissan — Salamon Mandel z"l לע״נ מרדכי שלמה בן בנימין אליעזר ז״ל
In loving memory by his wife, children and grandchildren

27 Av — לזכות ברכה והצלחה, פרנסה, רפאות, שידוכים
for our entire family and all of *Klal Yisrael*

Just Browsing ~ Asking prices under false pretenses

Chapter 11

Subtle Negative Statements

When we are trying to avoid a confrontation with someone, we might use vague, indirect ways of showing our negative emotions. In that case, our feelings almost always come through and hurt the other person, even though she may not be able to pinpoint why she feels hurt.

DAY 87

Beware the Undertone
~ Muttering

כ"ז כסלו
27 Kislev/Cycle 1

כ"ז ניסן
27 Nissan/Cycle 2

כ"ח אב
28 Av/Cycle 3

When Shlomit got married, she left behind in her family's home a coveted possession: her private bedroom. Zev, the next-oldest child, shared a small room with two brothers. Miriam, the next oldest sister, shared a room with a 2-year-old sister. Both were desperate for Shlomit's abandoned real estate. Their parents, recognizing that the situation was a pile of dry wood just waiting for a spark to ignite it, chose to stay out of the decision.

"You're two mature young adults," their mother told them. "Work it out."

Attempting to rise to the challenge, Zev and Miriam entered into negotiations worthy of international diplomats. However, they could not seem to come to a solution. Miriam stood firm in her belief that sharing a room with a baby was the greater misery, for she had to tiptoe around after 7:30 p.m. and was roused at 5 a.m. by the baby's cheery awakening. Zev complained that he was constantly losing important papers, sefarim and clothing in his crowded mess of a room.

The two siblings tried to keep their discussions civilized, but Miriam, the more aggressive of the two, tended to dominate. When Zev felt he was not getting his say, he would walk away shaking his head and muttering under his breath.

"What are you saying?" Miriam would demand. "Say it to my face! Whatever you're saying, say it to me."

"No, it's nothing. I'm just talking to myself," Zev would reply. All through their arguments and debates on the destiny of Shlomit's room, the muttering continued. For Zev it was a release valve for his built-up frustration, but for Miriam it was a detonator that made her want to explode.

206   Chapter Eleven: Subtle Negative Statements

Zev knew better than to let out angry words at Miriam, and so he used his muttering to say what was on his mind while avoiding a direct conflict. He thought he was doing a good thing, holding down his voice even though he could not hold back his words altogether, or better yet calmly say his piece in a way that would enable him to work through the conflict with his sister.

From Miriam's point of view, however, **the muttering itself was *ona'as devarim*, no matter what the words were**. She realized that it was an expression of anger, or at the very least, sharp disapproval of her position. She also understood that if her brother was muttering the words, they must have been too hurtful to say to her face. Knowing that Zev even thought such angry words upset her, and she was still more upset because Zev was not giving her the chance to hear and respond to his complaints.

Would it have been better for Zev to shout his hurtful statements into Miriam's face? Obviously it would not. But a person does have to realize that when she resorts to muttering inaudible words under her breath, the other person is still being hurt. In fact the other person might be even more deeply upset by the muttering, because she might imagine that the comments are much worse than they really are.

The real solution to this kind of *ona'as devarim* is to learn basic communication skills: how to present our own point of view clearly, calmly and firmly, even in the face of opposition. In this way, disagreements can be productive. Each side can present her point of view and respond to the other person's comments without having to suffer a secret attack of words that she cannot hear and that do nothing to resolve the conflict.

Reality Check:

Do I have a habit of muttering under my breath when I am upset? I will pay attention to this habit and try to channel my frustration more productively.

What If...

Zev knew how to assert himself? What could he have done or said to Miriam to make sure that he had an equal chance to express his side of the argument?

---

27 Kislev — לע"נ שרגא בן יעקב ז"ל
Dedicated by Miriam & George Fleischman

27 Nissan — In memory of our beloved grandmother Sarah Avrukin *a"h*
Dedicated by the Avrukin family

28 Av — לע"נ אברהם בן חיים ז"ל
Dedicated by Mr. and Mrs. Chaim Mordechai Abramson

DAY 88

Get the Hint?
~ Insulting hints and sayings

כ"ח כסלו
28 Kislev/Cycle 1

כ"ח ניסן
28 Nissan/Cycle 2

כ"ט אב
29 Av/Cycle 3

Sixteen-year-old Shari and 11-year-old Temmy had spent an entire Sunday baking for their brother's bar mitzvah kiddush. Now they worked together in the kitchen, washing the bowls and pans, sweeping the floor, and scrubbing the flour-and-cocoa-spattered counters. While Temmy had been gung ho during the baking part of the program, by cleanup time her energy and her interest were both spent. So she worked without much enthusiasm, and it seemed to Shari that her sister hoped to get away with doing as little as possible.

"I knew a girl in elementary school who was so lazy that she hired her friend to clean her room for her every Friday afternoon," Shari told Temmy.

"I'm not lazy. I'm tired!" Temmy protested. "We've been baking all day long. And you better not say one more word to me or I'm quitting."

"I didn't say you were lazy," Shari answered with a convincing dose of disbelief that her sister could have misjudged her so harshly. "I just said that I heard about a girl who was lazy. But you know what they say: 'If the shoe fits, wear it!'"

"What's that supposed to mean?" Temmy asked.

"It means whatever you think it means," Shari answered. Her younger sister seemed ready to burst with frustration. She knew she was being criticized, but she couldn't pinpoint the insult well enough to fight back.

When we criticize another person indirectly by a hint or a quote or a well-known saying, we deliver a sneak attack that is not only damaging, but also difficult for the other person to oppose. Telling a friend,

208 Chapter Eleven: Subtle Negative Statements

"I'm sure there are people who take longer to get a joke, but I can't think who," is not any less insulting than saying, "You're so slow!" Saying, "You've got a face only a mother could love" is easily translated into "You're ugly."

Using "wise sayings" to put another person down is especially insidious. The victim feels that she is foolish or wrong not only in the eyes of the speaker, but also in the eyes of the world, which has accepted the "wise saying" as truth.

For instance, if someone who has caused problems to others suffers a setback of her own, she might hear from an unsympathetic friend, "What goes around comes around." This makes her feel that she is a bad person who deserves the bad fortune that has come her way. Using quotes to hint at our displeasure or even our constructive criticism of another person is very rarely received as an effort to help the victim make positive changes. **Usually it is seen as what it often is: the urge to display our sense of superiority at another person's expense**.

People sometimes choose this means of making their statement because they feel that it is less insulting than stating their criticism outright. Who can argue with "What goes around comes around?" Everyone knows that this is true; the energy we send into the world, whether positive or negative, tends to come back to us. Nevertheless, a person hearing this statement in a time of trouble will neither learn from it nor take comfort in it. The speaker may feel she has done nothing but state the obvious; but in fact she has committed *ona'as devarim*.

When we know that what we want to express would be insulting if we were to say it directly, we can be fairly sure that saying it indirectly would be insulting as well. Subtlety is usually a good thing, but subtle sourness still tastes sour.

---

28 Kislev — In memory of Rabbi Ernest Rothschild *z"l* לע״נ אליהו בן מאיר ז״ל
Dedicated by his children

28 Nissan — In honor of Rabbi Yechezkel Kornfeld *n"y*
Dedicated by John Sindorf and Mary Ann Bolte

29 Av — לע״נ דוד יוסף בן הרב יהודה לייב יבלחט״ט
By his wife, Gloria Pearl and children, Sara, Asher Zelig and Chananya Yisroel

Reality Check:

Do I sometimes use hints or sayings to deliver a negative message? I will try instead to phrase my opinion in an informative, positive way.

What If...

Shari sympathized with Temmy's tiredness but wanted her to know how much she needed her help to finish the job? How could she state this in a way that would make Temmy feel valuable rather than insulted?

DAY 89

The Cutting Edge
~ Sarcasm

כ"ט כסלו*
*29 Kislev/Cycle 1

כ"ט ניסן
29 Nissan/Cycle 2

ל אב
30 Av/Cycle 3

> "Look! It's Little Miss Sunshine!" Ilana announced as she walked into the lunchroom. She approached her moody classmate Gila, who was sitting at a table hunched morosely over a cup of coffee. "How can we stand so much happiness?"
>
> . . .
>
> "You get an A-plus for customer service," said the irate customer to the clerk, who refused to accept the merchandise she wished to return. "No wonder everyone loves this store."
>
> . . .
>
> "Great job cleaning the room," Chani said to her sister. "Maybe if you keep going, we'll find the floor."
>
> . . .
>
> "You're a genius, aren't you," Miri said coldly to Gitti, who had just knocked over her bottle of Coke. "I'm so glad I sat down next to you."

* When this month has only 29 days, the lesson for 30 Kislev should also be studied today.

All these comments have two things in common. First, their meaning is the opposite of what it seems to be. Secondly, the people on the receiving end of the comments will end up feeling either foolish or angry. What they will *not* feel is remorse.

Sarcasm is a form of *ona'as devarim* that comes in a thin disguise, because the words used in a sarcastic comment are often, when taken at face value, either positive or neutral. It is the circumstances and tone of voice that supply the insult. **In addition, most sarcasm carries a spirit of disdain that would be absent from the same criticism if it were stated in a direct way.**

For instance, Chani could tell her sister, "You got a long way on the cleanup, but the job isn't done until everything's off the floor." The sister might not like hearing the criticism of the job she's done, but she would not feel demeaned by it. She would simply understand that she has not completed the task that was expected of her.

Some people use sarcasm to disguise their displeasure, thinking that a little ironic humor will carry the message in a less painful way. For instance, a girl who is tutoring an unfocused student might think that it is better to ask, "How are things in outer space?" than to say, "Shaindy, pay attention to the work!" In reality, however, the second comment gives the child direct instructions she can put to use, while the first comment simply ridicules her personality. With children, specifically, sarcasm is hurtful and confusing because they often do not even understand the irony in the comment, but they do feel the disapproval it carries.

A person who makes sarcastic comments sometimes does so because she is afraid that a direct comment will arouse anger. The problem with this approach is that it delivers a highly negative message to the listener. If she cannot accept direct criticism, it is usually better to say nothing or wait for an opportune time for straight talk.

People also use sarcasm because they find it funny. Clearly, however, the prohibition against *ona'as devarim* leaves no room for entertaining ourselves or others at the expense of another person's feelings.

A sharp comment is a dangerous weapon. It cuts and wounds, but it is not nearly as powerful as a direct, softly and carefully stated comment in conveying the message we really want to convey.

---

29 Kislev — In honor of our grandchildren Sara Nessa, Odelia and Shylie Efrat
Dedicated by Mr. and Mrs. Boris Gulko

29 Nissan — שלום וברכה לכל המשפחה, ולכל בני ישראל
Dedicated by Naomi Scheier

30 Av — In memory of Mike Greenfield *z"l* לע"נ מאיר בן ברוך ז"ל
Dedicated by his children Sari and Ari Bacon

Reality Check:

Is there someone who arouses in me a desire to be sarcastic? I will work on communicating with that person in a sincere and direct way.

What If...

the recipient of a sarcastic comment also finds it funny? For instance, what if the tutor's comment to Shaindy makes her giggle? How can we distinguish sarcasm from good-natured humor?

Teves

לע"נ דוד יעקב בן שמואל חיים ז"ל נלב"ע י"ז טבת

לע"נ יונה בת נור ע"ה נלב"ע כ"א אב

Dedicated by the Badani family

לע"נ רב יעקב צבי בן רב מנחם ז"ל

כזכות לברכה והצלחה, בריאות והליכה

בדרך ישראל סבא לכלל ישראל

Iyar

לע"נ שלוה ראכל ע"ה בת ישראל מנחם ע"ה
נלב"ע א' אייר
לע"נ ישראל מנחם בן שלום ז"ל
נלב"ע כו' טבת

As a z'chus for our family

Dedicated by Rabbi and Mrs. Shmuel Rochkind

לזכות בריאות והצלחה ברוחניות ובגשמיות לילדינו
בתוך כלל ישראל

Dedicated by Mr. and Mrs. Yakov Shadrooz

Elul

In loving memory of Darrel Parks z"l
נלב"ע יד' אלול תשס"ד
*Dedicated by his Mom and Dad,
Larry & Jana Parks*

In gratitude to the Lubavitcher Rebbe

In honor of my mother, Chaviva Tashkadi

and two Jewish chassidic women who showed me the meaning of love that was so sorely lacking in my family life

---

לע"נ אהרן בן סלומן ז"ל
In memory of Dr. Aaron Friedman z"l
לע"נ ברכה בת יוסף ע"ה
*In memory of Beatrice Friedman Presant a"h
Dedicated by their loving family*

DAY 90

A Day at the Zoo
~ Comparing people to animals

ל כסלו*
30 Kislev/Cycle 1

ל ניסן
30 Nissan/Cycle 2

א אלול
1 Elul/Cycle 3

> *"I can't believe you read my class journal!"* the girl said to her classmate. *"You're such a snake!"*
>
> • • •
>
> *"You eat like a pig!"* a girl told her brother. *"Why don't you save something for the rest of the family?"*
>
> • • •
>
> *"You're a bunch of wild animals,"* the baby-sitter scolded the rowdy children.
>
> • • •
>
> *"You have a mouth like a sewer,"* the boy told his friend.
>
> • • •
>
> *"Stop acting like a monkey!"* the boy told his study partner. *"Sit still and get serious for a change!"*
>
> • • •
>
> *"How can you hang around with such garbage?"* the girl scolded her brother. *"What does that make you?"*

* When this month has only 29 days, the lessons for 30 Kislev should be learned together with 29 Kislev.

When a person wants to make a strong point, she sometimes chooses strong, jarring words that leave no room for doubt. She takes out the "big guns" to make sure that the shot is heard. When we compare people to gross, frightening or repulsive animals or objects, no one can miss our point. With just one word these comparisons paint an ugly picture of subhuman behavior, which immediately delivers our message of total disgust with the other person.

The person who is the subject of such a comparison gets the message: "I am horrible in her eyes. I am like an animal to her: a mindless, loathsome creature."

That message may succeed in shocking someone for a moment, but it is very unlikely to inspire her to change. Instead,

216 Chapter Eleven: Subtle Negative Statements

her self-image will have been brought so low that change will appear impossible. A "pig" will never be able to control his appetite. A "sewer mouth" can never get rid of its stench. Someone who has the poor judgment to befriend "garbage" does not have it in him to attract better friends.

This is labeling of the most drastic kind. We are not just labeling someone as a flawed type of person; we are labeling her as a non-person. We are identifying her with the most animalistic part of her personality and completely ignoring her *neshamah*. **Instead of showing a person a window through which she can repair her mistakes, we are closing the window tightly**.

The Torah teaches that at all times we should speak in as mild a form as possible to accomplish our worthwhile goals. **Harsh, ugly words and images should not be used where softer words will do the job.** Comparisons to animals and vile objects violate this principle, for there are always softer ways to make the point.

The bottom line is that the Torah prohibits us from hurting each other with the words we use. However, it recognizes the fact that we must sometimes deliver a negative message; in that case it stipulates that we must deliver the message in the least hurtful and most effective way possible. Ugly comparisons can be extremely hurtful and are definitely not effective. Therefore they have no justifiable place in our conversations.

The question we should ask ourselves is, "What do I really want to accomplish?" If the answer is "to get the other person to realize her error," then the way is not paved with harsh, ugly metaphors. The words we choose should instead be words that open the other person's heart and let him see the potential that is within him.

> *30 Kislev* — לע"נ יוסף שמעון בן אלטער ישראל יונה הלוי ז"ל נלב"ע א׳ טבת
> פון זיין פרוי מרס חנה בראזדה און קינדער
> *30 Nissan* — As a זכות for our children, ושושנה מלכה, יצחק יונתן, אסתר מיכל
> Dedicated by Yankie and Amie Braun
> *1 Elul* — לע"נ חנה פערל בת שלום ופעסל ע"ה
> Dedicated by Isaac and Wendy Shulman

Reality Check:

Do I sometimes choose words for their shock value? I will think about the images and messages those words actually deliver, and approach my goal in a different way.

What If...

softer words do not get the message across? Don't shocking words sometimes cut through someone's defenses and make her face the truth? In that case, can those words be used despite their hurtful nature?

DAY 91

Music to Their Ears
~ Tone of voice

א טבת
1 Teves/Cycle 1

א אייר
1 Iyar/Cycle 2

ב אלול
2 Elul/Cycle 3

Without checking the caller ID, Dalia picked up the phone. "Hello?"

"Dalia! Sweetheart! It's Tanta Zeldy!"

Dalia's heart sank. Tanta Zeldy. That meant at least half an hour, maybe longer if she couldn't think of a way to end the conversation. But what could she do? Tanta Zeldy was alone and she needed people to talk to.

"Hi, Tanta Zeldy. It's so good to talk to you! How are you?"

"Well, sweetheart, I wish I could say I'm fine. Baruch Hashem I can say that I'm still here. I spent three mornings this week at the doctor; Monday the cardiologist, Tuesday the orthopedist and Friday I sat waiting for the eye doctor until two hours before Shabbos!"

"Oh, that doesn't sound like much fun," Dalia said. As Tanta Zeldy went on with her account, Dalia began reading her book for her English Literature class. It had to be finished by the next day, and who could tell when she'd be off the phone?

With her ear to the phone but her eyes on the book, Dalia made sure to respond with "uh-huh" or "oh, wow," or "that's nice" or whatever fit Tanta Zeldy's general topic. She amazed herself at her ability to keep up her end of the conversation, all the while working her way through her 400-page novel.

"Dalia sweetheart, is everything all right?" Tanta Zeldy finally asked. "You don't sound right. It's like you're distracted or something."

218   Chapter Eleven: Subtle Negative Statements

How did Tanta Zeldy know that Dalia was distracted? She couldn't see her niece reading the book. Dalia didn't miss a cue for responding to her aunt. The secret was betrayed by her tone of voice. The little bit of distance, the extra split second of response time, was enough for an elderly woman who was doing almost all the talking to realize that she did not have her audience's attention.

Tone of voice often says more than the words themselves. That is why there are some people with whom we especially love to share good news. Their tone shows that they are as excited as we are, and that makes us even happier. Usually these are the same people to whom we turn with our bad news, because their sincerely sympathetic tone makes us feel that they really share our burden.

On the other hand, an angry or cold tone of voice can undo words that would otherwise seem positive. For instance, you tell your friend that you are very disappointed with the role you got in the school play. Perhaps she would respond, "Don't worry about it. Just wait until next year." If she looked at you sympathetically and spoke warmly, you would feel comforted. With a cold, annoyed tone of voice, however, her words could be interpreted, "It's no big deal. Get over it."

We can't hide negative emotions behind neutral or positive words if our tone of voice quickly gives our true feelings away. We often hear that when offering constructive criticism we should "criticize the action, not the person." However, if we criticize the action in an acid tone, "I don't like what you did" will not sound any better than "I don't like you."

Tone of voice makes an immediate impression. When people feel that they are being addressed sincerely, they listen. We don't just hear the lyrics; we listen closely to the tune.

> **Reality Check:**
> What do I express with my tone of voice? Does it vary depending on the person to whom I am talking? Do I ever use my tone to express dislike or disinterest?

> **What If...**
> you are not generally aware of your tone of voice? What can you do to make sure that it does not cause other people to feel hurt or insulted?

---

1 Teves — In honor of our daughter and granddaughter שיינדל רבקה שתחי׳
Lani & Dovid Harrison and Stuart & Randy Rubinson

1 Iyar — In memory of Jack Friedman z"l לע"נ יעקב יוסף בן נתן נטע ז"ל
Dedicated by his children, grandchildren and great-grandchildren

2 Elul — Dedicated as a *z'chus* for Elisheva *bas* Elianora for good health
As a *z'chus* for Alla Chana *bas* Marina for a זיוג הגון

Music to Their Ears ~ Tone of voice

Chapter 12

Nonverbal Ona'as Devarim

A person can send a destructive message to another person without using one word. Facial expressions, body language and even silence can speak volumes.

DAY 92

In Your Face
~ Angry expression

ב טבת
2 Teves/Cycle 1

ב אייר
2 Iyar/Cycle 2

ג אלול
3 Elul/Cycle 3

"What's wrong with Vered?" Toby asked Yehudis as the two saw her coming down the hall. "She looks like she's mad about something."

"I don't know," Yehudis replied as Vered came near. She gave her two classmates a quick look and a weak smile and continued on her way.

"Is she mad at one of us?" Toby suggested.

"What for? I didn't do anything to her. Did you?"

"No, nothing. In fact I gave her my granola bar at lunch."

As Vered continued toward her next class wearing her unfriendly expression, several others of her friends were having conversations similar to that of Toby and Yehudis. They wondered what they did to deserve their friend's sullen nongreeting.

What was wrong with Vered? Nothing. She was just thinking about an argument she had with her sister that morning, stewing over what was said and what wasn't said and wearing her anger on her face. In doing so, she spread her bad mood wherever she went.

Without saying a word, a person's facial expression can tell someone "I'm happy to see you," "I'm interested in your story," "I'm proud of you," or any of thousands of other messages. A face can also say "You bore me," "I'm angry at you," or "You're strange." Being "literate" in face-reading is a vital tool for responding appropriately and understanding others' feelings. It is also a vital tool for social success, and sometimes even survival, because it can tell us whether we are facing a friend or an enemy.

Because this skill is so important, we are born with an ability to understand faces. There are studies that show that even an infant will become upset if his mother looks at him with a frown, and then will relax when his mother smiles. If even an infant can read an angry face, certainly older children and adults can just as instantly read what is written there.

Because faces say so much, we must take control of the messages our faces are sending. The easiest way to do this is to make a pleasant expression our "default setting." In other words, we should try not to look like something is wrong when everything is fine. Even when things are going wrong, there is no need to advertise our misery on our face. Rav Yisroel Salanter, the great *mussar* figure, went so far as to define the face as a *reshus harabbim*—public property—which we are obligated to keep pleasant and safe.

Sometimes, as in the opening story, a person's sour expression comes from a nonstop negative conversation running through her mind. She may be thinking about her problems or her grievances against other people, even when those issues are not right there in front of her. Her "self-talk" is angry and negative, and it shows on her face.

When we do this, we bring others down. Equally as damaging, we carry our problems around with us, increasing our level of stress and draining our energy. The best thing we can do is to change the "self-talk" to a focus on the good around us, and save our worries for a specific time and place.

By mastering this ability, we fulfill the Mishnah's directions (*Pirkei Avos*) to greet each person with a pleasant expression. We can then lighten others' moods and make them feel welcome, loved and appreciated, without saying a word.

> **Reality Check:**
>
> What is my "default" expression? I will try to avoid dwelling on negative thoughts so that my inner world and the face I show the world will be pleasant.

> **What If...**
>
> Vered had a serious problem she could not get off her mind: for instance, someone in her family was very ill?

---

2 Teves — לע"נ פייגא בת ר' יעקב שלמה ע"ה
Dedicated by Atara Grenadir

2 Iyar — לע"נ הרב משה גרשון בן הרב חיים ז"ל נלב"ע ב' אייר
לע"נ מלכה בת ר' צבי ארי' ע"ה נלב"ע כ"ז אלול

3 Elul — לע"נ אפרים בן חנוך ז"ל
Dedicated by Mr. and Mrs. Steven and Myrna Hoenlein

DAY 93

Unsend
~ Written communications

ג טבת
3 Teves/Cycle 1

ג אייר
3 Iyar/Cycle 2

ד אלול
4 Elul/Cycle 3

Atara had always wanted to tell Yocheved just what she thought of her. However, in the interest of avoiding an awkward feud with a girl she would have to see every day, she held herself back. She couldn't help feeling that brilliant, popular Yocheved looked down on her. Even Yocheved's smiley, singsong "How are YOU?" seemed like condescending "chesed" friendliness. In the six years the girls had lived next door to each other, Atara never felt she could be a part of Yocheved's inner circle.

And now the proof was in. Atara heard the happy splashing sounds of a pool party in Yocheved's backyard. What would it have taken for Yocheved to have invited Atara—her own next-door neighbor—to the party? Even if the party was just for Yocheved's close friends, how could she leave Atara out?

Still, Atara did not want a face-to-face confrontation. She knew she would never be able to keep her cool and have her say in an argument with Yocheved. Instead, she decided to write Yocheved a letter telling her exactly what she thought of her, and then never speak to her again.

She pulled out a sheet of paper and began writing. Two bitter, angry pages later, she was done telling Yocheved what a cruel, snobby, miserable person she was, and how she was surely headed for a life of unhappiness. Now all that was left was to sign it, seal it, stamp it and send it on its way to the house next door.

If Atara sends this letter, she will have created *ona'as devarim* no less than if she had knocked on Yocheved's door and yelled the same biting words into her face. In some ways the harm could be worse, because a letter can be read over and over again, stinging the recipient anew each time.

Sometimes people turn to written *ona'as devarim* because they are afraid to face the person with whom they are angry. This indirect method, they feel, will protect them from the other person's reaction. However, the voice inside us that says, "I can't say this to her face," is telling us something valuable. If the words cannot be said to the other person's face, they probably should not be said at all.

In our age of email and texting, the challenge of holding back our written words can become enormous. Both of these methods of communication are instantaneous, so fast that we can hardly think through what we are saying. The responses come almost instantly as well, leaving little or no time for really understanding the message. Especially in texting, the rapid-fire back-and-forth lends itself to a war of increasingly sharp "witty" comments that result in real insult and pain.

With "snailmail," people have time to cool off before they send their letter. Often, once they have vented their anger, they choose to throw the letter away. But with email and texting, that barrier of time is gone. There is no chance for second thoughts.

When used properly, writing can be a tool for avoiding *ona'as devarim*. Since it is less immediate than spoken communication, it gives us time to frame our statements in a positive, sensitive way. We can review our words and think about how the other person will receive them. We can erase and rewrite. If our goal is to address a challenging situation while avoiding insult to the other person, writing gives us a great opportunity to do so.

> **Reality Check:**
> How careful am I with my written communications? Do I stop to re-read what I've written to "hear" how it will sound to the other person? I will force myself to wait an hour and re-read any potentially negative message before I send it.

> **What If...**
> Atara wanted to use written communication to improve her relationship with Yocheved? Do you think that a letter could accomplish this? What might it say?

---

3 Teves — May today's learning be a זכות for our family on this special day.
Dedicated by David and Raisy Barnett

3 Iyar — Dedicated as a *z'chus* for the Rowner family

4 Elul — לע״נ משה דוד בן יוסף ז״ל נלב״ע ט״ו כסלו
לע״נ פייגא בת אפרים ע״ה נלב״ע ט׳ אלול

Unsend ~ Written communications

DAY 94

In Your Hands
~ Hand gestures

ד טבת
4 Teves/Cycle 1

ד אייר
4 Iyar/Cycle 2

ה אלול
5 Elul/Cycle 3

> As Tova asked another one of her clueless questions of the teacher, Aviva smirked at Tirtzah. Aviva pointed to her temple with her finger and twisted it back and forth. Tova noticed the gesture.
>
> "You know, that was really very babyish of you," Tova told Aviva later.
>
> "What?" Aviva said, pretending not to understand the accusation.
>
> "Saying I'm crazy or whatever to Tirtzah."
>
> "I never said a word. Hey, Tirtzah," Aviva called to her friend, who was standing nearby. "Did I say anything about Tova?"
>
> "You didn't say a word!" Tirtzah testified.
>
> "I saw what you did," Tova tried again. "You put your finger to your head like this, like to say 'She's nuts.' I saw it!"
>
> "Maybe I was just scratching an itch," Aviva suggested. "Touching your head is not an insult! Don't be so paranoid, Tova. Really."
>
> Tova walked away hurt and confused, certain that she had been insulted but unable to defend herself. Aviva, walked away triumphant, believing that even though she may have insulted Tova, she had not "said" anything wrong.

Unable to pin down the meaning behind the gesture, Tova will probably remained confused. But Aviva knows just what she did. She knows that her gesture was the exact equivalent of an insulting word, whose meaning had been understood by Tirtzah and any other classmates who had seen it.

226 Chapter Twelve: Nonverbal Ona'as Devarim

Insulting gestures hurt those at whom they are aimed, and therefore are included within the prohibition of *ona'as devarim.* They may be *devarim*—words—but they do what words do, which is to communicate an idea. Therefore, whether a person uses actual sign language or informal gestures that send a message, **her hands can speak** *ona'as devarim* **just as surely as her mouth can.**

Hand motions can also hurt others when they transmit a negative feeling. For instance, when we stand close to someone and point a finger at her, we make the listener feel that she is under attack. Pointing at someone while we speak is guaranteed to make her feel uneasy, and the message is bound to be perceived as negative.

The same is true if we pepper our comments with loud thumping on the table or other aggressive gestures. These motions are meant to manipulate other people's emotions without having to verbally make the threat that the gesture carries with it. For instance, if we say, "I need this done right now!" and bang on the table in anger, we are saying, "I need this done right now *or else!*" The "or else" is meant to scare people into doing what the speaker wants. Even if we don't say it, our gesture implies it.

Because our hands can speak as loud or even louder than our words, we have to become aware of what our hands are saying. We cannot hide behind the excuse that we have not "said" anything insulting if we have managed to deliver an insulting or angry message through gestures. If we want our message to come across as caring and sincere, we must measure not only what we say with our mouths, but what we say with our hands as well.

Reality Check:
Do I ever use gestures to communicate something negative? If so, I will take note that this, too, is *ona'as devarim* and is equally hurtful.

What If...
Tova had not noticed that she was being ridiculed? In that case she would not have been hurt. Would the gesture still have been *ona'as devarim*?

לע״נ אריה זכריה בן אביגדור ורעיה נוימן ז״ל — *4 Teves*
לע״נ מרדכי בן אשר הלוי ז״ל ואשתו רבקה בת יוסף חיים ע״ה
לע״נ יעקב ישראל בן יחזקאל שרגא ז״ל נלב״ע כ״ט אלול — *4 Iyar*
ואשתו אסתר לאה בת דוד ע״ה נלב״ע ד׳ אייר
5 Elul — Dedicated as a *z'chus* for our daughter

DAY 95

The Deadly Stare
~ Scornful looks and expressions

ה טבת
5 Teves/Cycle 1

ה אייר
5 Iyar/Cycle 2

ו אלול
6 Elul/Cycle 3

When other mothers complained about their difficulty waking their daughters up for school, Rachel's mother would silently thank Hashem that her daughter had no such troubles. Rachel woke up every morning alert and ready for the day. She was rarely sick and never late.

Then one morning, it all changed. "I don't know, Ma, I feel like I'm coming down with something," she complained. Her mother assumed that Rachel must have really felt sick; otherwise, why would she miss school? As the day wore on, the symptoms disappeared. The following morning, however, the "illness" was back.

As the weeks wore on, Rachel stayed home from school many more times, due to many more mysterious symptoms: stomach pains, headaches, dizziness, nausea. Yet nothing blossomed into a treatable illness. "O.K., Rachel," her mother said one day. "Something is going on. What is it about school that makes you sick whenever you think of going?"

After a long conversation, Rachel finally confessed. Her old gang had turned against her. She didn't know why, but she often saw them looking at her and smiling at each other, or staring at her and whispering. She felt as though she had three heads. School was impossible.

No one had laid a hand on Rachel. No one had even said a mean word to her. However, the humiliation she went through because of glances, stares, smiles and whispers did no less damage than the most aggressive words or actions might have done. Rachel's former friends had mastered the art of the wordless attack.

228 Chapter Twelve: Nonverbal Ona'as Devarim

Critical looks and condescending smiles, stares and disapproving expressions show disdain. In fact, most people read these expressions even more clearly than words, because they cut straight into the heart without first being interpreted by our minds.

No matter how old or mature a person is, this type of *ona'as devarim* hurts. Most of us can think of someone in our lives who makes us feel uncomfortable without saying one negative word. The discomfort comes from the way the person looks at us, as if we were a creature from another planet or a clumsy child.

Disdain is so powerful that it can block a person's spiritual growth. The *Shulchan Aruch* takes this type of insult very seriously. In the very first *halachah,* it recognizes disdain as one of the most likely causes for someone to give up her effort to stand up for a *mitzvah* and grow in her service to Hashem. By opening the entire code of Jewish law with a warning to the Jewish people not to allow themselves to be discouraged by other people's ridicule, the *Shulchan Aruch* shows how overpowering this force can be.

Once we recognize the pain that expressions of disdain cause in our own lives, there is just one short step to recognizing that we can inflict this pain on others as well, with no more than a sly smile or a hard stare.

On the other hand, sincere warmth can shine through our eyes even more powerfully. When we wear that expression, we open our lives to a world of *chesed*. We become a trusted friend that others can confide in, knowing that whatever they tell us, we will never respond with ridicule.

---

5 Teves — לע״נ שמואל בן ר׳ מאיר יחזקאל ז״ל
לזכות יעקב יוסף בן אהובה רבקה נ״י
5 Iyar — Bell Gildar *a"h* לע״נ בילא בת חיים שאול הכהן ע״ה
לע״נ חנה גלדא בת לייב ע״ה
6 Elul — לע״נ ישראל יעקב בן ר׳ מרדכי הכהן ז״ל

Reality Check:

Do you ever look at someone in a way that might make her feel uncomfortable? Think about the message you are trying to convey to her, and if it is a worthwhile message try to deliver it in a respectful, direct way.

What If...

Rachel's former friends were angry at her because of something she did wrong? How could they confront her in a way that would not cause her so much pain?

DAY 96

Is Somebody Saying Something?
~ Ignoring someone

ו טבת
6 Teves/Cycle 1

ו אייר
6 Iyar/Cycle 2

ז אלול
7 Elul/Cycle 3

"So then, just as the chassan was about to put the ring on my cousin's finger, my 2-year-old nephew ran down the aisle singing "Dreidel dreidel" at the top of his lungs. Everyone was hysterical laughing and then my nephew tripped and fell flat on his face and started bawling!"

Rikki's story brought a burst of laughter from the five girls who were sitting with her, working on a class presentation. All the girls were friends, except Shuli. Shuli had no real group of friends. For this project the teacher had stuck her with Rikki's group.

"Wait, I have a better story," said Naama. "At my uncle's wedding, the kallah's train fell off as she was walking down the aisle. Her friend started walking behind her, pinning it up as she went. The kallah went on like nothing was happening."

"If that was me," Fraidy responded, "I'd have started crying."

"Not this kallah! Nothing got to her!" Naama said.

Shuli knew a great wedding disaster story, but should she tell it? Shuli never felt comfortable with these girls. She summoned up some courage.

"My friend's sister was like that," Shuli put in. "There was a huge storm the day of her wedding and it caused a blackout in the middle of the dancing. The band's equipment went dead, so a bunch of the chassan's friends got up on stage with the singer and they sang. The kallah danced like crazy and all her friends got into it and it was the best dancing ever!"

The group was silent for a moment. No one looked at Shuli as she spoke, and no one responded to her story: no laugh, no comment, no question. "Fraidy, do

230   Chapter Twelve: Nonverbal Ona'as Devarim

you think we've done enough for today?" Rikki asked. "I'm getting kind of tired of this."

Reality Check:

Do I acknowledge everyone, even those who are not my type?

Most people, when they walk past a mirror, take a glance at their reflection. It's as if we need reassurance that we exist. That is why we love to get mail, phone calls, gifts and visitors. They prove that we are on others' minds and agendas. **One of the deepest needs of the heart is to feel that we matter.**

Because of this deep need, acting as if someone is invisible is one of the cruelest acts a person can commit. The popular girl tells a story and the group hangs on every word; the unpopular girl tells a story and no one listens. The popular girl offers her opinion and everyone applauds it; the unpopular girl offers her opinion and no one responds. The message to the unpopular girl is "We don't want you here. If you don't have the sense to leave, don't expect us to be pleasant."

Why do people do this? Sometimes the group feels that the other girl doesn't meet their standards, that she tarnishes their image. So they make her uncomfortable.

While no one is obligated to laugh at someone's joke or find someone's story interesting, there is a level of response that simply acknowledges the other person's value as a human being. To deny someone that acknowledgment is the emotional equal of denying her food and water. It simply cannot be justified.

What If...

you were a girl in Rikki's group, and you chose to break the silence and respond to Shuli's story? How do you think the rest of the girls would have reacted?

---

6 Teves — In honor of Devorah Yudkowsky
6 Iyar — As a *z'chus* for our משפחה
Dedicated by the Fischer family
7 Elul — לע"נ יעקב אריה בן ר' יצחק פריילך ז"ל
Dedicated by Odel Freilich and family

DAY 97

The Silent Treatment
~ Silence as a weapon

ז טבת
7 Teves/Cycle 1

ז אייר
7 Iyar/Cycle 2

ח אלול
8 Elul/Cycle 3

When Yael came home from school, she had an unwelcome surprise waiting for her. Her sister Dina had stopped talking to her.

"What's wrong?" Yael asked her, although she was pretty sure she knew. Yael had run out of the house that morning wearing her sister's new winter coat. Even though Dina was four years older, the two girls wore the same size. Forgetful Yael could not find her coat in time to make the bus and so, without asking, she grabbed her sister's coat and dashed out the door. She knew it was wrong, but she was sure that Dina would have said yes if she had stopped long enough to ask.

Yael's efforts to open a conversation with Dina fell flat. Dina marched around the house taking care of her various chores. She put away her clean laundry, noisily slamming each drawer shut. She set the table for dinner, clanking the dishes as if she were angry at them.

"At least you can tell me what's wrong," Yael persisted. "Are you mad that I took your coat? I didn't have time to ask you, and I thought you wouldn't mind. But it wasn't right. I'm sorry. You can borrow my new scarf and gloves for a whole week, O.K.? They look perfect with your coat."

But Dina wouldn't relent. Her campaign of silence continued all night long and into the next morning as well. Yael left for school under Dina's silent storm cloud. By the time she came home, though, the sun was peeking through. "What's new in school?" Dina asked her sister. But now Yael was angry over the heavy feeling she had been carrying around all day; the fight would have to go at least one more round.

Silence can be a powerful, painful weapon. It tells a person, "Not only am I angry, but I don't even care enough about you to try to talk it out."

Sometimes we resort to silence because we are so angry that we are afraid of what might come out of our mouths. This is sometimes, in the right situation, a good temporary tool for handling an explosive situation. Although the silence itself may be painful, it might be less painful than the words that would come out in its place.

However, even under those circumstances we must work on calming our roiling emotions and reinterpreting the situation in a way that we can handle productively. We might use the period of silence to try to see things from the other person's point of view or to find a *"gam zu l'tovah"*—Hashem's inherent goodness—in whatever has upset us.

Most of the time, angry silence is used as a weapon: another way to hurt someone without having to take responsibility for speaking cruel words. We should not try to deceive ourselves into thinking that offensive silence is better than offensive speech, because both cause pain. Sometimes the words that are left unsaid are more painful than words that have actually been said. The other person is left to wonder, *What is she really thinking?* Her imagination might supply a more upsetting answer than words would convey.

On the positive side, if we have the ability to keep silent we most likely have strong self-control. All we need to do is take that power and use it to control our anger, so that we can speak to the other person in words that address the issue with directness, calmness and respect.

Reality Check:

Do I ever use silence to make someone aware of my displeasure? If my first impulse is to stop talking, I will try to use that silent time to figure out a way to address the source of my anger productively.

What If...

Dina had simply confronted Yael with her feeling that she wanted her personal property to be respected? What could Dina have said to address the problem firmly, yet without *ona'as devarim*?

---

7 Teves — לע"נ הרב דוד נח בן יהודה זצ"ל

7 Iyar — May today's learning be a *z'chus* for our entire *mishpachah*.
Dedicated by Rabbi and Mrs. Yossi Spanier

8 Elul — לע"נ אריה לייב הכהן פרסר בן ירחמאל שלמה ז"ל
Dedicated by Marilyn and Jaime Sohacheski

Chapter 13

Everyday Challenges

It might seem that the potential for *ona'as devarim* lurks around every corner of our lives. But if we analyze the situation we discover that a few common situations produce a large portion of the challenges to our self-control. By focusing on those situations, which are unique to each person, and developing ways to respond to them with kindness and respect, we can succeed in making a major change in our lives.

DAY 98

Hello, Goodbye
~ Cell phone etiquette

ח טבת
8 Teves/Cycle 1

ח אייר
8 Iyar/Cycle 2

ט אלול
9 Elul/Cycle 3

With three full grocery bags hanging on one arm and two on the other, somehow Brochi managed to reach into her pocket and answer her mother's cell phone that she had taken along on her errand.

Fumbling with the phone between her ear and her shoulder she answered breathlessly, trying not to drop the phone: "Hello?"

"Brochi! I can't believe I got you!" said an enthusiastic voice on the other side. "It's Suri!"

Suri was Brochi's longtime friend who had moved out of town two years earlier.

"Oh, Suri!" Brochi said. "But, but, wait a minute..." she adjusted the phone's position as it slipped. "Listen, I can't talk right now. I'm loaded down with grocery bags. I'll call you back later, O.K.? Bye."

To Suri, the conversation felt as if her friend had opened the front door, seen her face, said hello and then slammed the door shut. When she thinks it through, she will probably realize that no insult was meant; but still, she felt rejected.

Because people carry cell phones with them as they go about their day, a whole new set of telephone-etiquette questions has been created, along with a whole new category of *ona'as devarim*. Anyone may call at any time, but not all of those times are appropriate or even possible times to speak.

The tone of voice that people often use in these situations makes the caller feel that somehow she should have known what an inappropriate moment she has chosen for a phone call. When someone says, "I can't talk right now. They're taking my mother into surgery!" the caller feels as if she is an insensitive fool. Who expects to have a chat when her friend is in the middle of a crisis?

When we are with someone and our phone rings, another problem arises. We pick up the call and chat away, leaving the person in front of our eyes to feel as if she has disappeared. Further issues arise when we notice a new call coming in and abruptly cut off the first call.

What can we do when the cell phone is ringing but a conversation is out of the question? The simplest answer is to let the caller leave a voice-mail message, and then be sure to return the call at the earliest possible time. Most callers prefer that to a harried, inattentive answer.

If a person does pick up the call, she should be very careful with the words and tone she uses. She should try to make the caller feel that her call is welcome, even if it cannot be continued at that moment. It doesn't take much longer to say a few calm, explanatory sentences than it does to grumble a distracted hello and an abrupt goodbye. Obviously, if we are with someone, we have to treat her with courtesy if the phone rings: either we excuse ourselves to briefly answer the call, or we let it go to voice-mail.

It may seem extreme, but it is even worthwhile to rehearse words to say before these situations arise. There was once a Torah scholar who spent time in front of his mirror practicing his smile. Because smiling at others is a way of showing them respect, he wanted to give the *mitzvah* his best effort by giving others his best smile. Today, the tone with which we answer the phone serves the same purpose. It is a way of showing respect to others, a goal that is always worth our best efforts.

Reality Check:

How do I answer a phone when the call comes at an inconvenient time? I will remember that the caller has no idea what I am doing, and try to avoid making her feel awkward.

What If...

Brochi realized that Suri might be hurt that she couldn't take her call? What words might she have used when she picked up the call?

---

8 Teves — לע״נ ר׳ אהרן בן ישראל ז״ל נלב״ע י׳ טבת
לזכות שידוך, דבורה לאה בת חי׳ ריזל שתחי׳

8 Iyar — As a *z'chus* for our family
Dedicated by Dr. and Mrs. Eli Bienenstock

9 Elul — In honor of Adam Aaron R'bibo לזכות אדם אהרן רביבו נ״י
Dedicated by your parents Ben and Sandra R'bibo

DAY 99

Just Say "No"
~ Navigating the negative

ט טבת
9 Teves/Cycle 1

ט אייר
9 Iyar/Cycle 2

י אלול
10 Elul/Cycle 3

"Can you study with me for the math test?" Gittel asked Tamar. Tamar knew Gittel could really use her help. On the other hand, Gittel did not know how to settle down and study. Whenever they studied together, Tamar did poorly on the test. "Sorry, Gittel, I can't," Tamar answered. "I think I do better when I study on my own."

"You're so selfish!" Gittel replied. "I always study with you when you need help with Chumash."

• • •

Yaffa asked her friend Breindy, "Can I get a ride with you to the Bais Yaakov play?"

"Sorry, but I don't think so," Breindy said. "Malky's mother is driving and the car is all filled up."

"Well, why didn't you count me in?" Yaffa responded in a hurt tone.

• • •

"Everyone is wearing silver gowns to my cousin's wedding," Aliza told her friend Chava. "I was thinking, that long silver skirt you have would look really nice. Could I borrow it?"

"Borrow my silver skirt? After what you did to my gray sweater, my raincoat, my wool skirt and everything else you borrowed, now you want my new silver chasunah skirt?"

Sometimes we say "no" because the request being made is impossible for us to grant. Sometimes it is possible, but we choose our own priorities over someone else's. This is the situation in the first scenario, where Tamar refuses Gittel's request to study together. While the "no" is not meant as an insult, Gittel takes it as one and hits back with *ona'as devarim*.

238 Chapter Thirteen: Everyday Challenges

Most people avoid saying "no." We want others to like us and think of us as kind and caring, and so we feel that we should do what they want and give what they ask. In such a situation, though, our "kindness" can backfire. Sometimes we overextend ourselves to the point where we are tense and resentful as we deliver the favor that was asked of us. In that state, we may end up exploding in *ona'as devarim* at the person who has seemingly forced us to give more than we wanted or felt able to give.

Because hearing "no" almost always feels like a rejection, we tend to read into it more than is meant. In the scenario with Yaffa and Breindy, Yaffa's first response is to feel hurt and left out. She might go on to obsess about how many times she has been left out of plans, who is going to be in the car, why they are more important than she is and so forth. By the time she is done, this "no" will have sprouted pages of footnotes.

"No" does not have to be *ona'as devarim*, but it *can* be if it is said in a hostile, rejecting way. That is the case in the final scenario where a girl asks to borrow her friend's gown. Sometimes we answer harshly because we do not want any argument. We feel that a loud, sharp "no" will be the final answer. Other times, that aggressive "no" comes when a situation is getting out of control. For instance, in the gown scenario, if Chava is constantly lending Aliza clothes only to get them back damaged she may have been wanting to say "no" for a long time. This "no" contains all the anger produced by her previous, reluctant "yeses."

Nobody wants to hear "no" to a request. However, most people can accept that "no," said in a clear but gentle way, is a necessary fact of life. It need not be spoken nor heard as a fighting word.

> **Reality Check:**
> What is my tone of voice and facial expression when I say "no" to someone? What is my response when someone says "no" to me?

> **What If...**
> Chava has spoken to Aliza earlier about her treatment of borrowed items? What might she have said after the first one or two instances?

---

9 Teves — לע"נ דבורה בת אליעזר ע"ה
9 Iyar — לע"נ הרב אליעזר בן שלמה ז"ל
לע"נ פסיא פנינה בת אפרים מנשה ע"ה
10 Elul — לע"נ דוד בן אברהם ז"ל

DAY 100

Same Story, New Ending
~ Recurring challenges

י טבת
10 Teves/Cycle 1

י אייר
10 Iyar/Cycle 2

י"א אלול
11 Elul/Cycle 3

"Ready to review?" Edna's mother asked.

Edna felt like running out the door. Her mother, a teacher, had offered to help her review for an upcoming Navi midterm. There was a mountain of material to memorize and Edna needed the help. But every time Edna's mother helped her with homework, the result was disaster.

"Let's skip tonight," Edna suggested. "I think I can work on my own."

"No, no, we decided we would put in a good solid week of review," her mother reminded her. "Didn't we have a bet that if you did that you'd get at least a B?"

Edna sat down with her mother and they began. Her mother asked her a question from material they had reviewed the previous night. Edna couldn't remember the answer. "I can't do this!" she complained.

"Keep trying! You'll see, if you put in the effort, you CAN do this. You're a smart girl."

They reviewed some more, and then Edna's mother tested her again. But Edna's mind was elsewhere. The work was too confusing and she just couldn't stick with it.

"Let's go over this part again," her mother suggested. "We'll just keep at it until you get it."

"I don't want to do it anymore! Leave me alone! I can't stand this! Just let me flunk, I don't care!" Edna railed. She stomped away from the table, knowing she had insulted her mother yet again.

Edna's mother shook her head sadly. She only wanted to use her teaching abilities to help her own daughter succeed in school, but every time they studied together, Edna ended up furious and she ended up feeling hurt.

240 Chapter Thirteen: Everyday Challenges

Life is full of challenges, and some of them are particularly hard for some people to handle. For one girl, getting up in the morning is difficult. For another, getting homework done seems impossible. Getting to bed at a reasonable time can be another area of difficulty. For some girls, choosing clothes is an area of contention. In all these areas, we are bound to end up in conflict with parents and others who are trying to help us make the right decisions.

When certain challenges are part of our everyday routine, conflict becomes part of our everyday routine. With conflict comes rising tempers, creating the perfect environment for *ona'as devarim*.

No one wants to have the same old fight every day, certainly if it means that feelings will be hurt every day. **Therefore, it is worthwhile to think of new ways to handle these predictable situations that often result in harsh words**. Rather than simply accepting that these battles must be fought, we can consult with teachers, with more experienced friends, or with relatives to find better ways to manage these situations.

Often the difficulties resolve themselves as we mature and take more responsibility for our own lives. In 10th grade a girl might think she is doing her homework for her teacher or her parents. In seminary, she does it for herself, for her own growth. Likewise, a girl who avoids household chores when she is 16 might have a different view when she has her own home that she takes pride in.

But although these daily challenges may fade into the past, the hurtful things we say in the heat of the moment may not fade so quickly; they can damage our relationships with those who love us. If we come up with new ways to deal with the conflicts we can expect to arise, we can also expect a lot more peace and happiness in our lives.

> *10 Teves* — לע"נ צבי ארי׳ בן אלתר חיים ישעי׳ ז"ל
> Dedicated by the Steger, Jacobovitch and Wesson families
> *10 Iyar* — לע"נ חי׳ מלכה בת משה זלמן ע"ה
> *11 Elul* — לע"נ ר׳ חיים שלמה זלמן בן ר׳ נפתלי ז"ל
> Reb Chaim Shlomo Zalman Weisberg • Dedicated by the Weisberg and Berkowitz families

Reality Check:

Do I have predictable conflicts in my life? Instead of going through the same arguments over and over again, I will find a new approach.

What If...

Edna realized that she could not work well with her mother on homework, and yet she knew she needed help? What alternative solutions could she suggest to avoid conflict?

Chapter 14

Strategies

We speak tens of thousands of words every day. There are probably no habits we repeat more frequently than those involving our speech. Therefore, changing those habits can appear to be a monumental task too immense to even approach. The key is to find strategies that give us tools to succeed. By adopting new, positive ways of thinking, feeling, acting and reacting to others, we find that step-by-step, we develop new, positive habits to replace the old.

DAY 101

The Big Payoff
~ Envision your reward

י"א טבת
11 Teves/Cycle 1

י"א אייר
11 Iyar/Cycle 2

י"ב אלול
12 Elul/Cycle 3

Adira loved to shop. She loved it so much that she spent every penny of the money she earned on clothes, purses, shoes, coats and accessories she did not need. Her dresser and closet were filled to the bursting point, but she always reasoned that the new item was "something I'll use" and that "it's always good to have an extra."

While her expensive hobby earned her the admiration of her style-conscious friends, it disabled all Adira's long-term plans. She wanted to save up to help pay for a year in seminary in Israel, a luxury her parents had already told her they could not afford. She also knew that when the time came for her to get married, her bank account would be important in purchasing some of the "extras" she would want.

Hard-working Adira baby-sat after school three days a week and for a few hours on Sunday. She could have put away several thousand dollars by now, the middle of 11th grade. However, no matter how much she wanted to save, she couldn't resist the sweet call of the shop window.

Most people have as much difficulty controlling what they say as Adira has controlling what she buys. In both cases, the urge of the moment overcomes the truer long-term desire. Adira wants to save money, but when she is faced with temptation her higher self instantly wilts. In the same way, we might truly want to be kind and gentle; but when our immediate convenience or comfort is frustrated, we react instinctively with anger, which overrides our higher ideals.

But imagine for a moment that Adira found a generous person who promised, "Every time you resist walking into a store, I will put $10,000 into your bank account." This is an offer that promises her an incredible reward and leads her in the direction that she wants to go; she would happily walk by every store window with a firm "no" on her lips.

In the case of *ona'as devarim*, this strategy would also work well. Imagine that every time a person derailed a thought that would lead to a hurtful word, she automatically received a $10,000 deposit in her bank account. In no time at all, she would be eagerly batting down every harsh thought and critical comment that came into her head.

This fantasy scenario is not really a fantasy at all. As the Vilna Gaon teaches, the Midrash promises *"Kol hachosem piv, zocheh l'or haganuz"*—"Those who close their mouths (rather than insult another Jew) are worthy of the hidden light (the light of Creation, which Hashem reserves as a reward for the holiest *neshamos*)." **This means that a "deposit" of incalculable value drops into our heavenly bank account every time we restrain ourselves from hurting someone with our words.**

But are we capable of keeping this invisible "bank account" at the front of our minds in a moment of anger, envy or frustration? A good way to start is to choose one area of life that is particularly likely to test our self-control. For instance, the morning rush might be a time when someone commonly loses her temper. If we prepare a way to stay in control during that period, a large portion of *ona'as devarim* can be erased from each day.

It's not within our power to understand the exquisite treasure stored up for us when we hold our tongues to protect another person's honor. However, knowing that treasure is there for us can motivate us to do that which, in our deepest hearts, we really want to do.

---

11 Teves — In memoey of Polina Reznikov *a"h* לע"נ פאלינא בת יעקב ע"ה
Dedicated by Benzion and Masha Wellson
11 Iyar — לע"נ מנחם מענדל בן אברהם צבי ז"ל
12 Elul — In memory of Lillian Gamzon *a"h* לע"נ חי' לאה בת אהרן הכהן ע"ה
Dedicated by Mr. and Mrs. Sheldon Gamzon

Reality Check:

Is there a time or situation that comes up frequently in my life when I find it hard to control my words? If so, I will create a strategy to get me through that situation without falling into *ona'as devarim*.

What If...

I try to change how I act in a challenging situation, but the other people in my life do not change? How can I react differently when they react the same old way?

DAY 102

Prepared for Landing
~ Preparing our responses

י"ב טבת
12 Teves/Cycle 1

י"ב אייר
12 Iyar/Cycle 2

י"ג אלול
13 Elul/Cycle 3

As he flew over New York City, the pilot glanced out the window of his propeller plane and realized that one of his engines had gone dead. He wasn't worried, though; he was excited. What a great learning opportunity this was going to be for the student pilot sitting next to him in the cockpit!

The pilot and his student reported the problem to the air-traffic control tower and like well-trained soldiers went through a series of maneuvers to bring the plane to a safe airport landing. Unfortunately, the maneuvers were not effective, and it became clear that the airplane was not going to make it to the airport. No problem: They would go to Plan B, an emergency landing in the East River. The plan was so well prepared that the pilot was able to let his student fly the plane until it was just 300 feet above the river.

At that point, the pilot took over and steered the plane to a perfect landing. As soon as it came to rest in the river, the pilot shot off a flare, and he and his student jumped into the river and swam away. When they were rescued a few minutes later, they were calm and cool, as if nothing unusual had happened.

In life, as in aviation, preparation can be the difference between a safe landing and a disaster.

This is the Ramban's message when he advises us on how to avoid falling into sin: "Accustom yourself to *always* speak *all* your words gently to *all* people at *all* times" (*Iggeres HaRamban*).

"*Tisnaheig tamid*"—accustom yourself—implies practice. When we play out a potential scenario in our mind and plan an accepting, calm response based on the idea of "*gam zu*

246 Chapter Fourteen: Strategies

l'tovah"—this too is for the good—we create a flight plan for a soft landing when the unexpected happens. The more we practice this response, the more likely we will be to follow it automatically when difficult situations arise.

If we prepare to respond as the Ramban advises, we will be able to handle disappointment with a peaceful heart. When troubles come our way we will be focused on productive, future-oriented responses rather than wallowing in bitterness or blaming others and planning our revenge. We will reserve our energy for fixing the problem, rather than wasting our energy on anger.

The Ramban teaches that an angry response is not just unproductive and unpleasant; it is a real risk to our lives, equal to a crash landing in the East River. The trouble itself is like the dead engine: we didn't ask for it and we surely don't want it to happen. **However, our response to the trouble determines whether we survive the problem emotionally and spiritually**. If we heed the Ramban's words, our response will be like that of the pilot. Rather than panicking or blaming the mechanic who didn't check the plane properly, we will slide into a prepared, productive response that enables us to accept the trouble and bring it to the best possible solution.

If we see a hurtful response as a real, life-threatening and eternity-threatening risk, we are naturally inclined to put time and effort into preparing for potentially risky situations. Little by little, we can build an attitude of acceptance that enables us to stay positive, calm and focused no matter what life throws our way. From this wellspring of trust in Hashem, only good can flow.

Reality Check:

Do I ever give thought to how I will react if a situation does not turn out as I hope? I will consider one such situation and its possible outcomes, and prepare myself with a "*gam zu l'tovah*" response regardless of the outcome.

What If...

other people are to blame for my problem? How can I make sure the situation does not happen again if I cannot place the blame where it belongs?

---

12 Teves — לע"נ שמואל חיים אליעזר בן מרגליות ז"ל נלב"ע א' חשון
לע"נ לאה בת אברהם ע"ה נלב"ע י"ב טבת
12 Iyar — Serach Dena Friedman *a"h* לע"נ שרח דינה בת שלום דוד יבלחט"א
Dedicated in loving memory by her family, Philadelphia, PA
13 Elul — לע"נ יוטא בת צבי פרנקל ע"ה
לע"נ יצחק בן דוב בער שכטר ז"ל נלב"ע י"ד אלול

DAY 103

Fork in the Road
~ Thinking before speaking

י"ג טבת
13 Teves/Cycle 1

י"ג אייר
13 Iyar/Cycle 2

י"ד אלול
14 Elul/Cycle 3

Tikva Goldstein was riding back to New Jersey with her family from her cousin's wedding in New York. Sitting in a carful of cranky younger siblings, she urged her father to take the quickest route possible. They sped along until it was time to decide which bridge they would take to get from New York to New Jersey.

"I heard that there's some construction on the Outerbridge," Mrs. Goldstein told her husband. "Maybe we should take the Goethals Bridge."

"Sounds good," her husband said. "The last thing we need now is to be sitting in traffic." He veered quickly into the lane leading toward the Goethals Bridge.

They sped along the highway for a while, but then, as they approached the bridge, the traffic got snarled up and came to a halt. Noticing the flashing red and blue lights up ahead, Tikva announced, "Oh, no! There's an accident."

The one second it took for Mr. Goldstein to choose the Goethals Bridge ended up costing the family a full hour of travel time, accompanied by the whining and fighting of five overtired children. One second's decision produced an hour of aggravation.

Most people take no time to decide whether or not to say something to another person. In fact, we often do not think about it at all; our words just rush out of our mouths like water from a bathtub faucet. Yet just as Mr. Goldstein's split-second choice had long-lasting results, the decisions we make about the words we speak have results that last much longer: not just for an hour, but for an eternity.

For example, a girl named Ariella comes to school with a new haircut, so short that she looks almost like a boy. Obviously

248 Chapter Fourteen: Strategies

something went wrong at the hairdresser's, but nothing can be done about it.

Now, as each girl gets her first look at Ariella, she is at a "fork in the road." She can thoughtlessly burst into a laugh and say, "Ariella! What did you do to yourself?" On the other hand, she can take a second to think: *She has a lot of guts to come to school with that haircut. She must be nervous about what everyone is going to say.*

At that point of decision, each girl chooses which road to take. She can casually throw out some funny, insensitive remark, and bring all the negative consequences of *ona'as devarim* to bear on herself. She can make Ariella feel even more self-conscious and give her the sense that her friends only accept her when she looks "right."

If the girl decides to take the other road, however, she can say something kind and supportive: "You have to have a pretty face to look good in such a short haircut." That doesn't mean the girl likes the haircut; it simply gives Ariella encouragement to deal with her embarrassing situation. Other girls who hear the positive remark might pick up on it as well, and rethink any insensitive comment that might have popped into their heads. For Ariella the support means a great deal, because it shows her that her friends are true friends who accept her no matter how she looks. This colors the way she feels about school, friends, herself and her life.

Hundreds of times a day, we come to a fork in the road. Our words can take us on a road that leads to pain and tears, or a road that leads to happiness and friendship. In the split second between thinking and speaking, we must make that choice.

Reality Check:

Sometimes a certain comment seems irresistible. Do I find myself bursting out with comments that have no positive purpose and might possibly hurt someone? If so, I will picture the "fork in the road" before I speak.

What If...

Ariella wasn't really bothered by her haircut and found the situation funny? Would it then be all right for her friends to tease her about it?

---

13 Teves — לע"נ הרב מאיר בן אהרן מרדכי הלוי ז"ל נלב"ע י"ד טבת
Dedicated by Nathan & Dvora Liebster

13 Iyar — לזכות אהרן משה מרדכי בן לאה רייזל נ"י וכל משפחתו
לזכות יואל בן רבקה דבורה נ"י

14 Elul — לע"נ גדליה שלמה בן ברוך צבי ז"ל וזוגתו חי' רחל בת אליהו ע"ה
Dedicated by the Benson family

Fork in the Road ~ Thinking before speaking 249

DAY 104

Image Transplant
~ Cultivating love for others

י"ד טבת
14 Teves/Cycle 1

י"ד אייר
14 Iyar/Cycle 2

ט"ו אלול
15 Elul/Cycle 3

> *Objectively, Hadassah knew that her friend Michal was loud. People described her as "over the top." A lot of people found her embarrassing or annoying to be with. Hadassah, however, had known Michal since the two of them were in playgroup together. They were like sisters, and to Hadassah, Michal's overdose of personality only made her more lovable and fun to be with.*
>
> *On the other hand, Hadassah found Shoshi unbearable. She was always bragging about her brilliant father and famous grandfather. Yaelle was annoying in a different way; she ate too loudly. Sitting with her at lunch was impossible. Then there was Zahava: Where was that girl's personality? Plenty of people got under Hadassah's skin, but Michal was certainly not one of them.*

There is a saying that "love is blind," meaning that a person who loves someone cannot see that person's flaws clearly. On the other hand, dislike seems to give people microscopic vision, allowing them to see the smallest faults in the person they dislike. When that happens, the person puts on her "critic's glasses" the second the other person comes into view. "There she is, bragging about her grandfather again." "There she is, making a racket eating her apple." "There's Miss Stingy who won't lend anyone a dime...."

These thoughts might be based on real experiences with the person, or they might be based on nothing more than a superficial impression. **Either way, our negative view of someone is likely to end up causing us to speak *ona'as devarim*.** Unless she is someone we would not dare insult, there is bound to come a time when our negative thoughts will sneak out of our mouths.

The Torah, however, does not make allowances for insulting people we dislike. On the contrary, it demands that we try to love them. When a person seems very unlikable, this *mitzvah* can seem impossible to fulfill. However, with an open mind and an open heart, there is an effective strategy we can use.

First we have to realize that with rare exceptions, every person has people in her life who love her and think well of her. They see attributes in her that we may not see, or may see but choose to overlook. If we would sincerely want to let go of our dislike for this person, now is the time to think about her good traits.

The second step is to remind ourselves that everyone has flaws. Just as we may focus on someone else's flaws, she could do the same to us. She could see our working hard as workaholism, our refinement as unfriendliness, our enthusiasm as loudness, our spiritual growth as self-righteousness and so on. But that is not what we want others to see; we want them to accept us and share the vision we have of ourselves.

The other person—the one we can't stand—wants that too. She does not see herself as an annoyance to humanity; she sees herself as a good person doing her best to live a good life. **Choose some positive aspect of this person and vividly imagine it**. If she's friendly, for instance, imagine her smiling and laughing with someone. If she's generous, imagine her helping someone. Give her a new identity: Miss Friendly, Miss Helpful, Miss Mature. Now, whenever we see her, we should think of her by her "new name." By doing this, we will eventually be able to get past our negative image of this person. We may even develop enough love for this person to become "blind" to her flaws.

> **Reality Check:**
> Are there people who "get under my skin"? I will focus on one such person and create a new image for her in my mind.

> **What If...**
> your dislike for someone is not baseless, but rather is based on the person's hostile attitude toward you? Can you change such a relationship from dislike into love? If so, how?

---

14 Teves — In memory of my Aunt, Reb. Shirley Rosner לע״נ שרה בת ר׳ משה ע״ה
Dedicated by Shaindi Hirsch

14 Iyar — Dedicated as a *z'chus* for our children

15 Elul — לע״נ חיים ראובן בן ישראל צדוק ז״ל
Dedicated by Norman Freedman and family

Image Transplant ~ Cultivating love for others

DAY 105

Human Like Me
~ Developing empathy

ט"ו טבת
15 Teves/Cycle 1

ט"ו אייר
15 Iyar/Cycle 2

ט"ז אלול
16 Elul/Cycle 3

Ita glanced at her watch. It was 6:48 p.m. Her Wednesday night baby-sitting job started at 7 and she was 10 minutes away. She would be on time, but just barely. She imagined Mrs. Weissman's disapproving expression if she arrived late. "I have to be on time for my class, Ita," she would say. "If you can't be here at 7, then even though you're a wonderful girl, I just can't use you for this job."

Ita picked up her pace as she wove her way along the crowded sidewalk.

Just as she raced around the corner to Mrs. Weissman's block, another girl was rushing along from the other direction, carrying a large carton that blocked her view. The girl tried to pass someone walking in front of her, and she smacked right into Ita. The carton, the girl and Ita all went tumbling to the pavement. Ita heard the sound of glass shattering.

As the girls tried to stand up and brush themselves off, Ita noticed that her new sweater, which she had saved up for and bought with the money she earned from her job, had a giant hole on the elbow.

"I'm so sorry!" the girl said. "I was just in such a rush and you know…."

"Why don't you watch where you're going?" Ita said harshly, pointing miserably at her ripped sweater. "Now look what happened!"

The other girl's face collapsed. "I'm so sorry, really. I was just running this errand for my neighbor, picking up these wine glasses for her. She's making sheva berachos in half an hour and now I've broken all the glasses and ruined your sweater, too…"

Suddenly Ita saw the other girl as someone just like herself, rushing around trying to do what needed to

252 Chapter Fourteen: Strategies

be done. And now she was stuck in the middle of the sidewalk with a box of broken glasses, getting an earful of abuse from a stranger.

"Really, it's O.K. I'm sorry I lost it," Ita apologized. "Maybe my sweater can be fixed. I hope your neighbor won't be mad about the glasses."

When we lose ourselves in anger, we instantly forget one very essential fact: **It's another human being on the receiving end of our rant.** It's a person with a heart, feelings, hopes and challenges. It's a person like ourselves. Taking a moment to remember this is one of the most effective ways to reduce the *ona'as devarim* in our lives.

But it's not easy. When we lose our temper and we're in the middle of venting our outrage, it's hard to stop ourselves. It helps to plan the strategy we will use in that situation at a time when we are not being pulled by powerful emotions.

What can you do the next time you feel the urge to scream at someone? Look her in the eyes when you speak to her. See that there is a person there, with her own thoughts and her own problems. Will your words disturb her tonight as she tries to fall asleep? Will they make her angry and cause her to lose her temper with someone else? Will they damage her confidence in herself?

We don't have to hurt each other. If we try to relate to the other person's humanity rather than blocking it out of our minds, our natural reaction will be to find another way: a gentler, more sensitive and respectful way. The way we ourselves would like to be treated.

Reality Check:

When I respond in anger, do I have any concern about how the target of my anger is feeling? I will try the strategy of looking her in the eye as I speak, recognizing her as a fellow human being.

What If...

the girl who bumped into Ita had not been so apologetic? What if she had even blamed Ita for the accident? How should Ita respond?

15 Teves — לע"נ ר' שלמה שמואל בן ר' יצחק ז"ל נלב"ע י"ד טבת
Saul Gerszberg z"l • Dedicated by Drs. Neal and Marilyn Gittleman

15 Iyar — לזכות אריכת ימים ושנים טובים לאמי מורתי שיינע בת חנה פייגל שתחי'
Dedicated with all my love and admiration, Lisa Glenner

16 Elul — As a *z'chus* for our family
Dedicated by Mr. and Mrs. Adler

Human Like Me ~ Developing empathy

DAY 106

Variety
~ Accepting differences

ט"ז טבת
16 Teves/Cycle 1

ט"ז אייר
16 Iyar/Cycle 2

י"ז אלול
17 Elul/Cycle 3

Imagine meeting someone new. She is sitting next to you at a wedding and you begin to talk. You find out that she is from your old neighborhood. She knows many of the same people you know. In fact, her favorite pizza shop in the neighborhood is the one you used to love when you lived there—and for the same reason. You both like the spicy tomato sauce!

The more you talk to this girl, the more you discover things you have in common. You share your opinions with each other on school, jobs, music, books, clothes and much more. By the end of the night, you each feel that you've made a new friend.

Why? You feel connected because you are so much alike. You hear your own views seconded by this like-minded girl and see in her someone who really understands you. Very little is as comforting and comfortable as being with someone similar to ourselves.

This may explain why people have so much trouble accepting differences in other people. Since, as the saying goes, "the best defense is a good offense," there are some people who deal with differences by going on the attack, rejecting or insulting the other person and her views.

This way of thinking has caused unending misery for the Jewish people. Divisiveness, defensiveness and belittling of the "other" are all elements of our age-old enemy, *sinas chinam*—baseless hatred—which our Sages teach (*Yoma* 9b) is the root cause of our exile.

Our wish to be surrounded by people just like us will never be satisfied, because "just as no two people look exactly alike, no two people think alike" (*Yerushalmi, Berachos* 9:1). These words of *Chazal* teach us how to view differences among people. Their physical differences rarely bother us. We don't expect people to look alike; Hashem made each of us with our own physical traits. **Therefore, we are not angry at others for having different physical features than we do**. The words of *Chazal* teach us that our differences in thinking and philosophy are exactly the same thing—the product of Hashem's design of the world. So they should be just as acceptable to us as our physical differences are.

A person who cannot accept differences is someone who will always be finding fault with others, and most likely, expressing her disapproval through *ona'as devarim*. When she works with others at school or at her job, she will resist others' ideas if they are different from her own. At home, she will become angry when family members do things differently than she would. In the community, she will find fault with people whose customs or background are different from hers. Her world will be a narrow one, populated mostly by opponents.

By opening her eyes to the value of differences and acknowledging that Hashem put all of us into this world according to His design, we can live a completely different kind of life. Acceptance allows us to learn from others, expand our horizons and enjoy things that may not be "our cup of tea," but still add something valuable to the world.

Reality Check:

When I judge someone critically, is it because she is wrong, or because her ideas or ways of doing things are different from mine? I will try to make this distinction and work on appreciating, rather than rejecting, valid differences.

What If...

I believe that someone is not only different, but wrong? Where does acceptance fit into that situation?

---

16 Teves — In memory of my brother לע״נ אליהו אפרים בן שלום ז״ל
Dedicated by Avrohom and Miriam Hoffman

16 Iyar — לע״נ שלום דובער בן הרב יעקב ישראל זובער ז״ל נלב״ע י״ח אייר
Dedicated by Izzy Zuber and family

17 Elul — May today's learning be a *z'chus* for חינוך הבנים.

Variety ~ Accepting differences

DAY 107

Be a Visionary
~ Focus on others' potential

י"ז טבת
17 Teves/Cycle 1

י"ז אייר
17 Iyar/Cycle 2

י"ח אלול
18 Elul/Cycle 3

> When Rabbi Yochanan met Reish Lakish, the bandit, he came up with an unbelievable proposal right there on the spot. To get Reish Lakish to give up his life of crime, Rabbi Yochanan offered him a deal: If he would agree to learn Torah, he could marry Rabbi Yochanan's sister.
>
> How does someone dare to propose a match between his own sister and a robber? Rabbi Yochanan was able to make that offer with confidence, because from his high spiritual level he could see what Reish Lakish was really made of. He could see the man's neshamah, and he knew what greatness was hidden inside the rough exterior. Rabbi Yochanan was not dealing with Reish Lakish as he was at that moment, but rather as what he would become once his personality was refined by his Torah learning.

Even without the benefit of Rabbi Yochanan's high level of perception, we can be sure that every person put into this world was put here for a positive purpose, to perform the tasks that are hers alone to perform. **Hashem makes no mistakes. He does not create anything or anyone without a purpose.** Therefore, even if we come across someone in our lives whose only purpose seems to be to upset and annoy other people, we cannot go wrong by assuming that this person, too, is worthy of respect because of the potential she has inside.

Often we judge others' value according to our own way of behaving, dressing, speaking and acting. "Normal" and "good" are often defined in our minds as "just like me," and differences become "weird" and "bad." **Yet the Chofetz Chaim teaches that our different strengths and weaknesses are literally** what make the world go around. He explains that in the *berachah* of *Borei Nefashos*, we praise Hashem for creating a variety of people– *v'chesronon*, "and their deficiencies." No one comes complete in himself: the patient needs the doctor, the doctor needs the grocer, even the *gadol hador* needs his *gabbai*. By structuring the world this way, Hashem ensured that we would be bound together in a network of *chesed,* and *chesed* is what the world is built upon.

When we demean the differences or the flaws and limitations in others, the raw material for *ona'as devarim* is manufactured by the ton. It is only a matter of time before those heaps of negative thoughts turn into spoken words. Even if we manage to tone them down so that our own guilty conscience feels better, those words will deliver their disapproving message.

A higher and more productive approach is that of Rabbi Yochanan. If we try to acknowledge the worth of others, just because Hashem made them and put them into the world, we will be able to see other people's strengths. **We will realize that even their apparent flaws are just the signposts that mark their personal road to growth.** The shy person needs her shyness and the aggressive person needs her aggression. The soft-hearted person needs her softness and the tough girl needs her toughness. Each person has in front of her the opportunity to accomplish something unique with her specific collection of traits and abilities.

By validating a person's value rather than demeaning her for her faults, we can help her channel all her traits—those that are positive and even those that seem negative—into hope, growth and achievement. We need only look at the people in our lives and think, *She is who she is supposed to be. She is the right one for her job.*

Reality Check:

Do I try to see the value of people who arouse a negative response in me? I will look at such people now with an eye toward recognizing that Hashem put them in the world for a positive reason.

What If...

someone's negative traits have a negative influence on me? How can I focus on her value and purpose without exposing myself to harm?

---

17 Teves — לע"נ מאיר בן ר' שמואל ז"ל
לזכות שמשון יחזקאל בן אהובה רבקה נ"י
17 Iyar — לע"נ ישראל בן דב ז"ל
Dedicated by the Farkovits family
18 Elul — Dedicated as a *z'chus* for Yonatan Yehoshua *ben* Esther, *n"y*

Be a Visionary ~ Focus on others' potential 257

DAY 108

The Remedy
~ Caring for others

י״ח טבת
18 Teves/Cycle 1

י״ח אייר
18 Iyar/Cycle 2

י״ט אלול
19 Elul/Cycle 3

> Malkie tried hard to keep her room perfectly clean and neat. She had come up with the design for the room herself, choosing the paint, bedding, curtains and rug and then coordinating all the other details. Every time she walked into her room, she enjoyed it as much as she had on the day it was finished. Naturally, the carefully coordinated décor could not shine through if the room was a mess, and so Malkie made sure to always put away her clothes, make her bed and keep every item in its assigned place.
>
> When Malkie's sister asked if she could use the clean, clear homework table in Malkie's room to prepare a project for her art class, Malkie's answer was, "Absolutely not, no way." The idea was not, in her mind, even a possibility.
>
> Why not? The reason was that Malkie cared for her room scrupulously. She invested a tremendous amount of her time and energy in designing it and keeping it in pristine condition. Her room meant a lot to her, and so she would never be inclined to do anything that might mar it or detract from its beauty.

The same way, when someone takes great care of another person, damaging that person runs against her grain. **It makes no sense to hurt someone that we spend our energy nurturing**. A doctor does not want to see someone he has cured become sick. A teacher does not want to see someone she has tutored fail. What we invest in, we protect.

That means that if we invest in other people's happiness, we will not want to see them hurt. Therefore, a powerful way to prevent *ona'as devarim* is to use our words to

258   Chapter Fourteen: Strategies

bring encouragement, confidence and happiness to others. By strengthening our ability in this vital trait, we give ourselves the opportunity to become real VIPs (Very Important People): people who know how to provide a shoulder to lean on when our friends face difficulties.

We do not need to have the answer for others' troubles or the cure for their illness, but we can help people see that Hashem is there with them in their dark time. Someone may be in pain, but she does not have to feel alone when she has a friend who can be there for her and gently reconnect her with the real Source of comfort.

Becoming such a person is not as difficult as we may think. All that is required is an *ayin tovah*—an eye that looks for the good in others; and *lashon tov*—a mouth that speaks well of others. We often see something we admire or appreciate, but we don't mention it. For instance, someone makes a great presentation in class, but by the time class is over, we forget to tell her how much we admired her work. Or someone cooks a dish we particularly like, but we don't remember to praise it.

By learning to notice the good and then mention it, we can reconstruct our entire way of interacting with others. The positive words that come out of this mind-set are our investment in the people around us. Our world becomes our beautiful room, a place of our own design, and we will naturally keep from doing or saying anything to damage it.

Reality Check:

Do I make an effort to say to people the positive things I think about them? I will try to make a stronger effort to see and say good things to others.

What If...

Malkie's room had been an ugly old wreck? Would it then be all right to add to the mess? In other words, if we have not yet become invested in making others happy, does that mean we have nothing to lose by hurting them?

לע״נ אסתר ריזל בת חיים דוד ע״ה נלב״ע כ״ה טבת — **18 Teves**
לע״נ שרה דבורה בת חיים מרדכי ע״ה נלב״ע י״ז אייר — **18 Iyar**
Dedicated by the Strauss family
19 Elul — In honor of our dear son נ״י לזכות ארי׳ פנחס יחזקאל בן חנה רחל

The Remedy ~ Caring for others

DAY 109

Word Exchange
~ Choosing the softest words

י"ט טבת
19 Teves/Cycle 1

י"ט אייר
19 Iyar/Cycle 2

כ אלול
20 Elul/Cycle 3

When Esther's parents left her in charge of the household, there was one thing Esther knew for sure. She had to lay down the law with her noisy, messy little siblings. As the oldest of seven children, she had no problem using her authority to get things done.

On one such night, Esther was working hard to get her twin 7-year-old brothers off to bed. She walked into the playroom where they had been playing quietly, only to discover popcorn scattered across the floor and a puddle of spilled apple juice with dozens of Legos swimming around in it like a flock of colorful ducks.

Her first impulse was to scream at them. "You guys always leave everything such a mess!"

Imagine if instead, she wrote those words on a piece of paper and studied them carefully.

"You": It's an accusation. Better to start with "I."

"Always": Not true. Sometimes they cleaned up very nicely.

"Everything": Again not true. They kept their school bags neat and organized.

"Mess": Negative. Why not concentrate on the positive idea of "neat"?

When the twins came downstairs to get bedtime snacks, they saw Esther standing at the playroom door. "Guys," she said, "Mommy will be so happy if she comes home to a neat house. Can we get this room cleaned up?"

The imaginary scene stops here. But we know that Esther managed to pass along a positive picture to her brothers. They got the message that a clean room would make their mother happy, and whether they helped a lot or a little, they probably pitched in to get the playroom in order.

The *Medrash* in *Vayikra* (33:1) tells of a feast at which Rabbi Yehudah HaNasi served tongue to his students. Noticing that each of them ate only the softest parts, Rabbi Yehudah taught his students a lesson: Just as they preferred the softest part of the tongue, others prefer the softest part of *our* tongues. We must speak gently.

Sometimes when we are in a position of authority we feel we must "lay down the law" when people don't perform up to par. However, when Hashem rebuked Miriam and Aaron for speaking *lashon hara* about their brother Moshe (*Bamidbar* 12:6), Rashi states that Hashem spoke gently. *Sifsei Chachamim* explains that Hashem did so because otherwise Aaron and Miriam might not have accepted His rebuke; even the Ultimate Authority, Hashem, softens His rebuke when speaking to righteous people who would be expected to accept His words.

Once we realize that a soft approach is important, we need tools to help us use this approach. For instance, **we can start with words that prepare the listener for something she might not want to hear**: "Unfortunately…" or "I'm sorry to tell you this, but…." We can also **state the problem in terms that are not absolute**: "It seems that…" or "It looks to me like…." It also helps to **downplay the issue** with words like, "a slight problem," or "a little mistake."

As we enter adult life, we are increasingly put in positions in which we become responsible for correcting others. If we speak without thinking, these words can bring about disputes and hurt feelings instead of improvement. By exchanging each harsh word for a softer one, our rebuke may be received not as a blow, but as a helping hand.

> **Reality Check:**
>
> Do I tend to choose the strongest words I can find in order to make my point? I will exchange those words for softer ones so that my words will be accepted.

> **What If…**
>
> we say something in the softest way possible and no one pays attention? Are we then allowed to use stronger language?

---

19 Teves — Rabbi Yosef Kalter *z"l* לע"נ יוסף בן נפתלי שמעון ז"ל נלב"ע כ"א טבת • Dedicated by friends from Milwaukee

19 Iyar — As a *z'chus* for *brachah*, health and happiness for our family
Dedicated by Mr. and Mrs. Miller

20 Elul — Dedicated as a *z'chus* for our children

DAY 110

Reading the Signs
~ Picking up nonverbal cues

כ טבת
20 Teves/Cycle 1

כ אייר
20 Iyar/Cycle 2

כ"א אלול
21 Elul/Cycle 3

The world is filled with signs: "Stop," "Danger," "Welcome," "Go Slow." The wise person pays attention to the signs and acts accordingly. We would walk into a store marked "Welcome" wearing a very different facial expression and posture than we would wear entering a store marked "Beware of Dog."

People's facial expressions and body language also bear signs: "I'm tired," "I'm annoyed," "I'm relaxed," "I'm interested." Those signs act as a warning to others, letting them know where danger might lie and advising them on how to prepare themselves. A face that says "I'm exhausted" is telling us not to choose that moment to flood the person with requests or questions. A face that says "I'm angry" tells us not to push the issue further at that moment.

But what good does a sign do if we do not read it, or worse yet, if we intentionally ignore the warning? If we do not pay attention to the cues other people provide for us, we often find ourselves on the receiving end of an angry response. In our minds, we've done nothing wrong: "I just asked a simple question and she exploded!" But in reality, we ignored the person's unspoken request—made through the look on her face, her posture or perhaps the circumstances around her—to stand clear.

Why would we put ourselves in the path of the anger that we are bound to provoke by ignoring the "signs"? Sometimes we are so preoccupied with our own thoughts and needs that we don't really notice the other person. A child might come home every night and ask, "What's for supper?" without noticing that, on this night, her mother looks as though she hasn't slept in days. A girl might accost her older sister the second she comes home from work: "I need a new skirt for a wedding tomorrow

262 Chapter Fourteen: Strategies

night. Can you take me shopping?" She doesn't notice that her sister's face says, "I need to relax for a while."

Sometimes the situation surrounding a person is enough of a cue to tell us that our question or request would not be welcome. When someone is in the midst of a tense situation, handling a big job, dealing with a cranky child, studying for a test, speaking on the phone or anything that demands focus, this is also a "sign" to wait for a better moment.

None of this, of course, excuses a harsh response. If the person who posts the "sign" dumps a load of *ona'as devarim* on the person who ignored the warning, it is still *ona'as devarim*. She certainly has choices other than a verbal attack. She could say calmly, "I'm sorry, but I need a little time before I deal with this."

But by "reading the signs," we can avoid starting the drama in the first place. Furthermore, we avoid the possibility that we will be insulted by the other person's annoyed response and answer back with *ona'as devarim* of our own.

Being sensitive to other people's facial expressions and body language does not mean that we should have to "walk on eggshells" around people in our lives who are abnormally moody. If that situation exists, professional advice may be needed. But within the range of normal human relationships, sensitivity to others' ups and downs goes a long way to keeping the peace, showing empathy and ultimately finding the right time and way to express ourselves so that our words will be heard.

Reality Check:

Do I pay attention to people's expressions, body language and surrounding circumstances when I speak to them? I will focus on people when I speak to them so that I can recognize and respond to the "signs" on their face.

What If...

you know it's a bad time to make a request, but the request must be made at that moment? How can you show empathy with the other person's mood or circumstance while still having your need met?

20 Teves — לע"נ הרבנית רחל בת רב אהרן ע"ה נלב"ע כ"ב טבת
20 Iyar — לזכות לחינוך הבנים
21 Elul — Manya (Dulman) Weichselbaum *a"h* לע"נ מרים בת חיים ע"ה
Dedicated by Judith Rottenberg and Miriam Arnstein

DAY 111

Pass It Along
~ Relating others' praises

כ"א טבת
21 Teves/Cycle 1

כ"א אייר
21 Iyar/Cycle 2

כ"ב אלול
22 Elul/Cycle 3

Mrs. Schor was leaving the bakery on a Friday afternoon, holding heavy bags of cakes and cookies. As she was about to step out the door, she noticed Mrs. Kaufman standing in the cashier's line. She turned back into the store and made her way through the crowd.

"Mrs. Kaufman! I'm glad I saw you before I walked out the door," said Mrs. Schor.

"I came back inside just to tell you that your Sara is a delight to teach," Mrs. Schor continued. "She has such a good head on her shoulders. Whenever she raises her hand, I know a good question is coming. She listens and thinks and really adds to the class."

"Thank you!" Mrs. Kaufman replied. "That's so nice to hear."

When Mrs. Kaufman got home, Sara was sitting in the kitchen eating lunch. Mrs. Kaufman repeated Mrs. Schor's glowing words to her. "She came back into the store and cut through the whole big crowd just to tell me," Mrs. Kaufman added. Sara felt happy to hear that her abilities and her contributions to the class were really noticed.

When she went back to school the next week, she came well prepared for Mrs. Schor's class. She had read her homework material carefully and looked for some extra commentaries to deepen her understanding. She wanted to make sure that she could ask some good questions and get some good discussion going. If Mrs. Schor considered her such an asset to the class, then she wanted to make sure she kept up her reputation.

264   Chapter Fourteen: Strategies

We all know the negative impact of hearing unkind words passed along about ourselves. But people don't often think about the opposite: the ripple effect of positive words being passed along. **We all love to hear that something nice was said about us.** It builds our self-esteem, and more importantly, it deepens our desire to keep doing the good thing for which we were praised.

For instance, a girl who hears, "Your mother tells me that she doesn't know how she would be able to make Shabbos without your help," will want to keep helping. If she hears "Your campers say you're their best counselor ever," she will make a supreme effort to keep up her reputation. If someone tells her, "A girl from your school says everyone loves you," she will want to be even kinder toward her friends.

People long to feel appreciated. We can accomplish that by praising someone to her face, but the other person might suspect in the back of her mind that the words are being said "just to be nice." **When she hears that she was praised to another person the praise rings true, because there isn't likely to be an ulterior motive.**

Aharon HaKohen used this method to build peace and friendship among people. He would tell each person how highly the other person thought of him, and in that way he created warm feelings between people.

We often hear good things about someone. By becoming a little more aware of the positive effects these words can have, we can remember to stash the compliment away in our minds and give it as a gift to the other person at the right moment. **Hearing the praise from a third party takes the positive message of the comment and magnifies it many times**. It gives the other person the encouragement to keep on doing what she does well, and the blessing of knowing she is appreciated.

> **Reality Check:**
> When I hear a compliment about someone, do I pass it along? I will try to remember to do so.

> **What If...**
> Sara already knows that Mrs. Schor thinks highly of her? Is her mother's report still important?

---

21 Teves — In honor of Mayer Rose Viders - Meira Rochel *bas* Daphna Pesel שתחי׳

21 Iyar — May today's learning be a *z'chus* for Klal Yisrael.

22 Elul — לע״נ יוסף בן פנחס ז״ל
Dedicated by Laurence & Michal Mammon

Pass It Along ~ Relating others' praises

DAY 112

Going Another Round
~ Avoiding pointless conflicts

כ"ב טבת
22 Teves/Cycle 1

כ"ב אייר
22 Iyar/Cycle 2

כ"ג אלול
23 Elul/Cycle 3

Behind their backs, the two oldest Bluestein children, Reuven and Ruth, were known by the neighborhood kids as the "Battling Bluesteins." As one family friend put it, "They can't even agree if it's day or night." It didn't matter what the issue was; it caused a fight. It was a nonstop competition for a prize that didn't exist.

Reuven, 12, and Ruth, 10, both had hot tempers, loud voices and no shame when it came to displaying their fireworks in front of whoever happened to be visiting.

For the rest of the Bluestein children, the situation was no joke. They were embarrassed to invite their friends to their house for fear of the ridiculous drama they would surely witness, and very likely talk about to others. As much as the Bluestein parents tried to get control of the situation, it was like trying to get a match not to ignite gasoline.

The fighting lasted through their teen years, but eventually Reuven and Ruth grew up, calmed down and became quite close. When they got married, their spouses got along and their children were close.

One Shabbos when Reuven and his family were visiting the Bluestein parents, a younger sibling, Dovid, was also visiting with his family.

"Remember how Ruthie and I used to fight?" Reuven reminisced with his brother. "Boy, we could really get after each other. But then we stopped, and you want to know why?"

"Yeah. Why?" Dovid asked, trying to cover up the unwelcome stirring of his painful memories. Didn't Reuven realize how everyone else had suffered?

"Because we realized that it wasn't worth it. We never solved anything. It was just the same fight over

and over again for ten years. We just lost interest in it and moved on. I wish it would have happened sooner. We would have saved ourselves a lot of grief."

There are some people in our lives with whom we tend to re-enact the same script, with minor variations, over and over again. Nothing ever gets solved. For instance, siblings might compete for their parents' favor. As babies and toddlers, they fight over toys or who gets held on their mother's lap. They get older and now the fight is over who gets to ride in the front seat or tell her story first or get the first slice of cake. In the teen years, the fights revolve around still other issues.

In some cases, people outgrow their conflicts and build a more productive relationship; in other cases, the competition persists. Even though the theme and the conflict stay the same, the "characters" in the play keep feeling the need to go another round. **With each round, they create more hurt feelings and add more resentment to each other's bag of grudges.**

If a conflict can lead to a solution of a valid issue, then it is most likely valuable to calmly, respectfully play out the conflict to a conclusion. However, many arguments just go around in circles, getting nowhere.

There is only one way to prevent the pain and hurt that comes with pointless conflict. Refuse to give in to it. Realize that, you will eventually come to see that you've wasted a lot of time and energy on things that were not, after all, very important.

Reality Check:
Are there people with whom I am in frequent conflict? If so, I will try to figure out what the underlying issue is and either work to calmly resolve it or, if it can't be resolved, drop it.

What If...
Reuven had realized the fights with his sister were useless, but Ruthie kept picking fights? How could Reuven respond to end the cycle?

---

22 Teves — In memory of Seymour Fiedler z"l לע"נ שמעי בן אלידהו ז"ל
Dora Mandis לזכות לרפואה שלמה דבורה בת רבקה שתחי׳

22 Iyar — Dedicated as a *z'chus* for the Hess family

23 Elul — May today's learning be a *z'chus* for our משפחה.
Dedicated by Moshe and Shulamit Soleimani

Going Another Round ~ Avoiding pointless conflicts

DAY 113

Take 15
~ Cooling down from anger

כ"ג טבת
23 Teves/Cycle 1

כ"ג אייר
23 Iyar/Cycle 2

כ"ד אלול
24 Elul/Cycle 3

As Chavi walked up the pathway to her house, she could already smell the sharp odor of burnt challah.

"I asked Zehava to watch the challahs," she thought. "I asked her to do one simple thing and she forgot all about it. How can a 14-year-old girl be so dense?"

As she opened the door, a light fog of smoke irritated her eyes. The fan above the stove was on high and the kitchen door was open. "At least she tried to air out the house," Zehava thought. But when she looked on the counter and she saw that her carefully shaped loaves had turned into four braided lumps of coal, she felt like exploding. Now she would have to go back out into the Friday-afternoon crowds and buy challah from the store. So much for being ready for Shabbos early.

Zehava came running down the stairs and into the kitchen.

"Chavi, I'm sorry," she said sincerely. "I just completely forgot about…"

"No kidding, you forgot!" Chavi interrupted. "Do you ever think about anything besides yourself?"

She saw her sister's hurt expression, but that did not stop her. She believed that Zehava needed to know how angry she was, to learn that being irresponsible has consequences. After this, she would never forget again.

"I can't count on you for anything!" Chavi continued. "Even Miri (their 6-year-old sister) is more responsible!"

Zehava saw that there was nothing she could say to turn off Chavi's temper. But Chavi did not see anything. She was blind to the fact that her hurtful words were not teaching her sister responsibility. They were only expressing her disappointment over the ruined challahs.

Ten minutes later, as Chavi arrived at the grocery

268   Chapter Fourteen: Strategies

store, she began to regret her words. But they had already been spoken, and were churning miserably in Zehava's heart.

Reality Check:

The next time I get angry over someone's misdeed, I will refrain from responding right away. After I calm down I will ask myself, "Is what she did so terrible, or am I upset over the disappointment or inconvenience she caused?"

When someone disappoints us, our first reaction is often anger, directly followed by excuses for our anger. "She was wrong." "She deserves it." "She should know better." With these excuses, we convince ourselves that letting out our anger on the other person is the fair and right thing to do.

The problem is that, as the burning anger cools down, we begin to feel differently. We realize that the situation could have been addressed without *ona'as devarim*. The ego that was screaming, "How can you do this to me!" has a chance to settle down, and the wrong begins to appear in its true form, as a mistake or a single bearable inconvenience.

If we want to avoid the regret that always follows when we hurt others out of anger, we can use one simple strategy: to step back from the situation for 15 minutes. We can distract ourselves with some other activity. In that time our temper will subside, and we will see the situation from a calmer perspective. We will come to realize that the harsh words we wanted to say would not fix the problem. They cannot repair what was broken, recover what was lost or undo what was done.

Trying to repair a situation with hurtful words is like trying to repair a broken item with a sledgehammer. The Torah urges us not to make this mistake, but instead to choose words that strengthen and uplift ourselves and the people we deal with.

What If...

Zehava had been the one who made the challahs? Would Chavi have reacted so angrily? Why or why not?

23 Teves — לע"נ אסתר בת חיים הלוי ע"ה נלב"ע כ"ו טבת
Dedicated by her children Reuven Sarett and Devorah Berger

23 Iyar — לע"נ אסתר בת משה ע"ה
Dedicated by the Steger family

24 Elul — לע"נ חי' מלכה בת יעקב שלמה הכהן שכטר ע"ה
מאת משפחת פרנקל

Take 15 ~ Cooling down from anger 269

DAY 114

No Offense
~ Overlooking insults

כ"ד טבת
24 Teves/Cycle 1

כ"ד אייר
24 Iyar/Cycle 2

כ"ה אלול
25 Elul/Cycle 3

A long line of excited teens waited for a chance on the go-cart course. As they watched the lucky drivers who were already out on the track, a buzz began circulating up and down the line. "Look! That boy is racing with no hands on the steering wheel!" The boy was shouting and whooping with delight one minute, but the very next moment he flew off the track and flipped over onto the grass. His whooping was replaced by a low groan as he gripped his broken, bleeding leg.

A person whose emotions have overwhelmed her good sense is like a person who lets go of the steering wheel as she speeds along the track. Damage and pain are almost inevitable.

There is one strategy, however, that can go very far to keep our emotions under control and in that way reduce the chances that we will speak damaging, insulting words. That is to learn how to overlook insults. An insult is one of the most powerful forces that pull a person's hands off the emotional steering wheel. The sharp pain of an insult seems to flip a switch inside us almost before we've completely absorbed what the other person has said. We strike back with our own insult, and soon the situation spins out of control; we say things we will regret and inflict pain we would never have intended.

If we learn to shrug off insults, we provide ourselves with powerful protection against the verbal "accidents" that happen when we lose control of our emotions. **In fact, the *Sefer HaChinuch* (§338) teaches that by responding calmly or with humor to an insult, we little by little reduce the amount of insult that comes into our lives.** Eventually we find that if we are careful in how we speak to others, the

270 Chapter Fourteen: Strategies

only people who insult us are fools. Since fools' opinions are meaningless, we do not have to pay attention to their words or come back with an answer.

There is, however, one vital exception to this advice. We are never required to stand by and allow our dignity to be attacked by others. Even while advising a calm, cool response to insults, the *Sefer HaChinuch* emphasizes that if someone is being harassed, she is entitled to defend herself just as she would from a physical attack. This is crucial to keep in mind when dealing with someone who does not just toss out the occasional insult, but demeans another person to the point of verbal abuse. If we think that this may be the case, we are obligated to speak to a rav or mental health professional to find out how to handle it.

Normally, however, a tremendous load of conflict and hurt—even long-lasting feuds—can be avoided altogether by learning how to step back from an insult. **Being offended is a choice a person makes; she does not have to rise to the bait**. In fact, the *Sefer Hachinuch* teaches the valuable concept that if we are insulted and do not respond in kind, we merit tremendous blessings in life. All of us can earn these blessings if we let someone else's thoughtless words or careless comment evaporate into the air and disappear without leaving a nick, scratch or dent.

Reality Check:

When someone insults me, do I feel that I have to defend my pride and hit back with my own insult or other form of revenge? I will consider the benefits that would result if I just "let it slide."

What If...

you try to "let it slide" but your hurt feelings will not go away? How can you handle those emotions?

---

24 Teves — לע"נ שרה אסתר ע"ה בת ר' ישראל חיים יבלחט"א
Sorala (Follman) Krigsman *a"h* נלב"ע כה' טבת תשע"ב
24 Iyar — לע"נ ברכה בת ר' יעקב דוד ע"ה
Dedicated by the Sanders family, Passaic, NJ
25 Elul — In memory of Yirmiyahu Yitzchok *ben* Moshe Yechezkel *z"l*

DAY 115

Bouncing Back
~ Dealing with insults

כ"ה טבת
25 Teves/Cycle 1

כ"ה אייר
25 Iyar/Cycle 2

כ"ו אלול
26 Elul/Cycle 3

Months had gone by, and still Michal and Shiffy were at war. It all started when Shiffy began hearing from other girls in her class some private information that only Michal knew. Disgusted that her confidence had been violated, Shiffy angrily confronted Michal. But Michal denied saying anything to anyone.

Now, a week before Purim, Michal had decided to try to mend the friendship. She called Shiffy and told her, "I know you still don't believe me, but I think it's ridiculous for us to be walking around angry at each other. Why don't we just have a truce? We'll leave the subject of who told the secret to be solved when Mashiach comes."

"You know, you're really nuts. There's something really wrong with you," Shiffy said. "You don't take anything seriously. How can I ever trust you?"

Shiffy's words stung. But why? Michal knew she hadn't betrayed her friend's secret. She knew she could be trusted. So why did it matter what Shiffy said? Why did the insult hurt?

Why *was* Michal hurt? The reason was that somewhere inside her, she feared that Shiffy's words might contain a bit of truth. She never felt that she was quite like everyone else, so maybe she really was "nuts."

For an insult to deliver its sting, it has to hit a person where she is vulnerable. Otherwise the recipient would just shake her head and think, *I don't know what she's talking about.* For instance, if Michal had been so self-confident and well respected that other girls came to her for advice, Shiffy's comment that

272   Chapter Fourteen: Strategies

there is something wrong with her would not have meant anything to Michal at all.

Another factor that makes an insult hurtful is when it attacks an area that is important to the person's self-image. If Shiffy had said "Someone like you would never become president of the United States," that verdict would not have hurt her. Becoming president was nothing she ever wanted, planned or believed she could do. But being considered normal is important to a girl.

It is worthwhile to try to understand why an insult makes us feel hurt or angry, because being able to regain our footing after being insulted helps greatly in controlling our response. If we examine the statement and see some little kernel of truth in it, we can try to drop our defense and deal with the message. Even if the messenger made a big error in speaking hurtfully, the message itself can be valuable, just as a bad-tasting medicine might still treat an illness. [**Note: At times another person's hostility can be excessive or destructive. If this seems to be the case, it is important to seek help from a knowledgeable, objective person.**]

On the other hand, if we think about the insult and conclude that there is no truth to it, we can dismiss it as irrelevant. While we may be disappointed at the insensitivity of the person who insulted us, we can at least cool our response with the knowledge that her words were nothing more than meaningless noise.

The alternative to learning how to bounce back from an insult is to be locked into an endless round of *ona'as devarim*. She insults you, you insult her back, she says something even worse and you respond in kind. If instead we try to understand why we feel insulted, we can actually grow from the message hidden in the insult, or if the words are baseless, we can let them roll off our backs and out of our lives.

> **25 Teves** — In memory of Harold Groner z"l לע"נ צבי בן יעקב יוסף ז"ל
> Dedicated by his children Zev & Chavi Groner and family
> **25 Iyar** — לע"נ הרב שלמה בן נפתלי מרגלית זצ"ל - נלב"ע יד' שבט
> והרבנית חוה רבקה מרגלית בת אברהם ע"ה - נלב"ע כה' אייר
> **26 Elul** — לע"נ הרב שמואל אליהו בן הרב רפאל אומן יבלחט"א
> Dedicated by Rabbi & Mrs. Refoel Auman and family

Reality Check:

How do I respond when someone says something I find insulting? Instead of responding with insults of my own, I will think about why I feel insulted, and honestly evaluate whether there was a message in the words that I needed to hear.

What If...

Michal did not want to let Shiffy's insulting statement stand? What could she have said without adding more *ona'as devarim* to the situation?

Chapter 15

Starting Now

We've come a long way together in our understanding of the power of our words. We know that our happiness in life depends on our success in building positive relationships. We have strategies to use as we try to make changes in our day-to-day lives, and now we are ready to start. Our first giant step is to wipe the slate clean of *ona'as devarim,* and commit ourselves to following the Torah's perfect wisdom on living a beautiful life.

DAY 116

Creating a Pearl
~ Teshuvah

כ"ו טבת
26 Teves/Cycle 1

כ"ו אייר
26 Iyar/Cycle 2

כ"ז אלול
27 Elul/Cycle 3

For an oyster to create a pearl, a small grain is inserted inside it. The oyster responds to the irritation by releasing nacre, the glowing white substance that hardens into a precious pearl. For Tehilla, teshuvah started the same way: A small, quiet thought began irritating the inside of her mind. This grain of doubt caused the release of a precious substance: sincere repentance.

The first thought of teshuvah did not occur to Tehilla on its own. As in the production of a pearl, the grain was forced into her. It happened in the process of a bitter argument with Avigayil, her closest friend.

"You think you're popular," Avigayil said bluntly. "But you know what? You're a girl who hurts other people. You make girls feel left out and you act like nobody's good enough for you. I'm only telling you this because I don't think you even realize what you're doing. But you have to know. Eventually this stuff comes back to you."

Since that shocking conversation, Tehilla's mind had been filled with pictures: hurt expressions, eyes tearing up, heads turning away to avoid her eyes, phony smiles of girls who were dying to be her friends. She really had made a mess, but could she still clean it up?

Hashem gives His imperfect creation—mankind—a way to work toward perfection through the path of *teshuvah*. **A person may never say, "That's the way I am and I can't change."** Change is wired into the universe, available to anyone willing to flip the switch.

The Sages teach (*Yoma* 85b) that sins between G-d and man can be erased by confessing the sin, regretting it, and committing ourselves to staying away from that sin. But when we sin against other people, there's a step we have to take before we can earn a clean slate: we have to ask forgiveness from the person we harmed. To do that, we have to do something that most people find very difficult: we must humble ourselves. That is what it takes to go to another person, admit we've done something wrong, and ask her to forgive us.

If we hurt someone with words, we must first realize that we have caused someone real pain. We cannot justify ourselves by thinking, *She didn't take it seriously*, or *She's said worse to me*, or *It wasn't really an insult* or any other excuse. Once we are able to feel real regret for the harm we caused, we must ask the victim to forgive us, and we must make a commitment to avoid speaking any more hurtful words. The Torah teaches that if the person does not forgive us, we are required to ask a second and even a third time.

For someone who has a habit of speaking harshly, it may eventually become impossible to get forgiveness because her apology will not be believed. In that case, she might have to ask for a chance to prove herself, perhaps by saying, "Give me a month and see if I keep my word." After that, she can ask for forgiveness again.

The sooner we realize that *teshuvah* is necessary, the less painful the process will be. Wounds heal far more easily before they've had a chance to become infected.

Because we have the gift of *teshuvah,* we do not have to leave behind a list of injured parties when we make our inevitable journey into the Next World. We only need to look inside ourselves and find in our hearts the humility and the optimism to begin again.

Reality Check:

Have I hurt anyone with harsh words? Even if said as a joke? I will think about this, and try to do *teshuvah* if I now realize it is needed.

What If...

I think someone might have been insulted by something I said, but she acted as if she did not feel hurt? Should I still apologize? Why or why not?

---

26 Teves — לע״נ שלמה בן ר׳ פסח ז״ל נלב״ע כ״ו טבת
In memory of Shlomo Kupetz • Dedicated by Shmuel and Chaya Esther Idler

26 Iyar — לע״נ אסתר בת יעקב ע״ה נלב״ע כ״ו אייר
Dedicated by Allan and Sheila Bleich

27 Elul — לע״נ שמואל בן משה ז״ל
Dedicated by the Metzger family

DAY 117

Sorry About That
~ Forgiveness

כ"ז טבת
27 Teves/Cycle 1

כ"ז אייר
27 Iyar/Cycle 2

כ"ח אלול
28 Elul/Cycle 3

Naomi couldn't sleep. Every time she thought about what she had said to Batya, her stomach churned. "Can't you do anything right?" she had exploded when Batya knocked over her coffee. Naomi could picture Batya's flustered expression as she scrambled for napkins to sop up the mess.

But, why couldn't Batya be careful? Naomi had to walk around the rest of the day in a damp skirt that smelled.

Still, Batya looked so hurt. Naomi wished she could be easygoing under pressure. She knew she needed to apologize, but it was so hard.

The next day, Naomi saw Batya at lunch. Instead of sitting with Naomi, Batya sat with her older sister. "I really better apologize," Naomi thought. It would be very embarrassing. Yet there was no other way to clear the air.

Naomi started walking toward Batya's table. Then she retreated. "I'll catch her alone later."

Later she saw Batya standing at her locker. She approached, but Batya was already walking away. "I'm not going to chase her down the hall," Naomi thought. "I'll get her while we're waiting for the bus."

After school, the girls stood outside as the buses arrived. Naomi spotted Batya standing alone. "Now or never," she thought. She walked over.

"Batya," Naomi said.

"What," Batya answered flatly, still staring straight ahead.

"Sorry."

Batya turned toward Naomi. "Accepted."

"I have a bad temper," Naomi said, "I gotta get a grip."

"I know. It's O.K.," Batya smiled. "We're still friends."

Despite our best efforts, there will be times when we hurt someone. Even as we become more sensitive to others' feelings, we can't expect perfection. Mistakes do not make us bad people; they simply reflect the fact that we are human. **Admitting our mistakes is what sets us free to grow**. So how do we repair *ona'as devarim*?

As we have learned, a key step in *teshuvah* is to ask forgiveness of the person we've hurt. For most of us, however, this is difficult. In the story above, Naomi made several false starts before she got over her embarrassment and said the word "sorry." By saying that one word, she gave Batya a chance to acknowledge the hurt and set the friendship back on solid ground. Rather than trying to brush the insult under the rug, Naomi was able to alleviate her guilt and Batya was able to let go of her hurt. **For the apology to do its job of wiping the slate clean, the guilty party has to accept blame without excuses**. If Naomi had said, "I'm sorry I hurt your feelings but you should have been more careful," that would not have been a true apology. "I was wrong" is the only relevant message.

On the other side of the equation is the imperative to forgive. When someone apologizes to us, we have the opportunity to earn incredible merit and Hashem's forgiveness of our sins if we accept their effort to make amends. We also benefit ourselves by gaining peace of mind and preserving our friendship.

It takes humility both to say and to accept "I'm sorry," but a small dose of humility is the nourishment for many, many of the *middos* that feed our spiritual growth.

Reality Check:

Do I ever apologize when I'm wrong, or do I tend to justify myself by blaming the victim or deciding that the insult was not really insulting? I will plan a better approach and think of words I would be comfortable saying when I need to apologize.

What If...

Naomi could not bring herself to say "I'm sorry" to Batya's face? Are there any other ways she could achieve forgiveness?

---

27 Teves — לע"נ פייגא נעשא פרסר בת בנימין הכהן ע"ה
Dedicated by Marilyn and Jaime Sohacheski

27 Iyar — Marty Halpern z"l לע"נ מאיר בן ישראל ז"ל
Dedicated by his grandchildren and great-grandchildren

28 Elul — לע"נ הרב ישראל איסר בן כתריאל ז"ל
Dedicated by the Farkovits family

DAY 118

The Sure Cure
~ Daily learning

כ"ח טבת
28 Teves/Cycle 1

כ"ח אייר
28 Iyar/Cycle 2

כ"ט אלול*
*29 Elul/Cycle 3

*On 29 Elul, the lesson for Day 119 should be learned together with today's lesson.

> "Sit outside in the sun for two hours a day and the pain will go away," the doctor told Tzippi.
>
> Each day, Tzippi did what the doctor ordered. She sat on a lawn chair by her camp's beautiful swimming pool as the sun blazed in the sky. A few weeks went by, but her pain was not going away. In fact, it seemed to be getting worse.
>
> She returned to the doctor. "I don't know why it's not working," she said, "but it isn't. I'm doing exactly what you told me to do, sitting two hours a day in the sun, and I'm only getting worse."
>
> "That's strange," the doctor said. "This always works. Tell me, what time of day are you sitting outside?"
>
> "From 2 to 4 in the afternoon," she said.
>
> "And where exactly do you sit?"
>
> "By the pool under a big umbrella."
>
> "I see," said the doctor. "But how do you expect the sun to help you if you block it?"

Hashem gave the world a cure for everything that ails us, and that is the Torah. A person who learns and lives by the Torah exposes herself to its unequalled powers to cure our souls and give them health and energy. With a healthy soul, we find that negativity and cruelty are repulsive to us. A person who absorbs the Torah is filled with light, and she naturally wants to radiate light, not pain and darkness, into the world.

Therefore, if a person attaches herself to the Torah and spends her energy doing its *mitzvos*, she will find herself greatly strengthened in her fight against negative, hurtful speech. She will become someone who is not easily angered, and therefore not easily pushed into displays of temper. She will develop an appreciation for all that Hashem has given her, and steer clear of the jealousy that sometimes motivates us to insult another person.

Most importantly, she will build a love of Hashem, His Torah, and His people. She will naturally want to live in a way that pleases Hashem.

Despite the Torah's tremendous ability to cure us of spiritual ills, we all know those who learn and keep the *mitzvos* and yet still fall into the habit of *ona'as devarim*. We might wonder how that can be. Why doesn't the light of Torah fill this person and change her into someone who spreads light?

The answer can be found in the scenario above. **For the Torah to work its cure, we have to expose ourselves to it.** There are people who sit under an umbrella, with the Torah shining all around them but little of it reaching their souls. What makes up the umbrella? Sometimes people perform the *mitzvos*, but their hearts and minds are not involved. Then Torah becomes nothing more than an obligation that feels like a bother. The negative feelings block the light, and the Torah cannot reach the person's soul.

Hashem gave us the Torah as a way to become close to Him. Otherwise there is no way a person would know how to do this, or even believe that she has the power to do it. When we see the Torah and *mitzvos* as a way to bask in Hashem's light, the light is sure to penetrate our hearts. We become higher, happier people: people who bring light into the world.

Reality Check:

Do I really take the Torah's messages into my heart? I will try to think of positive speech as a way to please Hashem, and let the Torah become a bigger part of who I am.

What If...

some groups of girls are not so serious about the Torah's *mitzvos* on interacting with other people? How can a girl become more sincere if her friends might see her as strange?

---

28 Teves — In memory of Alex Lowinger z"l — לע"נ ישראל חיים בן נחום הלוי ז"ל
Dedicated by his sons Robert and Eddie Lowinger

28 Iyar — In honor of the Chofetz Chaim Heritage Foundation

29 Elul — לזכות חנה בת רבקה גיטל שתחי'
לזכות נחמה פיגא רחל בת שרה שתחי'

DAY 119

In Other Words
~ Test your understanding

כ"ט טבת
29 Teves/Cycle 1

כ"ט אייר
29 Iyar/Cycle 2

כ"ט אלול
29 Elul/Cycle 3

Over the course of the past 118 days, we have learned to recognize *ona'as devarim* and we've studied how it seeps into our lives and our relationships. We've seen how it damages the self-image of those around us, and we have reviewed strategies to help keep this destructive force out of our lives.

Now we invite you to test your understanding. Below are 14 *ona'as devarim* statements. Try to find the constructive purpose hidden in each statement, and propose a way to say what needs to be said without causing unnecessary pain to the listener.

1. Two high school seniors are discussing where they will be going for seminary the next year. "I'm going to Bais Yalda Tova," says one girl. "It's right in the middle of Yerushalayim, very close to the Kosel. I can't wait!" The other girl says, "Not me. I'm staying here in the city. I'm not interested in going to *Eretz Yisrael*." The first girl gapes at her. "That's not normal! Nobody's staying here!" (DAY 36)

2. Graduation is just a few days away. Meira, the yearbook editor, excitedly opens up a carton of the yearbooks which has finally arrived. The first thing she sees as she opens the box is the yearbook cover, which reads "Baid Yaakov Sarah-Rivka-Rochel." Frantically she dials Leah, her co-editor and the proofreader-in-chief. "You messed up big time!" Meira screamed. "Didn't you proofread the cover? We look like total fools! All our effort is wasted because you did a sloppy job. I hope you're happy!" (DAY 44)

3. It's 12:45 p.m. on Sunday afternoon, and Brochie has been waiting a half-hour for her friend Estie to arrive at Bagel Heaven, where they agreed to meet for lunch. Estie is always late, but Brochie has made it very clear to her that this time she, Brochie, has to be home by 1:30. That doesn't seem to matter to Estie, though. At last she glides into the store,

282   Chapter Fifteen: Starting Now

looking like she has just rolled out of bed. "Hi, Brochie!" she says cheerily. Brochie responds, "Estie, really, you're so self-centered! Don't you ever think about other people?" (DAY 49)

4. The Chanukah *chagigah* is tonight, and Leora has offered to stay for an hour after school to help set up. The only problem is that she is supposed to be home to relieve Malkie, the girl who watches her little sister after school. "I'll call Malkie and ask her if she can stay a little longer," Leora decides. She goes to the office and dials her home number. "Hi, Malkie, it's Leora. I have to stay late at school today, so would you mind watching my sister for a little while extra?" Malkie pauses. "Well, O.K.," she agrees. "But come home as fast as you can. You know I can only take your little sister for so long until she starts driving me crazy." (DAY 50)

5. Shoshana lost her father a few years ago. Even so, she is a happy, friendly girl who tries not to feel resentment over her difficult situation. One day a few weeks before Pesach, Shoshana is talking about the coming holiday with her friend Kaila. "I love Pesach," Kaila says. "My father runs such an awesome *Seder*. He has an amazing way of keeping everyone interested and he makes it so much fun…." She stops in her tracks as she looks at Shoshana's eyes. "Oh, sorry," she mumbles, and tries to change the subject. (DAY 58)

6. It's a small thing: Temima's sister's recently dry-cleaned sweater, draped across Temima's bed. "Before you go to school today, could you please put your sweater away?" Temima asks her sister Debby, as the two girls eat their breakfast. Afraid Debby will forget, Temima reminds her again as she gets up to put her dishes in the sink. "The sweater," she says. "Don't forget. I don't want to come home from school and find it still on my bed." As Debby climbs the stairs to the girls' bedroom to gather her school books Temima shouts, "Are you putting the sweater away?" (DAY 66)

7. "Did you get your cavity filled yet?" Shira asks her friend Chana. "I don't have time now," says Chana. "I'm way behind on studying for finals and I still haven't found a dress for my brother's bar mitzvah." "Well, don't forget about it," Shira warns. "My cousin got blood poisoning from a rotten tooth and he almost died! He was in the hospital on IV for a week!" (DAY 68)

8. Eliana always has a little friendly advice to offer her classmates. Whether they want her advice or not, the other girls just accept it. "That's Eliana!" One day, a few months into 11th grade, a new girl joins the class. The new girl, Shaindy, is very thin. At lunch, Eliana sits herself down next to Shaindy and strikes up a conversation. "You really should eat more!" she says. "You're gonna starve!" Later, Eliana finds out that Shaindy is under treatment for a serious illness. (DAY 74)

9. Michal has just spent the past 20 minutes pouring out her complaints about school to her older sister Nechama. Nechama is tired of hearing it; she stomps her foot like a toddler having a tantrum and whines, "It's not fair! I can't take it!" She makes her voice babyish and squeaky in imitation of Michal, a 14-year-old who is tiny for her age. (DAY 81)

10. "Don't feel bad about your father losing his job," Shuli says in a kindly way to her friend Bina. "It happens to lots of families. I shouldn't tell you this, but Chavi told me that her father has been unemployed for the past two months. He's looking for a new job, just like your father is. That's just between you and me, O.K.?" (DAY 83)

11. Raizy's heart is breaking for her friend Mindy. Everyone in their group of friends got a job at the same overnight camp for the summer, but when it came to Mindy there were no positions left. Now she will be home alone, miserable, while all her friends are together at camp. "Wait, I know!" Raizy lights up. "My cousin Sima has been a secretary for that camp for the past five years. I'll bet if she put in a word

for you, they'd be able to find *something* you could do. I'm gonna call her!" Mindy feels hopeful for the first time in weeks. Every day she waits to hear from Raizy about the job… but Raizy keeps forgetting to make the call. (DAY 84)

12. Nava should know better than to put a cake in the oven and then go sit outside on the patio. How many Friday afternoons has she done that, only to be called in by the smoke alarm as her cake turns into coal? Today her brother arrives home from yeshivah, opens the door, and greets Nava as she is fanning the smoke out of the kitchen. "Good job, Nava! What a great wife you're gonna be!" (DAY 89)

13. "We need a superexciting theme for the Mother-Daughter Brunch," Ruchama tells her Special Events Committee. The other girls sit quietly for a minute, trying to come up with some inspiration. "I've got it!" Ruthie shouts. "This will be amazing! It will look gorgeous!" As she begins laying out her theme and her ideas for the decorations, she notices Ruchama staring hard at her. Ruchama's nose is wrinkled and her eyes are narrowed as if she is looking at something strange. Ruthie mutters a few more words and then says, "Well, maybe not." (DAY 95)

14. "My parents are going away this Shabbos," Sara tells Tova. "Can I stay with you?" Tova's house is always full of guests. But last week her brother asked her parents, "Could we have just a family Shabbos next week?" The whole family agreed that it would be a good idea. "Oh, I don't think so this week, Sara, sorry. Can you find someone else to stay with?" Sara shrugs. "Well, O.K. But I know you had Yaelle over last Shabbos. Now I know who your real friend is." (DAY 99)

29 Teves — לע״נ הרב ישראל איסר בן מנחם ז״ל נלב״ע ערב רח׳ שבט כט׳ טבת
Dedicated by the Indich families

29 Iyar — Dedicated as a *z'chus* for our family
By Ephraim and Devorah Rich

29 Elul — לזכות חנה בת רבקה גיטל שתחי׳
לזכות נחמה פיגא רחל בת שרה שתחי׳

In Other Words ~ Test your understanding   285

Don't Shut the Book Yet

On the Receiving End

This book shines a spotlight on the words we speak, opening our eyes to the massive impact they can have upon the people with whom our lives intersect. There is no exception or justification that reduces our responsibility to measure our words and make sure that they cause no unnecessary harm.

However, our relationships with others are two-sided. When we speak to someone, we are obligated to avoid hurting her with our words; but when we are the target of insensitive words, we have an obligation as well, and that is to make a sincere effort to overlook the slight and forgive the speaker, whether she has spoken out of anger, ignorance or misguided good intentions.

Before going any further into this topic we must give one vital warning: Our discussion here is about normal interpersonal relations, in which a certain amount of insensitivity can be expected. A situation in which one party **consistently** dominates, insults and belittles another is one which must be addressed by professionals. Such a situation is defined as abuse, and it must be stopped in order to prevent permanent emotional damage to the victim.

Leaving such situations aside, let's examine interactions between people who are generally emotionally healthy and well meaning. In any situation involving speech and interpersonal relationships, the pain a person feels is subjective. It is not like a broken leg, which, no matter how painful it feels, is still the same broken leg. With words, one person may take a certain comment as a terribly painful insult while another barely notices. Usually, the person who has a stronger sense of self-worth or a more easygoing, forgiving attitude toward other people will tend not to take negative words personally.

Whether we find a comment stinging and hurtful or just clueless and annoying, we are responsible for our response, reaction and behavior. Someone else's hurtful comment does not give us an excuse to feel sorry for ourselves and turn ourselves into the "victim." Even though the other person violated the law against hurting others, we still have the obligation to respond in a forgiving way.

In fact, the entire Jewish approach to interpersonal relationships, says Rav Chaim Shmulevitz, is based on this idea: each person must worry first about fulfilling her *own* obligations.

To illustrate this point, Reb Chaim would cite the statement of *Chazal*: "One should love his wife like himself and honor her more than himself." At the same time our Sages tell us that "a fine wife is one who does her husband's will." We may wonder how this can work. Who is obligated to honor whom? The answer is that if the husband focuses on honoring his wife and the wife focuses on serving her husband, they will have a good marriage. The trouble begins when the husband's first concern is that his wife fulfill her obligation to him, and the wife is primarily concerned with the husband's requirement to honor her.

The same applies to every type of human relationship. Although others are not allowed to speak hurtful words to us, if they do we are obligated to do our best to ignore the insult. If that is too hard, and sometimes it can be very difficult, we have to try our best to forgive and forget, even if the other person does not ask for forgiveness.

Every night when we recite *Krias Shema* before going to sleep, we announce that we forgive anyone who may have angered or antagonized us in any way, whether carelessly or purposely. It is not always easy to actually feel this forgiveness, especially if we are still angry.

We add to this prayer the request that no one be punished on our account. Even when we are insulted, would we really wish for the wrongdoer to suffer Divine punishment? Would we want to see the person ill, broken or worse? In nearly every case, the person who hurt us is someone whose serious troubles would greatly sadden us. Even if she is the snobbiest, most difficult girl in class, we would never want her to fall ill or suffer a serious challenge because of something she has said to us.

Being able to ignore hurtful words is not merely a "nice" character trait. There are powerful benefits for someone who develops this strength of character. *Chazal* (*Rosh Hashanah* 17a) stress that **Hashem forgives *all* the sins of "a person who overcomes his nature and overlooks insult and hurt."** In addition, the Gemara (*Chullin* 89a) tells us that **the world exists in the merit of "he who closes his mouth at a time of strife."** There have been more than a few authentic accounts of the unusual Heavenly blessings which come to people who have managed to overlook and forgive.

But how do we avoid the normal human reaction to an insult? The most effective way is to develop a healthy sense of who we are, along with a sincere belief that no one can really hurt us if Hashem does not want it to be. In addition, we must realize that by not responding or even taking the hurt to heart, we spur tremendous growth in our own spiritual and emotional lives. We develop the emotional strength to ignore hurtful words and insults, real or imagined, and make our journey through life equipped with a peaceful, loving heart.

Afterword
The One You Save May Be Yourself

By now you have read many scenarios and situations that come up in our everyday lives. Through these scenarios you've had a chance to peer into the hearts and minds of people who are coming under verbal attack, and you've seen the pain that is there. In our "What If" discussions, you've been encouraged to think about ways to avoid some of the pitfalls illustrated in this book. So far, this has been a book about how to avoid hurting others.

But there is one more vital point we still must take into account: **this book is just as much about how to avoid hurting ourselves.** That is because those hurtful words we speak, whether we are speaking to strike back at someone or just being careless and insensitive, are in fact a boomerang. The pain they inflict always comes back at us, perhaps not immediately, but eventually.

Most of us have heard remarkable stories about people who suffer from some trouble in their lives that no amount of prayer or *teshuvah* seems to alleviate. The trouble might be in the area of *shidduchim*, health, child-bearing, *parnassah, chinuch* or spirituality. Eventually, someone or something inspires these people to look back on their lives and search for someone they once hurt. When they find that person or people and gain forgiveness, their *yeshuah* finally comes.

Naturally, this does not mean that every person we meet who is dealing with a challenge in his life is guilty of hurting someone. There are many reasons for suffering, and very few people are capable of guiding someone to discover the source of his own difficult situation. Nevertheless, as these stories make clear, it is important to our own happiness and fulfillment in life to be as careful as possible with other people's feelings.

For most of us, though, it would seem to be impossible to be so careful that we never accidentally insult someone or mention a topic they find painful. We see from the scenarios in this book, which are very common, that we do not need to be cold-hearted villains to hurt others. We just have to be a little tense or impatient or inattentive. It would seem, then, that all of us are destined to fall into the trap of *ona'as devarim*.

In that case, we might wonder, what is the point of trying? The answer to that question is that our reward comes from our effort to improve, to become more sensitive and to rid ourselves of the false idea that our interactions with others are "just words." We are judged for who we are, rooted in the lives we've been given. How high we grow from those roots is the measure of our success.

Perhaps no *gadol* in our world today is more passionate about the problems brought by *ona'as devarim* than HaGaon Rav Aharon Leib Shteinman *shlit"a*. As the adviser and comforter to thousands of Jews facing difficult life situations, he has traced these difficulties time and time again to an episode, perhaps long forgotten by the individual, in which pain was inflicted on another. To prevent more of the great suffering he has seen as a result of *ona'as devarim*, he continually urges that an all-out effort be made throughout *Klal Yisrael* to raise people's awareness of the power of the spoken word and the serious repercussions words can have.

The following powerful words are a synopsis of a message endorsed by Rav Shteinman, written by his close *talmid*:

Point # 1: *Ona'as devarim* is a real *aveirah*

The first thing it is important for us to know is that *ona'as devarim* is far more dangerous than it seems at first glance. Because it does not carry the harshest penalties of *kareis* or *misas beis din*, we might assume that hurting someone or saying something hurtful is not considered a particularly serious *aveirah*. Yet the Midrash tells us otherwise.

The Midrash tells the story of Rabbi Shimon ben Gamliel and Rabbi Yishmael, who were taken to be killed by the Romans. When Rabbi Shimon lamented that he did not understand why he was subject to this decree, Rabbi Yishmael asked him if perhaps someone had come to him with a question and he had kept him waiting while he finished his drink or tied his shoe or put on his jacket. If that were the case, explained Rabbi Yishmael, then Rabbi Shimon would be subject to the Torah's dire punishment for afflicting a widow or orphan. But why?

This conversation is explained by the *Yalkut Shimoni*, which teaches that the phrase *kol almanah veyasom lo se'anun*—"you shall not cause pain to any widow or orphan"—includes any vulnerable people; Hashem will see their suffering, whether the affliction someone causes them is great or small. The verse ends with the measure-for-measure consequence of causing such pain: "My wrath will blaze and I will kill you with the sword, and your wives will be widows and your children will be orphans."

Obviously, we are not anywhere near the level of Rabbi Shimon and Rabbi Yishmael, and we are not judged with the same precision as they are. But the *Yalkut* is still speaking to us, telling us that there is a steep price to pay for hurting others, because they have Hashem on their side.

The repercussions may not seem real to us because we do not always see Hashem's justice right away, or even in our lifetime. Sometimes it appears that the wrongdoer goes on to win popularity and success while the victim suffers pain and humiliation. If we ourselves hurt others and do not seem to suffer as a result, we may delude ourselves into thinking that we have escaped responsibility. No matter how it seems to us in our limited view, however, the sin is real and the consequences of it are inevitable—in this world and in the World to Come. And punishment in the World to Come is infinitely more painful and enduring.

Point # 2: Avoiding *ona'as devarim* is central to our mission in life

Rav Shteinman often quotes the Chazon Ish, who said that a person's primary mission in life is to live the 70, 80 or 90 years Hashem gives him without hurting another person. And this is a difficult task. Life constantly places us in situations where our pride and will are challenged by other people.

Lashing out at those who seem to stand in the way of our goals and our happiness is a natural response. Living up to the Torah's standard of *bein adam lachaveiro* takes constant effort, because our natural tendencies will always take us downhill. But as we have just learned, the effort is really self-preservation. The hurtful words we mutter or hurl into the air will only come back to stab us.

On the positive side of the equation, working on this *mitzvah* is a sure road to a higher and happier life. The Talmud relates an incident in which Rabbi Pinchas ben Yair set out to redeem a Jewish captive. He reached a point where he had to cross a river; at his command, the waters parted. He explained to the students who accompanied him—who were also *Tannaim*—that they would be able to do the same thing, but *only* if they had never hurt anyone.

Rav Shteinman points out that Rabbi Pinchas ben Yair did not say that the river would split for one who was never *mechallel Shabbos* or never ate nonkosher food, but *only* for someone who had never hurt another person. It is no wonder, then, that when a gentile asked Hillel to summarize the Torah, Hillel answered, "That which is hateful to you, do not do to another."

Point #3: Good intentions do not prevent damage

Rav Chaim Shmulevitz would point out that the episode of Chana and Penina illustrates that good intentions do not save a person from the repercussions of speaking *onaas devarim*. When Penina taunted Chana about her childlessness, *Chazal* explain that her intention was to goad Chana into praying with more passion, so that ultimately she would merit children. Yet because Penina's taunts caused Chana such pain, Penina's own children died.

Rav Chaim Shmulevitz explains that this episode shows us that there is a cause and effect relationship between *onaas devarim* and troubles. **Just as someone who puts his hand into fire will get burned by it whether or not he intended to touch the fire or it was just an "accident," someone speaking** *onaas devarim* **will be hurt by it, regardless of what her intentions were.**

Point # 4: Seek and grant forgiveness

Unless we've lived the lives of angels, everyone in the world would seem to be on a dangerous road, according to Rav Shteinman's points above. But of course Hashem never places us in a hopeless position. *Teshuvah* is always available to us, and as we know, *teshuvah* for an *aveirah* between ourselves and another person has to start with seeking the wronged person's forgiveness.

That takes a large dose of humility, but it's the humility that gives *teshuvah* its power. As long as we hold our chins stubbornly in the air, our "sorry" doesn't accomplish anything. Therefore, it is worthwhile for every person to think about people in their lives whom they may have hurt, and sincerely ask them to forgive the insult.

The power of seeking forgiveness, even if it is difficult and inconvenient, is almost unimaginable. Rav Shteinman recounts numerous dire personal situations that suddenly resolved themselves after a person realized that he or she had wronged someone and went to the necessary lengths to gain forgiveness.

But what happens if it is no longer possible to find a person and ask forgiveness? What if it happened long ago and we have lost track of the person, or we are not even sure of the person's identity? **The Vilna Gaon said that when we have done absolutely everything we can to find the victim and seek forgiveness, and our heart is truly filled with regret for the incident, Hashem will put forgiveness in the victim's heart even without our asking.**

On the other side of the equation, we are also able to achieve great rewards for ourselves by granting forgiveness to those who ask. We are not allowed to hold onto our status as "victim" indefinitely; the *halachah* requires us to refrain from being cruel and to sincerely forgive those who ask. When we do that, we are helping ourselves even more than the person we are forgiving, for the Gemara tells us that a person who overlooks the respect and consideration due her and forgives the other person has *all* her *aveiros* forgiven.

Rav Chaim Pinchas Scheinberg once pointed out to a group of students that we ask Hashem every day to forgive us. Now, how can we ask Him every day to forgive us when we ourselves are unwilling to forgive others? To really succeed in life, one must be willing to forgive, to forget and to move on.

Point # 5: Find a better way

Rav Shteinman has gone to great lengths to alert us to the great damage *ona'as devarim* does to our own lives and souls. He has also shown us that seeking forgiveness, a process that every person finds difficult and humbling, is the only way to undo the harm. **Clearly, our very best strategy and goal should be to avoid *ona'as devarim* and keep our lives clear of its painful results.**

This book is meant to provide a pathway to an *ona'as devarim*-free life. First we have to realize that so much of what we think of as "just talk" has a major impact on others. Secondly, we have to examine our own motivations and assumptions to discover where these insensitive words are rooted. Then we must work on our hearts—our ability to accept, respect and care about every Jew—so that we will lose our desire to deflate and demean others. Finally, we must practice. New thought patterns and new ways of expressing ourselves take time to establish.

The daily lessons contained here will help you with all of these steps. May your journey be a successful one that brings blessing to you and to all those who are blessed to be part of your life!

The Positive Revolution

More Pathways to Happiness

Shmiras Haloshon Yomi:
~ A Beautiful View of the World!

Words. When you think about it, most of your day and all of your relationships revolve around what you say. If you get used to talking negatively, you'll start seeing the bad in people and life will turn bitter. But if you get used to speaking positively, life will seem wonderful—the world will be a great place to be, and every person will be a potential friend.

We now have a very clear picture of how our words affect the people to whom we speak. But there's another, huge part of the picture: *loshon hora*—the words we speak *about* others. In some ways, this is an even bigger challenge, because we can fool ourselves into thinking the other person will never know what we've said about her. We aren't really fooled, however, because we know from the youngest age that *loshon hora* and *sinas chinam* do tremendous harm. What we may not realize is that its opposite, shmiras haloshon, is a major source of every kind of *brachah, refuah* and *yeshuah* a person could ever need.

But the big question is, how *do* we take control of our speech? The Chofetz Chaim says that the best way to improve our shmiras haloshon is through learning the *halachos*. In just five minutes of learning a day, you can join the tens of thousands of people who have brought happiness, friendship and *brachah* into their lives through Shmiras Haloshon Yomi.

> The most **effective way to avoid forbidden speech** is to have a **set time each day to study** the *halachos* and *mussar* of proper speech.
>
> Chofetz Chaim—
> Chovas Hashmirah,
> Chapter 3

Here's What You Need to Know
~ Where does the concept of learning shmiras haloshon daily come from?

The Chofetz Chaim advised having a set time each day to study the *halachos*. Rav Yehuda Zev Segal, the Manchester Rosh Yeshivah, took this a step further and created a calendar with a clearly scheduled learning cycle of two *halachos* a day. He would encourage everybody he met to start learning *Sefer Chofetz Chaim* consistently.

~ How long does it take to learn all the halachos?

If you follow Rav Segal's cycle, you finish *Sefer Chofetz Chaim* every four months! New cycles start Rosh Chodesh Tishrei, Shevat and Sivan. There are many English *sefarim* that follow the same cycle.

~ How much time does it take?

Generally speaking, each day's learning takes less than five minutes. It's a small investment of time with a really big payoff both in *Olam Hazeh* and *Olam Haba*.

~ I already know what loshon hora is. How does learning the halachos help?

Like every mitzvah, the *halachos* are the key to success. For instance, we know what "work" is, but it's impossible to keep Shabbos properly until we learn the details of how the Torah defines "work" in relation to Shabbos. Otherwise, we might think that an enjoyable activity like drawing is fine, while a chore like clearing the table is forbidden. In the same way, we are bound to make mistakes in shmiras haloshon if we don't learn the *halachos*.

~ With whom should I learn?

Learn with a partner—you're more likely to keep your commitment and enjoy the learning!

~ How can I make sure I remember to learn every day?

If girls are not learning it in school, the best suggestion to remember Shmiras Haloshon Yomi is to attach it to something you do every day, i.e. when you drink your morning coffee, eat lunch, or right before you say *Shema* at night. If you make it a part of your daily routine, then you won't forget it.

~ I know Shmiras Haloshon Yomi is the right thing to do, but will I really see a difference in my life?

Rav Segal said that there is no family that has taken on the daily learning of shmiras haloshon that has not seen a *yeshuah*, whether for health, *parnassah*, *shidduchim* or children. Perhaps even more importantly, once you learn the *halachos* and become more careful with your words, you will find that your positive speech makes life incredibly sweet.

Machsom L'fi
~ The Power of Shmiras Haloshon – Multiplied!

Now that you know the power of shmiras haloshon, why not put it to work for someone in need of a *refuah* or *yeshuah*? When you form a Machsom L'fi group, you are taking the amazing merit of this mitzvah and multiplying it many times over as you and your friends work together to bring a giant dose of shmiras haloshon into the world.

~ What is a Machsom L'fi?

It's really very simple. A group of girls gets together and splits up the day into two-hour periods. Each girl takes one time-slot in which she commits herself, *b'li neder*, to be extra-careful with her speech. How do we know this works? Read the story below!

~ A Speech Problem and a Speech Solution: The Story of Machsom L'fi

About thirty years ago, Hindy H. had a young child who was being treated for a severe stutter, and she was very concerned. She contacted her sister, a well-known educator who lived in Eretz Yisrael, and asked her to please go to a *gadol* and ask for advice in finding a *refuah*. The sister approached Rav Meir Bransdorfer of the Eidah Hachareidis in Yerushalayim, and he suggested that the family focus on shmiras haloshon. Hindy's sister asked Rav Bransdorfer if he could be more specific, and Rav Bransdorfer proceeded to outline the rules for the Machsom L'fi:

A group of people should divide up the waking hours of the day, with each one committing to three hours of shmiras haloshon—being extra careful to refrain from loshon hora and all other forbidden speech (such as anger, hurtful words, and so on). The commitment should be taken on for a one-month period, b'li neder, and can be done as a z'chus for a shidduch, children, refuah, etc.

Hindy is more of a quiet person, and could not see herself pulling a group of women together, so she called her former teacher.

"Morah," she said, "I'm not the type…Can you help me?" And that was the beginning of the Machsom L'fi groups. *Baruch Hashem*, Hindy's son's stutter went away.

Over the years, this teacher organized many more groups. Seeing how difficult it was for women to keep three hours, she sent someone to ask

Rav Bransdorfer if the commitment could be for two hours. It took a long time, but eventually he agreed.

~ How does a two-hour commitment help? Isn't shmiras haloshon an obligation all the time?

Try telling yourself "I'll never speak *loshon hora* again!" You can be sure that the next voice you'll hear is that of the *yetzer hara*, saying, "Impossible! Never again is a long, long time!" But when you break down your commitment into two-hour periods, you will find that you can succeed. And if you can hold yourself back for two hours, you quickly realize that you really do have the power to control what you say. It's like strengthening a muscle: you start with lighter weights and build up as you become stronger.

So yes, of course, we are always obligated to guard our speech. But you are sure to find that two hours of special focus makes you much more aware of the words you say all day, every day.

~ How do I get a Machsom L'fi started?

The best motivation to get a Machsom L'fi started and keep it going strong is to do it as a *zechus* for someone in need of a *yeshuah*, *refuah* or *shidduch*.

- *Get enough girls together to cover the waking hours of the day in two-hour periods. (9 girls will cover the hours of 6 a.m. to midnight, and having 18 girls in the group will allow for each time-slot to have a backup.)*

- *Have each girl choose her two-hour slot until the entire day is covered. Each girl should commit herself, b'li neder, to be especially careful not to speak, hear or write loshon hora or hurtful words during her two hours. In fact, a good way to start your time-slot is to say the declaration (found at the bottom of the Machsom L'fi form on page 302). If you slip up (we're all human!) try again during the next two hours if you can, or give some tzedakah according to your ability.*

- *The Machsom L'fi usually lasts a month. If girls wish, they can recommit themselves for another month, perhaps as a z'chus for another person.*

Remember: The key to success in shmiras haloshon is to learn two *halachos* a day from *Sefer Chofetz Chaim* or an English version. Not only will you gain the knowledge you need to keep the mitzvah correctly, but you will also merit the *siyata d'Shmaya* everyone needs to really conquer *loshon hora* and bring Hashem's most beautiful *brachos* into our lives.

Machsom L'fi *Sign Up Sheet*

Date _____

Our Machsom L'fi is being done as a z'chus for: _____

HOURS	NAME	ADDRESS / ZIP	PHONE#
6-8 AM			
8-10 AM			
10 AM-12 PM			
12-2 PM			
2-4 PM			
4-6 PM			
6-8 PM			
8-10 PM			
10 PM-12 AM			

This form may be copied as needed for your Machsom L'fi group.

◆ Kabbalah/ Verbal Acceptance *(without a vow)* ◆

Please recite the following prior your Machsom L'fi hours: *I accept upon myself (without a vow) to observe the laws of shmiras haloshon, in regard to both what I say and what I listen to, during the hours of ____ to ____ as a merit for _____.*

א לומר נוסח זה קודם המחסום לפי:
אני מקבל על עצמי, בלי נדר, שמירת הלשון
בדיבור ושמיעה משך שעות _____ עד _____
זכות _____.

The Shmiras Haloshon Shaila Hotline
Call for answers to your halachic questions regarding proper speech. 718-951-3696 • 9-10:30 pm

How to Live a Happier Life

1. Daven to Hashem to see the good
—Rabbi Dr. Abraham J. Twerski

When we seek to grow spiritually our first line of action must be to ask Hashem to help us. R' Elimelech of Lizhensk composed a beautiful *tefillah* (which some say before davening) in which he asks Hashem, "Help me that I should see the good in other people, and not their faults and defects."

Fulfilling *v'ahavta l'reiacha kamocha* by seeing the good in other people is a wonderful way to prepare for *tefillah* and a great merit and virtue through which our prayers will be answered.

2. Understand people's motivations
—Rabbi Simcha Feuerman

A good way to cut down on frustration in relationships and to transform our negative view of others into a positive one is to seek to understand others. By seeking to understand why something is important to them or why they act or think a certain way, we open a new world of harmony, respect, and happiness within our relationships.

3. Be an easy grader—give partial credit
—Dr. Meir Wikler

It's not all or nothing! Learn to see the good in those around you by giving partial credit. When someone does a favor, runs an errand, etc.—even if he didn't do exactly what you wanted—it's important to give partial credit and express appreciation for the effort and for what he *did* do.

4. Accept differences
—Rabbi Doniel Frank

We need the humility to understand that just because *we* do things a certain way doesn't mean that's how others need to do it. Acceptance of these differences is key to keeping negativity out of our relationships.

5. We find fault... where *our* faults lie
—Rabbi Dr. Abraham J. Twerski

The Baal Shem Tov said that the world is a mirror in which the faults we see in others are really those within ourselves.

If you find a fault in another person, stop and consider, "Where is that fault in myself?"

6. Don't keep score
—Rabbi Simcha Feuerman

The notion that things have to be fair is an illusion that blocks our happiness. When people keep score and think or say, "I did this for you yesterday, why can't you do this for me today?" that's where negativity takes over and hijacks the relationship.

7. Everyone has faults... that's Hashem's design
—Rabbi Doniel Frank

The first principle of relationships is that people are born with deficits. Everyone has faults; that's part of being human. The quality of our relationships hinges upon our learning to embrace people as a whole with all their good points and their faults.

We gratefully acknowledge the following high-school girls who have responded with an extra level of commitment to the mission of promoting positive speech. May their involvement in this mitzvah bring them a lifetime of *brachah* and happiness.

Gitty Lefkowitz • לזכות רינה בת עליזה שתחי' • Pessy Heimfeld • לזכות פעסל מינקא בת ריזל שתחי' • Rena Cohen • לזכות אסתר נחמה בת רבקה רחל שתחי' • Tovah Chastkofsky • לזכות טובה גיטל בת חנה שתחי' • Esther Nechama Zoberman • לזכות אסתר נחמה בת רבקה רחל שתחי' • Adina Meth • לזכות יהודית עליזה בת לאה פעראל בילא שתחי' • Yehudis Frish • לזכות הדסה פראדל בת חי' אסתר שתחי' • Dassy Katzenstein • Chaya Devoiry Hirschler • לזכות חיה דבורה בת הינדל שתחי' • Etty Muller • לזכות אסתר בת שדה שתחי' • לזכות עטל בת זיסל לאה שתחי'

TIC TALK

It's always time for TIC Talk, the CCHF free Teen Inspiration and Chizuk hotline for high school girls. Innovative, intriguing and timely segments are uploaded daily on various features including Personal Stories of Wow!, Lessons for Life, The Playlist, Q&A, Spotlight on Schools and Serial Story. Listeners enjoy spending time in "The Auditorium" and "The Garage Sale" and have discovered a whole new meaning to "Global Warming". TIC Talk currently receives over 50,000 calls weekly from teens worldwide. CALL: 201. 855.8255

The Chofetz Chaim Heritage Foundation

Since 1989, the Chofetz Chaim Heritage Foundation has successfully launched innovative methods of promoting the Torah's wisdom on human relations and personal development. The foundation utilizes a vast array of effective communication tools including books, tapes, video seminars, telephone classes and newsletters, designed to heighten one's awareness of such essential values as judging others favorably, speaking with restraint and integrity, and acting with sensitivity and respect. The Chofetz Chaim Heritage Foundation's programs reassert the Torah's timeless recipe for building a world of compassion and harmony.

WONDER WORDS CHILDREN'S STORY LINE

WonderWords, a free children's story line, puts the power of a good story to work, conveying lessons of Shmiras Haloshon in an entertaining and engaging way—with daily features and weekly contests— hosted by Rabbi Yosef Pruzansky. WonderWords currently receives over 40,000 calls weekly.
Call: 212.444.1119

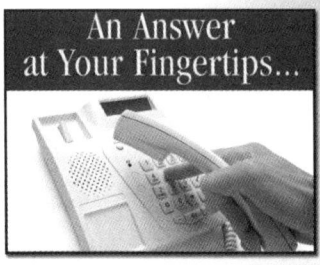

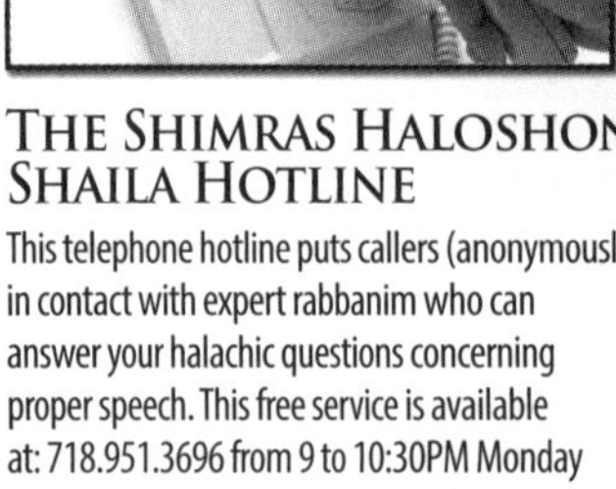

CD & TAPE BINDERS

A wide array of audio CD's on a variety of timely topics by renowned speakers inspire and guide you on your own journey of growth.
Call to order: 845.352.3505 x 116

THE SHIMRAS HALOSHON SHAILA HOTLINE

This telephone hotline puts callers (anonymously) in contact with expert rabbanim who can answer your halachic questions concerning proper speech. This free service is available at: 718.951.3696 from 9 to 10:30PM Monday through Thursday and Motzei Shabbos.

To purchase or sponsor a book or CD or
for more information on our programs please contact:
The Chofetz Chaim Heritage Foundation 
The Zichron Yaakov Zvi Center for the Teachings of the Chofetz Chaim
361 Spook Rock Road, Suffern, NY 10901
845-352-3505 ext. 116 or email: catalog@chofetzchaimusa.org

SPREADING THE LANGUAGE OF AHAVAS YISRAEL

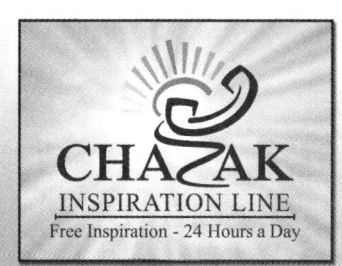

CHAZAK INSPIRATION LINE

A free inspirational telephone hotline is available 24 hours a day. Chazak offers chizuk and inspiration by some of the world's best speakers, including Rabbi Yitzchok Kirzner zt"l, and yb"l, Rabbi Yissocher Frand, Rabbi Paysach Krohn, Rabbi Abraham J. Twerski, and includes an array of topics for personal growth, better relationships, Torah thoughts and insights, facing life challenges, meaningful prayer and timely topics for every season. Chazak currently receives over 50,000 calls weekly.
Call: 718.258.2008 or 845.356.6665

EMAIL

Thousands participate in Shmiras Haloshon Yomi through one of our daily learning emails, which include three choices of text to study from and our new mp3 daily, 5-minute SHY audio. Additionally, more and more people are receiving our daily email reminders for the Morning Machsom L'fi as well as daily learning of Lessons in Truth, Loving Kindness and our popular biweekly newsletter, Chosen Words.
Email: editorial@chofetzchaimusa.org

BOOKS

With over 350,000 volumes in print, our best-selling books for daily learning, for both adults and children, have created a worldwide revolution of speech and deed. Building on that success, POSITIVE WORD POWER shows us how to harness the incredible power of words to nurture and uplift the people in our lives. Call to order: 845.352.3505 x 116

Prayer for Proper Speech
תפילה על הדיבור

מאת מרן החפץ חיים זצ"ל

רִבּוֹנוֹ-שֶׁל-עוֹלָם, יְהִי רָצוֹן מִלְפָנֶיךָ אֵ-ל רַחוּם וְחַנּוּן שֶׁתְּזַכֵּנִי הַיּוֹם וּבְכָל יוֹם לִשְׁמוֹר פִּי וּלְשׁוֹנִי מִלָּשׁוֹן הָרַע וּרְכִילוּת: וְאֶזָּהֵר מִלְּדַבֵּר אֲפִילוּ עַל אִישׁ יָחִיד, וְכָל שֶׁכֵּן עַל כְּלַל יִשְׂרָאֵל, אוֹ עַל חֵלֶק מֵהֶם וְכָל שֶׁכֵּן מִלְּהִתְרָעֵם עַל מִידוֹתָיו שֶׁל הַקָּדוֹשׁ בָּרוּךְ הוּא. וְאֶזָּהֵר מִלְּדַבֵּר דִּבְרֵי שֶׁקֶר, חֲנוּפָה, מַחֲלוֹקֶת, כַּעַס, גַּאֲוָה, אוֹנָאַת דְּבָרִים, הַלְבָּנַת פָּנִים, לֵיצָנוּת, וְכָל דִּיבּוּר אָסוּר. וְזַכֵּנִי שֶׁלֹּא לְדַבֵּר כִּי אִם דָּבָר הַצָּרִיךְ לְעִנְיְנֵי גוּפִי וְנַפְשִׁי, וְיִהְיוּ כָל מַעֲשַׂי וְדִיבּוּרַי לְשֵׁם שָׁמַיִם.

Master of the World, may it be Your will, compassionate and gracious G-d, that You grant me the merit today and every day to guard my mouth and tongue from speaking loshon hora and rechilus. May I be zealous not to speak ill of an individual, and certainly not of the entire Jewish people or a portion of it; and even more so, may I be zealous not to complain about the ways of the Holy One, Blessed is He. May I be zealous not to speak words of falsehood, flattery, strife, anger, arrogance, hurt, embarrassment, mockery, and all other forbidden forms of speech. Grant me the merit to speak only that which is necessary for my physical and spiritual well-being, and may all my deeds and words be for the sake of Heaven.

> "Sometimes people learn the halachos and they still have a hard time keeping them. It's because they forget that they have to ask Hashem for help."
> — Rabbi Moshe Mordechai Lowy

This volume is part of
THE ARTSCROLL SERIES®
an ongoing project of
translations, commentaries and expositions on
Scripture, Mishnah, Talmud, Midrash, Halachah,
liturgy, history, the classic Rabbinic writings,
biographies and thought.

For a brochure of current publications
visit your local Hebrew bookseller
or contact the publisher:

Mesorah Publications, ltd

4401 Second Avenue
Brooklyn, New York 11232
(718) 921-9000
www.artscroll.com

YOU can be a part of the Positive Revolution!

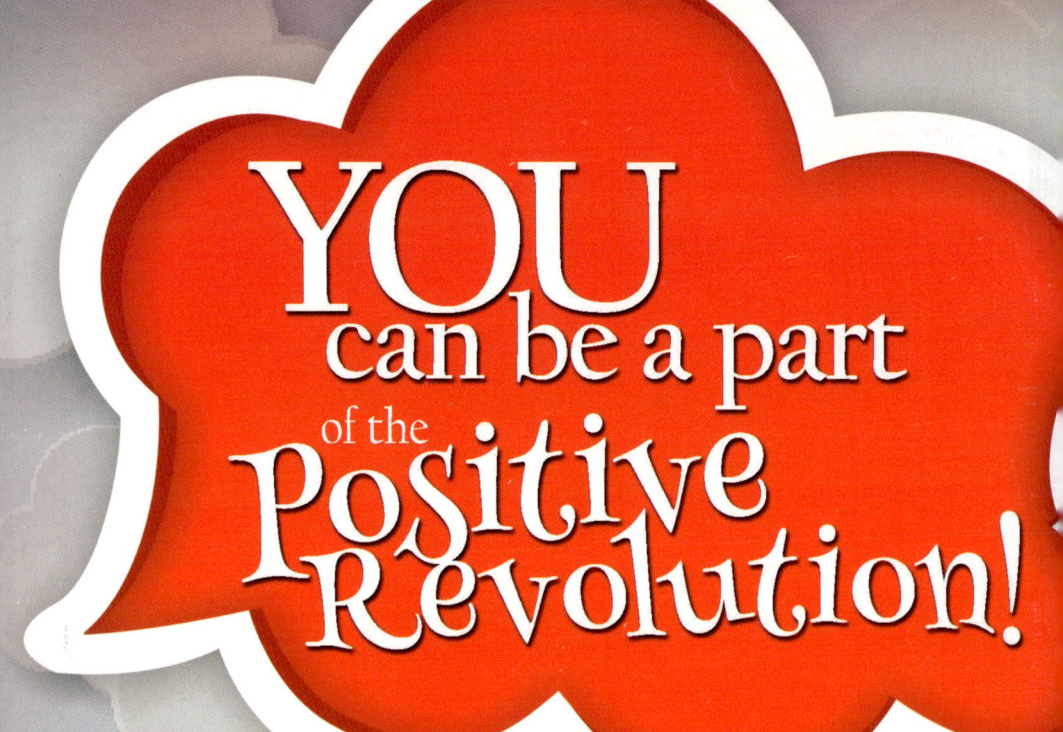

Teen Inspiration and Chizuk

TIC TALK
Inspiration & Chizuk Hotline for Girls
It's always time for TIC Talk!

Call the TIC TALK Inspiration Line
The Chofetz Chaim Heritage Foundation's Free Teen Hotline